laughing
HYSTERICALLY

film and culture

JOHN BELTON
general editor

FILM AND CULTURE SERIES

A series of Columbia University Press
Edited by John Belton

What Made Pistachio Nuts?
Henry Jenkins

*Showstoppers: Busby Berkley and
the Tradition of Spectacle*
Martin Rubin

*Projections of War: Hollywood,
American Culture, and World War II*
Thomas Doherty

*Laughing Screaming:
Modern Hollywood Horror and Comedy*
William Paul

laughing
HYSTERICALLY

American Screen Comedy

of the 1950s

ED SIKOV

columbia university press

NEW YORK

Columbia University Press
New York   Chichester, West Sussex
Copyright © 1994 Columbia University Press
All rights reserved

Library of Congress Cataloging-in-Publication Data

Sikov, Ed.
    Laughing hysterically : American screen comedy of the 1950s / by
Ed Sikov.
        p.   cm.—(Film and culture)
    Includes bibliographical references and index.
    ISBN 0–231–07982–6
    1. Comedy films—United States—History and criticism.   2. Motion
pictures—Political aspects—United States.   I. Title.   II. Series
PN1995.9.C55S49   1994
791.43'617—dc20   93–48900
                                                                              CIP

Casebound editions of Columbia University Press books are printed on
permanent and durable acid-free paper.

Printed in the United States of America
c 10 9 8 7 6 5 4 3 2 1
p 10 9 8 7 6 5 4 3 2 1

For my parents,
who met in 1953,
got married in 1956,
had a baby in 1957,
and still managed to
keep a sense of humor.

contents

"My subconscious was battling against my conscious, and the basic intelligence of my mind wouldn't allow myself to comprehend some of the problems that were forethought prior to sleeping."

—Jerry Lewis in *Artists and Models* (1955)

"Mental health is successful, efficient resignation–normally so efficient that it shows forth as moderately happy satisfaction... In the long run, the question is only how much resignation the individual can bear without breaking up."

—Herbert Marcuse, *Eros and Civilization* (1955)

preface

Taste is always debatable, particularly on the volatile subject of movies. One might question why I focus on the 1950s comedies of Howard Hawks, Billy Wilder, Alfred Hitchcock, and Frank Tashlin rather than those of Stanley Donen, Vincente Minnelli, Douglas Sirk, and Blake Edwards, or, on the film buff fringe, those of Norman Taurog, Michael Gordon, George Marshall, and Hal Walker. Or why, at a time when director studies continue to be dismissed as "auteurist" and passé, I am still choosing to discuss comedy in the context of directors' visions. The answer is simple: a relatively complex film is relatively more interesting than a relatively simple one, and these four directors made some of the funniest and most complex films of the decade. With strong authorial voices as well as literate scripts, talented stars, often magnificent art direction, and clever musical scores, these films are as richly detailed as any film made at any time by any filmmaker. They are unusually articulate, and therefore they are optimal choices for cultural study.

This selection of directors and films hardly precludes further looks into the period. In fact, I hope this book encourages others. There is a general impression both in film studies and in journalism that Hitchcock, Hawks, and Wilder have been so thoroughly worked over that nothing more needs to be said about them. I have found instead that the quantity of words devoted to their work tends to bear an inverse relation to the number of things that have actually been said. For this reason, one of the secondary projects of this study will be to confront a history of critical discourse, in particular the normative and, I will argue, repressive tendencies within the canon of writing about Hollywood cinema.

Ideally, a study of fifties comedy would also tackle television series as well as many more films. It would integrate comedy into a pattern of other genres. And it would compare contemporary art and literature more extensively to films of the period. I have opted instead for a much more limited study of works that concretely expose a certain rebelliousness in a period of widespread conservatism, comedies that comment on their era through satire and caricature and thus offer social critiques. In the 1970s and 1980s, film critics and theorists enjoyed qualifying their own work by calling it "Notes on . . ." or "Notes Toward . . ."—as though the resulting criticism was somehow more tentative and less positivistic than it would have been had it been given a real title. This study is not "notes on." This is a book-length analysis of Hollywood film comedy of the 1950s. Still, it remains necessarily incomplete, a fact I am pleased to acknowledge.

Why these directors? Evading restrictions, representing people as caricatures, undercutting drab normality—these characteristics of film comedy are not limited to the work of Hawks, Wilder, Hitchcock, and Tashlin. Some of Buster Keaton's and Charlie Chaplin's films fit the description as well, as do many others. But one can certainly see these traits in peculiar abundance in the works of these four disparate talents throughout the 1950s, from "clean, direct, functional" Howard Hawks to flaming, loud, uproarious Frank Tashlin.[1] Subversion is especially potent in broad comedies like *The Girl Can't Help It* (1956), where representational excesses bring the tension between repressed and repressor to the breaking point. But from the satirical comedy of *Sunset Boulevard* (1950) to the pastoral morbidity of *The Trouble with Harry* (1955) to the lurid Technicolor farce of *Will Success Spoil Rock Hunter?* (1957), all of the Americas represented here seem to be in imminent danger of comic dissolution and the effect is, to me at least, liberating.

Freud saw the rebellious quality of jokes and of caricature as the basis of their freeing appeal: "The joke then represents a rebellion against that authority, a liberation from its pressure. The charm of caricatures lies in this same factor: we laugh at them even if they are unsuccessful simply because we count rebellion against authority as a merit."[2] Since the widespread perception of the 1950s as a time of humorless conformity has all but erased a generation of comedy from America's collective memory, it may come as a shock to rediscover the wild lengths to which fifties comedies went to be rebellious. At this point in the study—and in history, too, for that matter—one can only wonder idly whether the erasure of fifties comedies from the register of culture *itself* has something to do with repression. Just look at Jerry Lewis.

Equally to the point is the fact that, with one or two exceptions, each of the films discussed here combines narrative intricacy and comic risk with commercial success in mainstream America. While box-office receipts are not in any sense a sign of artistic quality, they do indicate a form of cultural acceptance, a statement by millions of people regarding the actual as well as the presumed content of the work. Audiences pay *before* seeing the film rather than vice versa, and the fact that a given release generates a healthy income for its producer and distributor probably has as much to do with the way the film is sold as with what it contains. Audiences buy the whole package, and in the case of these films, the directors' track records, together with their technical and stylistic competence, gave them enough artistic clout in Hollywood that they could afford to take some chances with the jokes they told. They were popular directors who made films that both embraced and challenged contemporary norms, they worked within the artistic and moral confines of Hollywood filmmaking, and they usually made money doing so.

I began this study with the vague idea that these films were anomalies of their era, that these four directors perceived elements of their society that eluded most others. Although each of the directors treated in this book offers visions of America that depart significantly from what we have come to accept as the period's putative values, by opening up their work to meanings that have previously been hidden, the membrane of conjecture that surrounds the 1950s also began to perforate. As it turns out, Hawks, Hitchcock, Wilder, and Tashlin were very much a part of their era, which suggests that it is now time to reconsider not only our view of what constituted the social norms of the period but also, implicitly, the idea that any set of social, sexual, and political values can be *effectively* dominant and exclusive.

A historian is a detective—the simile may be worn, but it is no less accurate for wear—and the question here is not so much who done it but what happened. We know who done it. Whether one cares to describe, say, *Gentlemen Prefer Blondes* (1953) as a Hawks film, a Fox film, a "Hawks" film, or a Hawks-Fox-text, or whether the critic needs to descend further into the exclusive language of film studies experts and talk about signatures, inscriptions, and palimpsests, the fact is that Howard Hawks *did* direct *Gentlemen Prefer Blondes*. I think that we can begin again to talk about what Hawks's films might mean, not only as reflections of Hawks's worldview but as articulate cultural artifacts—visions of the world Hawks and everybody else lived in.

Beyond this very traditional beginning, there are two ways of proceeding. One may either deduce the specifics of what happened—the meanings of the artwork—from general principles regarding the cinema and this particular period, or one may induce a general idea of cultural meaning in the period from the evidence on the screen. Previous studies of films of the fifties have tended to follow the former model, and since the general principles that result from those efforts are more or less unsatisfying, this particular study will be inductive as well as deductive. It's true that I begin with some broad observations, most notably that these four directors all worked at the same time in the same place in the same medium; that they all made comedies; that these comedies tend to involve sexual repression and frustration; and that in theory, at least, comedy can be a liberating response to repression as well as a means of expressing it.

In analyzing films, I have tried to work as close to the texts as possible, to shed light on the specifics of the art as well as of the era. The following analyses are thus more detailed than the capsule reviews with which many readers are familiar. By so doing, I hope to let the cultural evidence mount for itself. Still, I find myself using broad theory to justify quirky film practice, a critical mode with which I am somewhat uncomfortable. Freud couldn't have been more vocal in his belief that comedy served a therapeutic function, a means of pleasurable escape from civilized repression. And yet what Freud saw in comedy has completely eluded those who have ignored or impugned Jerry Lewis. If Lewis, Hawks, Mansfield, Hitchcock, Wilder, Lemmon, Ewell, Monroe, Grant, Tashlin, and yes, even Gloria Swanson—if the comedians of the fifties have become so remote from the critics of the eighties and nineties that they need snippets from Freud, from cultural historians, and from film theorists to bolster their reputations and explain their art, the cost to the films on the one hand and to Freud et al. on the other will be minimal. I hope that such theoretical support will be justified by the revival of gleeful subversion that these comic visions offered at the time—and continue to offer now—to anyone, that is, who is willing to suspend propriety long enough to hear the deep, raucous laughter that such visions compel.

There is a personal political agenda behind this book, and I want to make it explicit here. For me, sexuality—its repression as well as its expression—plays a large role in defining the nature of fifties film comedy, and my concern with this issue is not abstract. Throughout the book, I keep bringing up the specific topic of homosexuality in the 1950s; I do so because I am a child of the late fifties whose self-esteem was nearly destroyed by the fierce antigay assaults of my own culture—assaults which began in earnest in the early 1950s and continued full force through my adolescence in the early 1970s, if not to the present day. I believe that a restoration of mental and social health—my own as well as that of other gay men and lesbians—can be achieved through a sort of cultural talking cure in which the critic-historian repeats, often in a tone of shocked familiarity that is all too recognizable to any analytic patient, the metahistory of his or her own traumas. Given the excesses of the traumatic history in question, I can hardly talk about it enough.

A note about film stills and frame enlargements: this book is illustrated entirely with stills. There are no frame enlargements. Film historian Richard Koszarski once described frame enlargements as having been "ripped untimely from the film," and I tend to agree. Films exist in time; frame enlargements don't. They do have limited uses, but often film historians use them merely to prove that their prose is accurate. Aha, one says, peering at a scratched and blurry frame enlargement—the writer has told the truth after all. Stills, meanwhile, have several advantages. The image quality is far superior, even if the photos only approximate the film's content. As long as a still isn't being passed off as an actual frame of the film, there is no inaccuracy in using a still to illustrate a point. More important, stills reveal what frame enlargements cannot—namely, how the film was sold.

They are images designed, produced, and widely *re*produced to entice people into the theater, and therefore one can see in them what *the studio* found meaningful and marketable. Since this book is a cultural study, stills are especially appropriate as illustrations of a film's cultural appeal. Film stills are gorgeous photographic come-ons, and I like the way they look.

I am grateful for the help and advice I received throughout this project's life. In several cases, I received generous assistance from some of the very people whose work I criticize in the book. Foremost among these is John Belton, whose knowledge of the art, technology, and cultural meaning of the American cinema is unsurpassed. I take issue here with John's reading of *Monkey Business* (1952); I do not take issue with John's command of film history, and I am tremendously grateful for the help, encouragement, and information he has given to me—even after I attacked him.

Andrew Sarris, too, comes under fire here despite his benign and generous reading of the text. I would like readers to know that I value Andrew's work very much. He remembers more about films than anyone I have ever known, and he knows what's important. I attack and admire Molly Haskell as well, for many of the same reasons. William Paul, on the other hand, doesn't get attacked here, and readers may thus be fooled into thinking that I don't admire him. I do. And I thank him for guiding this project, for pointing out its weaknesses and nudging me toward solutions, and also for helping me through writer's block.

There are many other scholars whose ideas I criticize, sometimes sharply, but who nevertheless have provided me with a great deal of information and insight. Critical disagreements aside, I owe these scholars a profound debt of gratitude. They include Robin Wood, Thomas Doherty, Peter Biskind, Nora Sayre, Maureen Turim, Ian Cameron, Richard Corliss, Douglas Miller, Marion Nowak, Raymond Durgnat, Jonathan Rosenbaum, Claire Johnston, Paul Willemen, Stephen Heath, Laura Mulvey, and many others.

I want to express special gratitude to Philip Rosen, Edward Said, Tzvetan Todorov, Richard Koszarski, Stefan Scharf, Frank Daniel, and Terry McAteer, all of whom helped make graduate school lively and engaging. Many of the ideas behind this book were born in their classes. Thanks also to Jennifer Crewe, Anne McCoy, Roy Thomas, Chris Bram, Draper Shreeve, Matthew Mirapaul, Mason Wiley, Damien Bona, Howard Karren, Sandra Archer, Robert Cushman, Howard Prouty, Steve Garland, the late Vito Russo, Howard Mandelbaum, Ron Mandelbaum, Eric Ashworth, Neil Olson, Edward Hibbert, Ron Caldwell, Michael Kaniecki, Troy Alexander, Frank Roma, Irving and Betty Sikov, and, most of all, Ethan Scheuer, who sometimes laughed at my jokes and whose spirit continues to lighten my heart.

laughing
HYSTERICALLY

introduction

HEARING THE LAUGHTER

Only jokes that have a purpose run the risk of meeting
with people who do not want to listen to them.
—Sigmund Freud[1]

Hollywood or Bust

Pointless jokes speak to everyone, but only the willful ones have the
nerve to risk disapproval. What gives comedies of the 1950s their
peculiar flavor—some might call it an acquired taste—is that certain
directors, writers, and stars took these risks in an era of widespread
conservatism. An enormously popular Republican military hero
occupied the White House for most of the decade and, so a certain
vision of American film history suggests, the strict moral codes of a
nation bent on producing bigger cars and better babies set the tone
for popular art. In this trite scenario, darkness appears in the form of
either Joseph McCarthy or communists, depending on one's political
affiliation (it's almost always the former), and Hollywood, caught
between the official propriety of the Eisenhowers and the official terror of the House Committee on Un-American Activities (HUAC)
and its aftermath, produced a decade of dull and strenuously witless
films. As one movie reviewer declared a few years ago:

Something went seriously wrong with American movies in the '50s. In one decade, Hollywood seemed to forget everything it had learned in the preceding three: the visually elegant '20s, the fast and fuzzy '30s, the gritty, noirish '40s all gave way to the clumsy, stodgy, emotionally dishonest '50s.[2]

The charge of dishonesty cuts both ways. Films of the 1950s really aren't the products of a massive attack of amnesia that managed in its fury to strike every producer, director, actor, screenwriter, studio boss, costume designer, technician, distributor, and theatergoer from coast to coast and beyond our shores to the worldwide market as well. Hollywood did not suddenly forget how to be Hollywood. On the contrary. As every film textbook tells us, the fear of television and the breakdown of the studio system provoked the film industry to step up its efforts to entertain the public by making films that looked and sounded like nothing had ever looked and sounded before. A quick glance at the decade's roster reveals not only new technologies—CinemaScope ("the modern miracle you can see without glasses"),[3] VistaVision, Cinerama, stereophonic sound, and 3-D—but also the quick and appreciative (if exploitative) inclusion of rock 'n' roll music into soundtracks, a distinctive style of art direction featuring some of the best streamline design of its age, the baroque flowering of the science fiction genre, and the ascendance of a whole new generation of stars like Marilyn Monroe, James Dean, Jerry Lewis, Marlon Brando, and Montgomery Clift, all of whom played neurotics, hysterics, or infantile grotesques as fictional extensions of their own highly publicized personalities. This widespread elevation of emotional trauma to the level of star status was nothing if not a extraordinary innovation.

In the history of American popular culture as it has been written *by* American popular culture, Hollywood in the 1950s was an entertainment matrix from which conformism, complacency, single-minded corporate ambition, and tattle-telling anticommunism emanated. Family values reigned, or so we're told. Film academics may like to pepper their courses with Douglas Sirk and Frank Tashlin, but then again film academics haven't successfully defined American movie tastes. For the rest of the country, *Father Knows Best* and *Leave It to Beaver* still sum up everything that was wrong with Hollywood in the 1950s; never mind that they were TV shows. In the national myth of the past, Doris Day's virginity is an all-defining metonymy for the era's sexual values. Only the buffs remember that Doris and James Cagney rip each other apart throughout the 1955 musical *Love Me or Leave Me* in one of the most severe depictions of a wretched marriage Hollywood has ever produced. But in popular memory, there's no *Love Me or Leave Me*. It's all a desexed version of *Pillow Talk* (1959).

It isn't hard to find films that fit the bill of stodginess and emotional dishonesty, at least on the surface: Leo McCarey's notorious commie-catcher, *My Son John* (1952); Jean Negulesco's slick, forced *How to Marry a Millionaire* (1953); Robert Wise's businessman's weepie, *Executive Suite* (1954); Mervyn LeRoy's ridiculous *Quo Vadis?* (1951); William Wellman's *The Next Voice You Hear* (1950), in which future First Lady Nancy Davis plays a pregnant suburbanite who, like everyone else in the world, turns on the radio to hear God broadcasting from Heaven, and so on. From the competent to the idiotic, examples of reactionary, repressive, or even simply dull films can be dredged up from the archives of the 1950s just as they can be dredged up from any decade's.

In terms of film and national politics, Victor Navasky, Larry Ceplair, Steven Englund, and others have been more than convincing in their descriptions of how Hollywood first suffered, then developed, and ultimately refined blacklisting and political persecution. And a quick look at a history book tells the story of America's consolidation of corporate interests at home and abroad as well as the rhetoric of nuclear arms and the popular revival of religion that coincided with it. Still, to limit one's vision of the films of the fifties to those that readily relate to HUAC, anticommunism, corporate development, and ideological conformism is to see only a small part of the story. To put it another way, there is no reason not to treat *The Girl Can't Help It* (1956) as having at least as much or more to say about the 1950s as *On the Waterfront* (1954). In fact, *The Girl Can't Help It* says things about the 1950s that *On the Waterfront* could never say. It's a comedy. And comedy of the past is like a foreign country. They do things differently there.

Given the outrageous excesses of many fifties comedies, it is remarkable that neither of the two book-length studies of films of the 1950s and their politics—Peter Biskind's *Seeing Is Believing: How Hollywood Taught Us to Stop Worrying and Love the Fifties* and Nora Sayre's *Running Time: Films of the Cold War*—gets into the decade's comedies. Both writers analyze the political nature of Hollywood's collective representation of the period, yet they limit their field of inquiry mostly to trenchant dramas and an occasional sci-fi film, all of which just seem to have "the fifties" written all over them: *The Thing* (1951), *High Noon* (1952), *From Here to Eternity* (1953), *On the Waterfront* (1954), *Rebel Without a Cause* (1955), *Invasion of the Body Snatchers* (1956), *12 Angry Men* (1957), and others. Both Sayre and Biskind share an overly sober tendency to ban comedy from the realm of meaningful culture. One gets the sense they're avoiding something. Sayre writes:

> There were notably few comedies in the Fifties, and the occasional farces, such as the labored *The Seven Year Itch* and the sublime *Some Like It Hot*—both directed by Billy Wilder—shrank from subtlety. Joseph Mankiewicz's *All About Eve*, one of the few really *written* movies of the period, was a time-traveler: the style of rapid riposte and jubilant wisecrack belonged to the Thirties. Screen comedies thrived during the Depression due to the very harshness of the era, which augmented the public's appetite for amusement, for laughter as an engine of survival. But in the Fifties survival was hardly at stake.[4]

It's not only Hollywood that suffers from periodic amnesia but also its critics. The comedy team of Martin and Lewis turned out "occasional farces" at the rate of one, two, even three per year, and they were enormously successful at the box office. The fact that in 1955 the Internal Revenue Service presented Dean and Jerry with a tax bill for $650,000 is only one indication of their vast commercial appeal.[5] Bob Hope was knocking out comedies as well, as were Danny Kaye, Abbott and Costello, and Francis the Talking Mule. In fact, Francis starred in more fifties films than either Laurence Olivier or James Dean. On a more culturally upscale level, *The Seven Year Itch* (1955) and *Some Like It Hot* (1959) are subtle enough to withstand and encourage many viewings—but even if they didn't, a lack of subtlety is scarcely a good reason not to listen to them and hear what it is that they are screaming.

Screenwriters like James Agee and John Huston (*The African Queen*, 1951), Betty Comden and Adolph Green (*Singin' in the Rain*, 1952), Garson Kanin and Ruth Gordon (*The Marrying Kind*, 1952), Budd Schulberg (*On the Waterfront*), Frank Nugent (*The Searchers*, 1956), and Ernest Lehman (*North by Northwest*, 1959) produced these and a sizable number of other "written" scripts in this period. These films are grounded on exemplary, classically literate screenplays, and there were certainly many others. Why *All About Eve* "belonged to the Thirties" when it was released in 1950 is obscure. The logic apparently goes something like this: *All About Eve* is a witty comedy, so it's really a thirties film. If it were gritty, it would scoot into the forties. Since it isn't dull or unsubtle (i.e., since it fails to fit the preconception), Sayre simply hurls it back in time and moves on to discuss yet another drama. Even someone like Ian Cameron, who really *likes* films, falls into a similar trap: "The best comedies of the 'fifties—*Pat and Mike* or *Gentlemen Prefer Blondes* or *Designing Woman*—could just as well have been made any time between the late 'thirties and the early 'sixties."[6]

All this time-shuffling aside, Sayre's comment about the social genesis of comedy does get to the heart of the issue. If we take the testing of the atomic bomb, the invention and subsequent testing of the hydrogen bomb, the omnipresence of the Cold War, the brute fact of the Korean War, the resulting boom in bomb shelters, and the nationwide dissemination of pamphlets about how to remain alive in a nuclear holocaust to be even moderately pertinent to the decade, we can safely say that sheer physical survival was "at stake" during the

1950s. The attacking-mutant subset of the science fiction genre provides the most impressive example of how fears of obliteration reached the screen in narrative form, but Sayre's forgetting the obvious (until the end of the book, when she minimizes it) is not as self-damning as the idea that audiences in the fifties weren't after "amusement" the way their parents' generation was. It's not much of a surprise to learn that people watched a lot of television in the 1950s. By 1956, according to one report, Americans spent as much time looking for amusement on TV as they did earning a living.[7] Some of their favorite television stars and shows, of course, were comedians and comedies: Jack Benny, Milton Berle, Sid Caesar, Imogene Coca, Ernie Kovacs, Lucille Ball, Jackie Gleason, Phil Silvers, *Father Knows Best* (1954–1962), *Mr. Peepers* (1952–1955), *The Goldbergs* (1949–1955), *The Burns and Allen Show* (1950–1958), and on and on. The abundance of popular comic talent and product strongly suggests that audiences of the 1950s were indeed amused by comedy and that the handiest, most accessible, and above all most domestic medium of comedy was not the cinema but television, the brand new gadget that brought laughs directly into the living room and kept them there for the duration of an evening, a season, even several years. Taken as a whole, TV comedy tended to be somewhat tamer and more domestic than film comedy. Again, this isn't surprising; it hit people literally where they lived.

Like any Hollywood decade, what took place on the big screen between 1950 and 1959—in every film, in every genre—reflects an exceptionally rich field of historical and aesthetic meanings that cannot be quickly traced back to self-evident generalizations about real-life America. Because films are not made in a void, because they appear out of a clutter of real events and circumstances, their representations of life may directly contradict our simplest and most cynical impressions of life on the street, in the kitchen, and in corporate offices in the 1950s. Politics takes many forms, some of which aren't terribly obvious. Because comedy is a formal occasion to which audiences are invited with the hope that they will take belly-laughing pleasure in seeing standards of normality inverted (often rather viciously), all comedy is political. By dismissing comedy, Sayre,

Biskind, and others have ignored an entire political arena. They have missed the flip side of the 1950s.

Biskind is a funnier writer than Sayre, and he enjoys poking holes in American social values. Still, he devotes a total of two independent clauses to *Some Like It Hot*, one of the decade's top commercial successes and a critical hit as well. In the first, Biskind notes that Marilyn Monroe "tells Tony Curtis . . . that she likes men with glasses," a point he concludes later in the book with the statement, "in films like *Some Like It Hot*, transvestism had become a harmless and humorous metaphor for the feminization of men."[8] Blaming comedy for emasculating ideas as well as protagonists, Biskind renders this popular film literally meaningless; because Wilder succeeded in being funny, his work necessarily fails to mean anything. A much more sweeping dismissal comes from historians Douglas T. Miller and Marion Nowak, who take a very informative but selectively joyless look at ten full years of American culture: "Certainly there was some fun in the fifties—the Coasters' songs, Lenny Bruce's nightclub routines, Sid Caesar's TV antics. But in retrospect it was essentially a humorless decade."[9]

By looking for cultural meaning only in more or less direct, seemingly unmediated "statement" films like *Marty* (1955) and *12 Angry Men*, or pretentious westerns like *High Noon*, or problem dramas like *Rebel Without a Cause*, these critics have tended to isolate one strain of fifties culture to the exclusion of all others. Paradoxically, critics who have taken more limited views of the films of the fifties and their sociocultural meanings—Thomas Doherty looks at fifties teenpics, Jackie Byars analyzes gender in fifties melodramas—tend to produce much richer views of the period and its culture. Still, looking for social consciousness and cultural significance in the *comedies* of the 1950s has never been a priority. At best, these comedies have been seen purely as directors' visions, as divorced from the cultural flux from which they arose as they are from the audience to which they were aimed. A closer look at the culture that produced *Gentlemen Prefer Blondes* (1953), *Artists and Models* (1955), *Some Like It Hot*, and other fifties comedies may provide some balance. To do so, I want to offer a few contrarian glimpses of American life during the period, alternative snapshots of the culture in question. Films of the fifties are nowhere near as complacent as their reputations, and neither were American consumers.

All Shook Up

The consumption of tranquilizers, from Milltown (meprobamate, used to relieve mild anxiety) to Thorazine (chloropromazine, used to treat severe psychotic disorders), went from nothing in the early fifties to 462,000 pounds of pills in 1958 to 1,159,000 pounds worth about $4.75 million in 1959.[10] Since by all accounts the 1950s was the decade of American consumption par excellence, statistics on what the ballooning bourgeoisie of the fifties consumed, especially physically, give an eloquent testimony to the spirit of the times. While these stark figures may not be enough evidence to commit the entire decade to the psycho ward of history, they do suggest that there was something more than slightly forced about the era's complacency. On the basis of the types and amounts of drugs and alcohol consumed in the fifties, it appears that Thorazine, like thermonuclear weapons and the Salk vaccine, hit the marketplace in the nick of time.

Patients in mental hospitals formed only part of the tranquilizer market, for the pressure to perform and conform in urban business and suburban leisure was difficult if not impossible for many people to bear. Businessmen were notorious pill poppers, grown children had doctors prescribe them for elderly parents who were not acting the way the children wanted them to, women took them with great regularity (one imagines for a variety of reasons), and teenagers took them as well.[11] "Life in growing suburbia, specifically in Englewood, New Jersey, is giving people ulcers, heart attacks and other 'tension-related psychosomatic disorders,'" one *New York Times* reporter wrote near the decade's close.[12] Anxiety flourished, psychiatry boomed, and alcoholism was rampant, especially among the families of businessmen and professionals who had found their lucrative niches. As more people earned more money, the percentage of drinkers skyrocketed.[13]

Although clearly tongue-in-cheek, the following want ad in the February 5, 1956, issue of the *New York Times* presents a grim picture of the price one paid for a key to the executive washroom: "Salesmgr: Intangible exp, must be able to move effectively at top mgmt level and effectively understand 'Big Business' problems. Should be able to handle 12 martinis."[14] The omnipresence of alcohol in corporate life was an open secret. When Frank Tashlin adapted George Axelrod's 1955 Broadway hit, *Will Success Spoil Rock Hunter* (1957), he dispensed with practically the entire play except for sexpot Rita Marlowe (Jayne Mansfield) and incessant drinking, moved its locus from the entertainment industry to the high-powered world of New York advertising, and spotlighted the man in the gray flannel suit in the form of Rufus (Henry Jones), the corporate cog who achieves his greatest success when he devises a line of alcohol-flavored cosmetics: Stay-Put Lipstick in martini, scotch, and Manischiewitz. Watching films from the 1950s, one often gets the sense that heavy drinking played a fundamental role in enabling daily life to be performed. In George Marshall's horserace comedy *Money from Home* (1953), even the nag gets drunk before the big race.

Anxiety wasn't confined to office buildings. Historian Reuel Denney, coauthor with David Reisman of the influential sociological study of late 1940s America, *The Lonely Crowd*, reported in 1953 that "self-vanishing is what ten-year-old children wanted most according to a recent survey." Denney understood this mass, wish-fulfilling disappearing act as a direct consequence of an impossibly constricted culture: Americans, he wrote, "feel themselves pressured into social conformity, so that it satisfies them to involve themselves in fantasies of beating the world by vanishing from it."[15]

The towering possibility of instant cremation by nuclear bombs was of course a factor in the public's perception of its own precariousness and was largely responsible for the pervasive sense of paranoia in the decade. The postwar years were a period of alternately rising and falling fear of mushroom clouds, and on the level of conscious awareness overt terror mostly took a downward trajectory. Historian Paul Boyer, author of *By the Bomb's Early Light*, has charted these hills and valleys and, not surprisingly, found that Americans' initial alarm in the year or two after we slaughtered the civilian populations of Hiroshima and Nagasaki gave way to a kind of neurotic resignation: "By the end of the 1940s, the cultural discourse had largely stopped. Americans now seemed not only ready to accept the bomb but to support any measures necessary to maintain atomic supremacy." According to Boyer, nuclear boosterism was able to supplant dread only because another dread was looming large: "Fear of the Russians had driven fear of the bomb into the deeper recesses of consciousness."[16]

In the 1950s, Americans transformed themselves from victors, aghast and terrified at the power they had unleashed, to paranoid crusaders bearing a hideous atomic torch. As his language demonstrates, Boyer understands this transformation to be a psychological maneuver, a matter of repression rather than resolution. As with any form of repression, this pressured burial of nuclear knowledge was periodically pricked by current events. When radioactive rain fell on Chicago in 1955, for example, the question of nuclear consequences found its way quickly back to consciousness. The same thing happened in 1959 when, damn it to hell, strontium-90 turned up in milk. These eruptions into consciousness were rude but intermittent, and yet the fear of mass death was *never* far from consciousness. Boyer quotes "What the Atomic Age Has Done to Us," a *New York Times Magazine* article from 1950, which opined that the bomb's "most important effects are those in the minds of men." As Boyer notes, "Those who died in Hiroshima and Nagasaki would surely not have agreed with this shift of emphasis from the reality of seared flesh and radiation-ridden corpses to the abstract realm of consciousness," but he acknowledges that the *Times* had a point. The article's author, Michael Amrine, argued that the fact that "civilization can perish attacks directly the belief almost unconsciously accepted by Western man: progress is inevitable." Because the idea of progress runs deep in the American psyche, the trauma of its destruction was especially bitter: "It is very difficult to judge the long-range effects of the largest piece of bad news the race has had since the fall of Rome."[17]

Boyer also mentions a timely 1948 self-help guide, *The Art of Staying Sane*:

Many people are already minor neurotics, worrying about the falling atom bomb. "When the atom bomb falls!" "When the atom bomb falls!" "When the atom bomb falls!" It echoes through living rooms and lecture halls and over bar tables and on the quiet beach like the tragic refrain of some chorus in a Greek tragedy."[18]

In 1945 the *Ladies' Home Journal* had predicted that nuclear arms would cause "a worldwide nervous breakdown." This is the sort of discourse that led to the neurotic Greek chorus period. But by 1950 an exemplary country western tune called "When the Hell Bomb Falls" "mingled images of nuclear destruction with the wish that God would 'lend a helping hand' in Korea." As historian of popular culture Charles Wolfe puts it, a future atomic holocaust was becoming "an inevitable, almost natural occurrence."[19]

Such surface complacency had fissures. And by seeing the cracks, one was invited to crack up—not to dismiss tension, but to acknowledge it. In 1952, the year in which the United States began testing atomic bombs in the atmosphere, the barely suppressed but naturalized terror of the bomb found comic expression in (of all places) that most conformist journal of the middle class, the *Reader's Digest*. Mrs. L. F. Van Hagen of Madison, Wisconsin, wrote the following yarn in one of the *Digest's* true-to-life humor columns, "Life in These United States":

> My son and his family, who live in California not far from the atomic-bomb testing grounds in Nevada, are becoming used to seeing a flash and some minutes later feeling the house rock. One night recently he woke from a sound sleep and asked, "What's that?" "Oh, go back to sleep," said his wife. "It's only an atomic bomb." My son settled back. "All right. I was afraid one of the kids had fallen out of bed."[20]

To this classical *Digest* family, atomic bombs are as much a part of everyday life as kids tumbling out of bed, yet their horrifying joke shows that they and any reader who found the anecdote even mildly amusing knew quite well that atomic bombs were dangerous and threatened their lives at all times. The joke's double punchline, delivered by Mom and Dad but appreciated as comedy by Grandma, depends on the self-evident contrast between two extremes: the bomb is next door and normal, yet the bomb, as everyone knew, could lay cities to waste in a matter of seconds and fry not only this particular family but, more devastatingly, the entire way of life promoted and exemplified by *Reader's Digest* and its many advertisers. The force of the joke, the sting of its failed complacency, comes from the family's strained naïveté regarding this nearby risk and from the ironic comparison of the enormity of the risk with the insignificance of a child's three-foot drop to the floor. In short, Dad's mild reaction contradicts his literally dreadful experience of American life.

A similar and just as subtly grisly joke appeared later in the decade in the *Saturday Evening Post*, which featured a weekly cartoon called "Hal Block's Inventions for a Better Tomorrow." On January 11, 1958, the drawing whimsically depicted an "atomic high chair for kids"; "no fall out" was the punchline. Here, too, the bomb's grotesque effect on children was the underlying comic point. Block's cartoon baby sits trapped in a sort of enclosed nucleus, its hands, legs, and head protruding like spokes from tiny holes, its face contorted in an amusing expression of sadness and irritation. The *Post's* cartoon message is more easily condensed than that of the *Digest*. Though the atomic high chair prevents "fall out," the joke comes from an essential contradiction—an atomic high chair might also prevent the baby.[21] Two weeks later, the *Post* brought this unstated contradiction into the realm of blunt consciousness in a feature story about an "atomic garbageman" who made a modern living through the collection and disposal of atomic waste. The article openly stated that overexposure to radiation (a hazard to which the cartoon child would necessarily have been subjected) would cause "sterility, blindness, or malignancies." Later, the article noted that "besides radioactive waste, the captain and his hearties cheerfully fetch and carry a variety of chemical leftovers, any of which could blast them into eternity."[22] Humor in the fifties was oftentimes not especially lighthearted.

Indeed, fifties comedy sometimes took on the tone of gallows humor. One must keep in mind that these magazine anecdotes are just compact comic expressions of the panicky "Watch the skies!" rhetoric of contemporary science fiction films in which, among other things, alien pods could drop from the heavens and change humans into emotionless vegetables, if not specifically due to atomic energy then at least as the result of nuclear age dream work and Cold War paranoia. Judging from the regularity with which popular movies and magazines reiterated the public's barely suppressed fear of radiation-induced mutation, death by instant immolation, or more generally— and therefore more terrifyingly—of the giant question mark of the nuclear future, it appears that worrying was not confined to isolated intellectuals but was rather more widespread.

The "learned-to-stop-worrying" version of life in the fifties weirdly ascribes blissful ignorance to the whole population. Was complacency really embraced by a nation of mindless bourgeois who were just too full of the fat of the land to notice what was happening to them? I don't think so. By discounting the not-so-hidden signals of popular dissent, signals which are every bit as confessional about the social world as, say, statistics on 4-H Club memberships and the hula-hoop craze, this view of the period distorts the 1950s beyond recognition. The fact that much of the population took great pains, not to mention tranquilizers and martinis, to suppress their incipient hysteria only shows that people knew a great deal more than they cared to.

Crazy Man Crazy

The *Oxford English Dictionary* defines *crazy* first as "full of cracks or flaws; damaged, impaired; liable to break or fall to pieces; 'shaky'"; then as "diseased" or "sickly"; and finally, in respect to the meaning most generally accepted in the United States, "insane, mad" and "demented."[23] In the 1950s, however, "crazy" came to mean "the best," "personally satisfying," "excellent," and "admirable."[24] Crazy had acquired a positive spin in the music world as early as 1927, and while it appeared throughout the 1930s and 1940s in the language of jazz and bop musicians, it didn't reach general usage until the 1950s.

Why large numbers of American teenagers latched so enthusiastically onto the word *crazy* as a description of their aspirations and joys is a complicated question best left to sociologists, but it is nonetheless worthwhile to note that the era witnessed meaningful changes in linguistic as well as pharmaceutical consumption.

In terms of the evolution of *crazy* as well as the ongoing spill of history, 1953 was a turning point in many ways. In January, Gen. Dwight David Eisenhower was inaugurated as president; three months later, he issued Executive Order 10450, which forced new government employees and government-related workers to undergo intensive loyalty investigations. "Any derogatory information, no matter what its source (always kept secret), was grounds for dismissal."[25] In June, Elizabeth II took the throne in London, the Rosenbergs were strapped to the electric chair and burned to death at Sing Sing, and the Korean War was terminated at Panmunjom. Later that summer, the Soviet Union revealed that it had built its own H-bomb, and the Central Intelligence Agency helped to overthrow the elected prime minister of Iran. The year 1953 also saw *crazy* making two appearances in popular music—one widely felt, the other taken more or less for granted. In the song "When Love Goes Wrong," written by Hoagy Carmichael and Harold Adamson for Howard Hawks's *Gentlemen Prefer Blondes*, a chorus of French and Algerian bystanders laud Marilyn Monroe and Jane Russell with cries of "Crazee! Crazee! Oui! Oui!" Of much greater musical significance as well as of greater impact on the English language, American young people began to articulate their position in the ongoing world drama by responding with their bodies as well as their money to rock 'n' roll—specifically to Bill Haley's hit single, "Crazy Man Crazy," the first rock 'n' roll song to rank on *Billboard*'s chart of best-selling records.[26]

Bill Haley and his Comets quickly gained a large following, significantly widening what had been a "minority audience" of rhythm and blues cultists and, in the process, broadening the more or less subversive appeal of black and black-based music. Such subversion did not go unnoticed. Major record companies much preferred to produce "cover" versions of songs that sounded too black for their comfort, and consequently record stations tended to fall into line by refusing to play the originals.[27] On a more analytical level, some observant people were seeing that teenage fans were responding to more far-reaching issues than a particular arrangement of chords and vocals. That claim had actually been spelled out three years earlier by David Reisman in an essay called "Listening to Popular Music," in which he commented on the teenage rhythm and blues fans' "rebelliousness," their "dissident attitudes towards competition and cooperation in our culture," and the tendency of the R&B minority "to polarize itself . . . from American culture generally." Rhythm and blues, from which rock 'n' roll derived in the early years of the decade, seemed to Reisman to be solidly bound to social and political ideas; his description is so direct that it deserves to be quoted at some length:

[These teenagers had] a sympathetic attitude or even preference for Negro musicians; an egalitarian attitude towards the roles, in love and work, of the two sexes; a more international outlook . . . ; an identification with disadvantaged groups . . . ; a dislike of pseudo-sexuality in music, even without any articulate awareness of being exploited; similarly a reaction against the stylized body image and limitations of physical self-expression which "sweet music" and its lyrics are felt as conveying; . . . a diffuse resentment of the image of the teenager provided by the mass media.[28]

In retrospect, the implications of Reisman's study are especially clear: what had begun as African-American music, the rebellious music of a defiant minority, was adopted first by a small group of alienated white teenagers and then, in a more watered-down form, by a huge segment of the white population which tended to identify—or wished to identify—with an oppositional culture that their own race actively continued to oppress. Given the overt schizophrenia of this mental maneuver alone, it is little wonder that *crazy* became a meaningful term of satisfaction and success.

By the mid-fifties, *crazy* had reached such levels of general acceptance that it entered the vocabulary of Madison Avenue with uses like "the crazy thing" about a new hi-fi or "the crazy new Kraft candy bar." It rapidly lost its rebellious appeal. But by that time, the attention of the more subversive consumers of popular art and culture had turned to other gratifying affronts—the amphetamine-ridden prose of Jack Kerouac, for instance. Referring to *On The Road*, published in 1957, Kerouac's biographer, Ann Charters, writes: "Once Kerouac had the idea about how to begin his narrative, he wanted to get right to work on the book. All he had to do when he got out of the hospital and back in the loft was pile up the benzedrine and sit down in front of the typewriter."[29] In *On the Road*, Kerouac has one character, Carlo Marx, tell the protagonist that drugs were the key to unlocking otherwise repressed ideas: "'Dean and I are embarked on a tremendous session together. We're trying to communicate with absolute honesty and absolute completeness everything on our minds. We've had to take benzedrine.'"[30]

Drugs weren't the only answer. You could just stare at Elvis Presley's phenomenal hips. Or at Jayne Mansfield's breasts. Or you could read Herbert Marcuse's *Eros and Civilization*, published in 1955. In this influential Freudian analysis of Western culture, Marcuse distinguished between basic repression, the necessary hindering of instincts so that civilization can be maintained, and "surplus-repression," the extensive "additional controls arising from the specific institutions of domination."[31] It was bad enough that at the peak of the Cold War the expatriate Marcuse was living in Massachusetts preaching Frankfurt School Marxism. To top it all off, his solution to the problem of surplus-repression was free love—Eros for everybody. Many of Marcuse's observations must have come as a shock to Americans of the mid-fifties. For instance, then as now, personal hygiene was a worry; you might be dressed for success, but you'd be nowheresville if you stank. Yet here is Marcuse on the liberating communism of BO:

[Smell and taste] relate (and separate) individuals immediately, without the generalized and conventionalized forms of consciousness, morality, aesthetics. Such immediacy is incompatible with the effectiveness of organized *domination*, with a society which 'tends to isolate people, to put distance between them, and to prevent spontaneous relationships.' . . . Their unrepressed development would eroticize the organism to such an extent that it would counteract the desexualization of the organism required by its social utilization as an instrument of labor.[32]

You didn't have to throw away your Mum to be free. You could just listen to Gene Vincent shouting "Be-Bop-A-Lula" over and over into a microphone. Or Screamin' Jay Hawkins and his 1956 song "I Put a Spell on You":

> Reputedly in a drunken stupor, the singer ranted and raved through the parts of the song he could remember, while equally drunk musicians laid down a beat as best they could. The performance had a compelling atmosphere, although the grunts and groans that originally began the record were wiped off when radio stations objected to their outrageous implications.[33]

Because Hawkins could not remember the recording session let alone his rendition of the song, he had to learn to sing the song again from the record, which eventually sold over a million copies. Hawkins was something of a comedian. A key facet of his act was his macabre comic persona—that of a black Vincent Price. Price himself was busily specializing in another type of black comedy in which two of the spectator's vicarious goals were to murder and be murdered. Following through on the Price/Roger Corman brand of popular amusement, Hawkins began opening his performances by emerging from a coffin.[34]

As in any period, humor in the 1950s was in the eyes and ears of the beholder. The coffins, pills, drinks, songs, breasts, and psychiatrists' couches that litter films of the period were not merely pervasive; they were, often deliberately, the sources of comic pleasure.

Hollywood Hysteria

Although writers like Jack Kerouac, singers like Screamin' Jay Hawkins, and actors like Jerry Lewis (*"le roi de crazy"*) owed their commercial success to a particularly strung-out zeitgeist, the use of psychological terms like *hysteria* and *schizophrenia* to describe popular culture of the 1950s has generally been limited to the so-called political witch hunts, perhaps in deference to that governing metaphor, and their effect not only upon the country at large but specifically upon Hollywood:

> (Michael Wilson): The degree of hysteria or fear or degradation depended on how close or how far away one was from Hollywood.[35]

> (Victor Navasky): Even before the blacklist, many members of the movie colony felt they were inhabitants of a political-cultural schizophrenia.[36]

> (Larry Ceplair and Steven Englund): The atmosphere of hysteria which HUAC utilized to sweep up the anonymous small fry from other industries and professions could not have been generated by a Congressional hearing which peered into the political past of, say, a "Harlan County Ten.[37]

These writers are describing a time of right-wing fanaticism and its effect upon American entertainment, but they also suggest that Hollywood—both the community and the industry, the place and the art—was by its nature susceptible to excessive emotional upheavals. One can no longer simply say that careers were ruined, trusts shattered, and ideas suppressed by the brutal congressional investigations, the concomitant blacklist and graylist, and the ensuing period of almost exclusively center-to-right politics. The passive voice does not accurately describe the very active role of the oppressors. But just as the urge to oppress and repress was not limited to specific people like

Martin Gang or Joseph McCarthy, nor institutions like the Federal Bureau of Investigation and the Congress, nor even to political categories like conservatives and corporate-liberals, hysteria was not confined to the witch hunts. Because the McCarthy era provided such extraordinarily sick political theater, historians have tended to find Hollywood blacklisting vastly more entertaining than Hollywood filmmaking during this period. After all, this was a time when Ginger Rogers' mother, Lila, was touted by one HUAC member as "one of the outstanding experts on communism in the United States."[38] No bit of movie dialogue could ever compare with that. Still, the shrillness of the period's overtly political discourse is only one element of a larger phenomenon. One look at Jerry Lewis "itching, twitching, and jerking" his way through Frank Tashlin's *Hollywood or Bust* (1956) is enough to prove, I think conclusively, that fifties hysteria had its roots not just in a surge of rabid anticommunism and not just in the threat of nuclear war, but in an extraordinarily powerful set of repressive systems intertwined with every strand of American life so thoroughly that it may itself be held to blame for both the nuclear threat and the right-wing extremism identified with the period.

The victims of the witch hunts had their hysteria thrust upon them, but the frenzy of the witch hunters and the delirium with which America built and tested nuclear warheads are the effects as much as the causes of generalized hysteria. The apparent symptoms of this warped hegemony take the form of witch-hunting and bomb-building on the most malevolent end of the spectrum, but one can also see the explosive popularity of rock 'n' roll and Jerry Lewis as benign symptoms of the same disorders. Indeed, it's not only tempting but practically unavoidable to see Lewis as nothing but a walking, babbling symptom of profound national insanity, but this is a topic that must be postponed until chapter 4. In any case, when we look back at the 1950s we see a culture of extreme neurosis and paranoia, an age that was defined by inner turmoil and external threat but that nonetheless never had the relaxing benefit of a full-fledged breakdown. Just as white teenagers responded to the often rough, always sexy sounds of black-inspired rock 'n' roll because it gave them a chance to dance away some nervous hormonal energy, so did audiences respond to Jerry Lewis, for here was someone whose anxieties were so excessive that they not only broke through the facade of the ordinary but virtually took control of his whole personality and caused him to physically convulse his way through the decade. Screamin' Jay Hawkins, too, was a product of his time as well as a means for his fans to mentally extract themselves from that time. Accordingly, one can see not only Lewis and Hawkins but a whole strain of disruptive fifties comedy not just as the product of a particular society but as a kind of therapeutic answer to it.

Before the Freudian age, doctors believed that hysteria was related to the movement of the uterus; hence its name. Freud, however, saw it not as a physiological phenomenon but as a psychological one. As J. Laplanche and J.-B. Pontalis put it, Freud "aligned himself with a whole current of opinion which saw hysteria as a 'malady through representation,'" an illness in which the symptom bears a specific though highly distorted resemblance to the cause. Laplanche and Pontalis go on to mention the greater importance hysteria played in the development of a wider theory of the mind—specifically, the theory that obsessed and informed American culture in the 1950s: "It was of course in the process of bringing the psychical etiology of hysteria to light that psychoanalysis made its principal discoveries: the unconscious, phantasy, defensive conflict and repression, identification, transference, etc."[39]

If hysteria is a malady through representation, a close look at Hollywood's comic representations of life should unearth a gold mine of symptoms. It may also show, as it clearly does with rock 'n' roll, that the symptom was itself a kind of therapeutic response to the underlying cause, a way for audiences to break out of the social, political, and sexual binds that by most accounts seem to have dominated their lives outside of the theater.

Psychoanalysis distinguishes between two types of hysteria—conversion hysteria and anxiety hysteria, the latter type characterized by phobias. Given the overtly phobic nature of much of fifties culture (its chief objects being communists, African-Americans, gay people, and mutants from outer space), it's not hard to see the connection between anxiety and hysteria during the period. But the former type, conversion hysteria, is if anything even more pervasive in Hollywood cinema of the fifties. As Laplanche and Pontalis put it, "Psychical conflict is expressed symbolically in somatic symptoms of the most varied kinds," not the least of which "may be paroxystic (e.g., emotional crises accompanied by theatricality)."[40] This may ring a bell with anyone who has ever seen a Douglas Sirk melodrama—say, for instance, *Written on the Wind* (1956), in which Dorothy Malone dances her father to death in a hysterical, quasi-jazz, quasi-rock 'n' roll paroxysm. To say that these "women's weepies" are hysterical and hilarious isn't to belittle them in the slightest; Sirk and his peers aimed at, and achieved, a high-pitched emotional state that hovers between melodrama and comedy—a space occupied by hysteria, the halfway acknowledgment of a repressed and disturbing truth.

For Sirk, this truth often has to do with the impossibility of fifties social constructs: racism in *Imitation of Life* (1959), family relationships in *Written on the Wind*, the suburbs in *All That Heaven Allows* (1955), and so on. Watching characters fall apart in a Sirk film can be refreshing. These moments represent on screen the shrill tensions of their era, and from the safe distance of almost half a century one can afford to laugh openly. But in *comedies* of the period, such safety was afforded by the narrative mode itself. After all, who takes comedy seriously? To put it another way, with melodramas audiences were encouraged to look at the world and break down. With comedies, they were asked to break up.

The Freudian Fifties

Retrospectively labeling the 1950s as "hysterical" flies in the face of the drearily deterministic tone of the traditional vision of complacency/naïveté/conformism in which the repressed, like Lefty, always fails to return. One can be smug when looking back on these years and see nothing but a nation held in thrall by an avuncular president and at bay by corporate expansion, but the vitality of the decade's artistic rebelliousness provides exactly the kind of messy contradiction that turns the social world into a carnival. Prominently featured on Hollywood's carnival midway was a new mode of satisfying rebellion: a proliferation of psychological, psychiatric, and specifically psychoanalytical rhetoric in films of the period. Nearly everyone has noticed the rise in the forties and early fifties of films in which psychiatry found positive popular expression, and psychiatry's impact on the cinema has been seen in any number of films that have little or nothing to do with actual psychotherapy. Peter Biskind cites *Spellbound* (1945), *The Locket* (1946), *Possessed* (1947), *Sleep, My Love* (1947), *The Snake Pit* (1948), *Home of the Brave* (1949), and others. Nora Sayre describes *Rebel Without A Cause, East of Eden* (1955), and *Tea and Sympathy* (1956) as bluntly "Freudian" because of their emasculated fathers and mixed-up sons. In their book *Psychiatry and the Cinema*, Krin Gabbard and Glen O. Gabbard are so impressed with Hollywood's positive portrayal of psychiatrists in the late 1950s and early 1960s that they dub it "the Golden Age of psychiatry"; they cite *The Three Faces of Eve* (1957), *Home Before Dark* (1958), *Anatomy of a Murder* (1959), and others.[41] More symptomatic is Janet Walker, who sweepingly derides Hollywood's representations of psychoanalysis and psychotherapy as "extremely crude," then goes on to analyze several of them so deftly and in such persuasive detail that they come off as anything *but* crude.[42]

Whatever one thinks of these films, whatever quality one sees in them, the central idea behind Hollywood's absorption with the rudiments of Freudian psychology is unmistakable. Psychoanalysis clearly distinguishes between two perceptual levels: the calm facade of everyday life is not only accompanied by *but actively opposed by* its darker underpinnings, the revelation of which was evidently gratifying in the postwar era. In "'Civilized' Sexuality and Modern Nervousness," Freud describes "neurotics" as a class of "naturally rebellious" people "with whom the pressure of cultural demands succeeds only in an apparent suppression of their instincts, one which becomes ever less and less effective." Not only were such rebellious characters *heavily* represented in Hollywood films of the time, but the fact that so many films used psychoanalytic rhetoric itself indicates a kind of rebellion on the part of popular art against normative "cultural demands."[43] Some films were more astute in their execution of this conflict than others, but the basic presuppositions of this particular narrative tension necessarily remained more or less the same in film after film as Hollywood endlessly reiterated the existence of an unconscious and its capacity to threaten everything and everybody. And if the accompanying mass faith in a simple Freudian cure seems naive, the equally mass belief in an underlying mass mental illness is particularly insistent.

Regardless of the degree of complexity with which individual films treated psychoanalytic concepts, most critics have tended to belittle their popularization. In what comes across as a misguided effort to rise above what they evidently see as an audience of dopes and vulgarians, critics haven't been able to hear what the sheer numbers of "Freudian" films resoundingly chant, namely that an unparalleled confession of national mental illness was occurring in theaters across America at precisely the moment when the economy was booming and everyone was supposed to be content. In marked contrast to previous periods, audiences of the late 1940s and 1950s seemed naturally to assume that the structures of psychoanalytic thought, originally developed toward the treatment of psychosis, neurosis, and perversion, now applied to their own quotidian lives—that dangerous and frightening secrets were lurking just below the surface. To the critics, though, it's just so much Hollywood hooey: "Naïveté and overstatement dominated many movies, which were drenched in floods of simplified Freudianism, and it appeared as though the wit and speed of the Thirties films had been unlearned, that the best grittiness of the social realism of the Forties was forgotten."[44]

There's that decade shuffle again. On one level, Hollywood did "unlearn" a few things here and there, the fine art of sexual censorship being one of the most liberating. But instead of being a matter of forgetting, it was a question of remembering what could no longer be repressed. Hollywood may have popularized psychology by turning it into entertainment for millions of people who never studied Freud, but it certainly didn't *create* the illusion that psychoanalysis was a quasi-religious tonic designed to soothe modern malaises. Philip Rieff, for instance, locates the seeds of Freud's popularity in Puritan New England rather than hedonistic Beverly Hills:

The most congenial climate for the training of the therapeutic has been in a waning ascetic culture like that of Protestant America. It is specially true of this Calvinist culture that it proved a breeding ground for remissive equivalents to the original ascetic motives in which the emphasis is on retraining for a fuller activity and not on the achievement of some new general meaning. . . . Freud taught lessons which Americans, prepared by their own national experience, learn easily: survive, resign yourself to living within your moral means, suffer no gratuitous failures in a futile search for ethical heights that no longer exist—if they ever did.[45]

The tonic's purely benign power was rather short-lived in Hollywood's Freudianism period. In *Spellbound,* one of the first films in the Freudian cycle of the 1940s and 1950s, it survives less than two hours before grave doubts creep in. By the end of that film, the cure is called radically into question when an apparently benevolent psychiatrist turns out to be a psychotic killer who commits suicide by pointing the gun directly at the audience—in a drastic point-of-view close-up—and pulling the trigger at everyone's head. Hollywood Freudianism is itself more conflicted than its detractors have ever admitted.

For the purposes of dramatic conflict, Hollywood's ambivalence was a frankly good thing, for in representing the war between the psyche and the social order as well as that of the ongoing battles within the psyche, Hollywood found in psychoanalysis the means by which to further complicate its already sophisticated narrative-generating apparatus. It ought to go without saying that ambivalence about psychoanalysis goes with the territory. On a mass level, though, the unconscious, when blown up to the size of the big screen, provided yet another way in which audiences could distinguish between various levels of meaning in any given character. Although we take it all for granted today, it is worth pointing out that audiences had already learned to distinguish between the star and his or her individual characters, between the present and the past through flashbacks, and between the supposedly objective camera's vision and an individual character's point of view. With the burst of psychoanalytic films, millions of moviegoers learned quickly to see that the obvious and up-front aspects of a given character might crumble into dust at any moment, with darker hidden elements taking their place. And they were asked to see *themselves* in these troubled characters—to identify with them and their mental illness.

For example, Joseph Mankiewicz's comedy-drama *All About Eve* doesn't dwell on psychoanalysis per se, but when kind, prim Eve Harrington (Anne Baxter) turns out to have trampled all over Margo Channing (Bette Davis) in a monomaniacal drive toward stardom, her transformation makes sense only by virtue of the character's implicit psychopathology. "Your name is not Eve Harrington. It's Gertrude Slojinsky," Addison DeWitt (George Sanders) declares in a comic revelation of her false facade, and he proceeds to describe in simplistic but no less logical terms the basis of her personality disorders: "a contempt for humanity [and] an inability to love and be loved" are the deficiencies that have made Eve/Gertrude what she is. By the way, the film's "Freudianism" was not lost on critic and future screenwriter Frank Nugent, who wrote admiringly that Mankiewicz "took a psychiatrist's view of the theater and introduced fascinated audiences to the Freudian compulsions which drive and beset the dedicated disciples of the stage."[46]

Even in its most superficial form, psychoanalysis set the stage for what in retrospect appears to be a widespread assumption that fictional heroes could be (and were almost necessarily) deeply unbalanced. Screen protagonists, like musical ones, no longer had to appear constitutionally stable in order to generate a following, and indeed the opposite may have been the case. The major figures of rock 'n' roll certainly didn't radiate stability by gyrating, moaning, and screaming nonsense syllables into the microphone, and the spirit of the times enabled even a relatively bland performer like Johnnie Ray to cause an empathic stir in 1951 by spastically weeping while singing "Little White Cloud That Cried." As *Melody Maker* put it at the time: "Johnnie Ray, a 25-year-old Oregon-born vocalist, has jumped from the $90 to $2,000 bracket by hitting on the excruciating formula of virtually breaking into tears while singing a song. . . . If an artist has to descend to this level to capture the masses, then the outlook for popular music is bleak indeed."[47]

When one looks at fifties film stars, too, one sees overwhelming psychic tensions built into *and exposed by* their personae. As stars, James Dean, Marilyn Monroe, Montgomery Clift, and Marlon Brando are fundamentally unlike, say, Lillian Gish, in whom the tension between virginity and sexual energy runs rampant but remains suppressed and seemingly beyond her characters' comprehension.[48] Closer to the period, not to mention the gender, are the big male stars of the 1940s—Tyrone Power, Errol Flynn, John Garfield, and Henry Fonda, to name a few, yet in certain ways they are as remote from the new breed of fifties neurotics as Gish was. All of them, Gish included, convey a psychological complexity that goes beyond individual characters and their foibles, but they still maintain an inherent stability. Stars of the fifties, in contrast, tended not only to make their characters' anxieties overt but also to incorporate their own interior tensions into their screen personae and publicize themselves as such. They could do so, in part, because audiences were being simultaneously exposed to many crude and not-so-crude depictions of the same "Freudian" psychological conflicts.

Sexual Subversion

In part because of this foregrounding of neurosis, the focus of screen politics changed thoroughly during the 1950s. One can see a stark difference in attitudes about the political assumptions on which Hollywood operated by contrasting what two prominent cultural figures had to say about the morality of the silver screen, a kind of before-and-after picture of the movies. In 1948 novelist Ayn Rand provided what has since turned out to be one of the crudest expressions of the radical right's censoring reflex, no small achievement considering how extensive political censorship was at the time. In a pamphlet put out by the Motion Picture Alliance (a handy volume with arresting chapter headings like "Don't Smear the Free Enterprise System," "Don't Glorify the Collective," "Don't Deify the Common Man," "Don't Smear Success," and "Don't Smear Industrialists"), the following rules of thumb—penned by Rand—appeared:

All too often, industrialists, bankers, and businessmen are presented on the screen as villains, crooks, chiselers, or exploiters. It is the *moral* (not just political but *moral*) duty of every decent man in the motion picture industry to throw into the ashcan, where it belongs, every story that smears industrialists as such. . . . It is the Communists' intention to make people think that personal success is somehow achieved at the expense of others and that every successful man has hurt somebody by becoming successful.[49]

By 1960, however, Bob Hope saw subversion on an altogether different plane: "Our big pictures this year have had some intriguing themes—sex, perversion, adultery, and cannibalism. We'll get those kids away from their TV sets yet!"[50]

The repressed did return during the fifties, and it returned with a vengeance—but not in the form American leftists have been looking for ever since. Perhaps because of the objectivity afforded by cultural distance, French and British leftist critics have typically been better able to perceive and appreciate the tensions of Hollywood films of the fifties than Americans have been. Whereas Biskind and Sayre focus their studies on overt political suppression, *Screen* critics (and their American followers) have centered particularly on the inherent contradictions in Hollywood's representations of sex and gender. Battles in film criticism aside, however, the period itself featured open defiance. Howard Hawks effectively tossed Rand's dicta into his own trash can in 1952 and 1953 and made industrialists out to be decrepit buffoons (not to mention villains, crooks, chiselers, and exploiters) in his two fifties comedies, *Monkey Business* (1952) and *Gentlemen Prefer Blondes*. In 1950, Billy Wilder showed wealthy landowner Norma Desmond corrupting and then killing impoverished young William Holden in *Sunset Boulevard*, and he followed suit in *Some Like It Hot* by characterizing the Mafia as a typical American corporation. And in 1956, Frank Tashlin specifically depicted recording industry executives as disreputable thugs with criminal records in *The Girl Can't Help It*. For the moment, however, one need only note that sexual rather than economic subversion became so overt during the decade that by 1960 one of the country's leading comedians could recite his list of outrageous "themes," knowing that they were precisely what fifties Hollywood had led up to.

The question is not one of simply labeling all of the decade's films as sex-ridden and rebellious. Some weren't. It would be just as foolish to wrap up the whole of the 1950s with pithy descriptive categories like "sexually subversive" as it is to proclaim the thirties the decade of wit and speed and the forties the time of grit. According to *Film Daily Yearbook*, a total of 2,949 American feature films were produced and released between January 1, 1950, and December 31, 1959. One could scarcely generalize about these films' one or two overriding characteristics with any accuracy whatsoever. Nor is it any more sound to say that the fifties saw the rise of an all-new comedy genre. In *Pursuits of Happiness*, film critic and philosopher Stanley Cavell takes several comedies of the 1930s and early 1940s and uses them to proclaim the birth of "comedies of remarriage." Cavell's observations are astute and often brilliant, but there is no new genre there. One could just as easily claim on the basis of the relatively few films discussed in this book that the 1950s generated a brand new category, "comedies of hysteria and fanatical discontent." It didn't. Scholars looking for the next new genre will not find it here.[51]

Still, sex played well during the 1950s. It sold. Anticommunist censors effectively squelched the possibility of Hollywood films that could explicitly attack the ideology of capitalistic growth and corporate control, but producers and directors were increasingly bold as far as the sexual content of films was concerned. In this light, crazy 1953 was the beginning of the end of sexual repression in Hollywood cinema. The end, of course, has never been reached; far from it. Sex scenes may be de rigueur, but when was the last time you saw two men or two women getting it on in a Hollywood film? Nevertheless, the fact remains that Hollywood's self-censorship system received a forcibly administered premonition of its own demise in the same year in which the Rosenbergs were electrocuted, for it was then that Otto Preminger decided to release *The Moon Is Blue*—a sex comedy— without the Breen Office's seal. While there would continue to be challenges and counterchallenges back and forth between the Breen Office and Preminger and others until the early 1960s, it was the

1950s that both witnessed and caused the de facto collapse of a certain kind of political suppression. If Hollywood was not explicitly testing America's economics, it was most definitely pushing sexual revolution further than it had been allowed to be pushed since the heyday of the Production Code Administration, which cranked itself up in 1934, a key year for the witty, speedy, and elegantly effervescent thirties.

In too many ways, the legacy of the 1950s is harsh and demoralizing. The CIA engineered yet another coup against an elected head of state (this time in Guatemala). As a result of Executive Order 10450, from nine hundred to one thousand gay men and lesbians were either fired or forced to resign from the State Department because of what the government called their "perversion." The U.S. Information Service banned *Walden* from its libraries because it conflicted too obviously with our way of life. And government harassment forced Charlie Chaplin into exile.[52] But all was not completely bleak, especially if one happened to be in a theater showing the latest Frank Tashlin movie. Looking back on it, the radioactive cloud of fifties hysteria appears to have had a silver lining, not to mention a good amount of sexual fallout.

Object Choices

Comedy—all comedy, from any period—takes a subject or several subjects and makes fun of it, uses it as a target, aims at it. Since the social world comes under deliberate attack in comedies, most strongly in satires, the target exists within the individual audience member as he or she sits in a theater and watches the screen, and yet it also exists at one remove from the spectator, who can watch the screen's representation of society from a safe distance, the position of a seemingly disinterested third party. Audiences at comedies are receptive, at least in theory, to seeing their world turned upside down and mocked because they assume—wrongly, I think—that they have nothing to lose but the price of a ticket.

When producers and distributors say that a film is aimed at an audience, they refer to the audience's pockets, but their attack is only the monetary form of a more diffuse kind of aiming that includes as targets the morals, ideas, and convictions that an audience brings to the theater. Unlike money, mental activity isn't surrendered at the ticket booth, even if that's what certain customers claim to want from their entertainment. Film reviewers, for instance, like to describe comedies—particularly broad summertime comedies—as "mindless," whereas they rarely talk about mindless melodramas or thrillers. But laughter is a profoundly mental exercise. There is never anything mindless about comedy.

In terms of an audience's conscious convictions, some remain intact at the end of the film, but some may not—at least not in the same form they had during the previews of coming attractions. This cultural transaction goes well beyond the director's intent. It depends on a society's receptivity to ideas and the form those ideas may take; it depends on the gratifications and fears of a given social moment; it depends on the greater workings of the world outside the theater. As a result of this cultural economy, films subtly but inevitably invest in their viewers ideas that may critique the social world or even directly anticipate social change but which, if they were to be stated explicitly outside of a fictional setting, would be met with a great deal more resistance. This process is especially—and literally—critical in a period of organized repression like the 1950s. In short, the sixties started at least ten years earlier.

In the darkness of theaters in the 1950s, audiences watched what could be described as extended dramatic jokes.* Not purely verbal, not purely visual, film comedy can be found in situations (a comic predicament, like Ginger Rogers' Edwina Fulton, in *Monkey Business*, holding an infant clad in a diaper and assuming without hesita-

---

*Freud distinguished between "jokes" and "the comic," but in the present analysis the distinction isn't terribly crucial. First for Freud, "the comic" could occur anywhere—on the street as much as in a theater. Second, many of the examples Freud uses for "jokes" were jokes that had been told to him informally—in conversation rather than from literature or from under a proscenium arch. Neither of these open-ended situations pertains directly to the movies, where nearly every detail is staged (or at least deemed acceptable for a final cut) and where "jokes" and "the comic" are thoroughly intertwined in dramatic form.

tion that he is her husband); in dialogue (Cary Grant's Barnaby Fulton describing youth as "a series of low comedy disasters"); or in physical gesture (Barnaby flying down a laundry chute and slamming his head against a wall). In each case, comedy lies in the expressive technique of the film joke, for the substance of any joke resides not in its content (which could be rewritten and reshot in such a way as to remove all traces of humor) but in the expression which the content has been given. As Freud had it, if this technique "is replaced by something else, the character and effect of the joke disappear."[53] In this particular study of comedy then, the emphasis will be on expressive details, the specifics that make the jokes funny.

Movies present a world of vicarious thrills, and one of the best reasons to study them is to try and see what kind of thrills people sought in a given period. In comedies, such fantasies bear the images of a society reflected in a fun-house mirror. The most dangerous elements of the fantasies may escape official censure by appearing stupid, exaggerated, and artificial. Comedy is certainly not the only kind of film to tap into unconscious fears and desires. The horror and science fiction genres both hinge upon manifestations of the repressed, and, like comedies, they both offer social critiques whether their directors mean them to or not. One might argue that comedies must obey the laws of the real world more than films about monsters and flying saucers, but this isn't always the case. A dog drives a car in *Hollywood or Bust*, a monkey invents a fountain-of-youth drug in *Monkey Business*, a corpse narrates the events that lead to his death in *Sunset Boulevard*, and everyone around them believes, quite idiotically, that Jack Lemmon and Tony Curtis are actually women in *Some Like It Hot*. Believability is not the issue as much as the fact that comedies, unlike horror and science fiction films, generally don't create monsters as a means of expressing human dissatisfaction. *Ghostbusters* (1984) actually does create comic monsters, the most preposterous of which is a pernicious marshmallow that stalks New York City; whether this mammoth phantasm is an expression of human discomfort in the Reagan years is a question better left to future critics.

Melodramas, like comedies, also criticize the foundations of society, as do crime films and many westerns, but these films' sources of pleasure are not as easily pinpointed as they are in comedies, where one can cite comic moments as being pleasurable to the extent that they cause or at least invite laughter and elation. Again, this distinction is blurred in fifties melodramas. One may be elated when watching Rock Hudson restore Jane Wyman's eyesight in Sirk's *Magnificent Obsession* (1954). The whole melodrama is certainly delightful. But people who describe their reaction as delight would most likely smile when they said it.

Only the stuffiest spectator would complain, when watching *Monkey Business*, that husbands and wives shouldn't splatter paint on each other and then viciously beat each other with the brushes. Such a person would be unable to find the sequence in question very funny. And if the image of Cary Grant speeding down a laundry chute were enough to trigger the violent return of some wretched and painful event from childhood, it would probably ruin your evening. But because all the films detailed in the following chapters stand in a deliberately defiant relation to standards of real-life propriety in the 1950s and, more subtly, that they depend upon an ambiguous but undeniably powerful relation to repression, they can be seen as dramatic extensions of what Freud called "tendentious jokes," jokes with a purpose, and the risks they took were often taken against the very people who paid to enjoy them. For Freud, tendentious jokes are therapeutic:

> The repressive activity of civilization brings it about that primary possibilities of enjoyment, which have now, however, been repudiated by the censorship in us, are lost to us. But to the human psyche all renunciation is exceedingly difficult, and so we find that tendentious jokes provide a means of undoing the renunciation and retrieving what was lost.[54]

Hostile jokes in particular are always a lot of fun:

> We are now prepared to realize the part played by jokes in hostile

aggressiveness. A joke will allow us to exploit something ridiculous in our enemy which we could not, on account of obstacles in the way, bring forward openly or consciously; once again, then, the joke *will evade restrictions and open sources of pleasure that have become inaccessible.*[55]

In a period of extraordinary surplus repression like the 1950s, when certain sources of pleasure were rendered especially inaccessible, comedy was absolutely critical.

Hollywood and Bust

Take, for instance, big breasts. The 1950s were obsessive on the subject. As Jane and Michael Stern observe in *The Encyclopedia of Bad Taste* (under the entry "Breasts, Enormous"), "one of the hallmarks of fifties culture was its fascination with so many things grown abnormally huge, from superwide CinemaScope movies and giant mutant monsters (*Them! Attack of the Fifty-Foot Woman*) to bloated, finned Cadillacs (which featured bosomlike protruding front ends)." As the Sterns note, "Whopping hooters were not a prerequisite for a woman who aspired to stardom," but in the 1950s a big bosom didn't hurt. They cite Jayne Mansfield's celebrity, Jane Russell's continuing appeal, the publication of *Playboy* in 1953, Russ Meyer's first film, *The Immoral Mr. Teas* (1959), and the wildly successful 1959 launch of Barbie, the plastic teen idol who not only has breasts but whose breasts are especially pert. As the Sterns helpfully note, Barbie's breast measurement works out proportionally to be the equivalent of 39 inches.[56]

What makes the fifties so fascinating are not only its excesses and foibles but the way in which it dealt with those excesses and foibles. Breast-bumpered Cadillacs are a fine example. The Sterns, being funny and astute cultural observers, look at the front of a 1957 Cadillac El Dorado Brougham and see two hilarious chrome and rubber-tipped breasts, but remarkably, *so did commentators in the 1950s.* Referring to the infamous "Dagmar" front bumpers, one automobile magazine editor joked at the time, "True, they have rubber tips, but they still amount to the most lethal pair of nursing bottles the poor young Chevrolet in the parking lot can ever encounter."[57]

This is the 1950s attitude toward women's breasts in a nutshell. They were big, they were comical, they required euphemisms, and they were simultaneously objects of desire and threat. This desire was seemingly never fulfilled, nor was the threat ever fully acted out and resolved, and as a result the fifties never tired of big breasts and big breast jokes. In her study of cross-dressing, Marjorie Garber notes the extraordinary popularity of Milton ("Mr. Television") Berle in the postwar era. Drag was a staple of Berle's comedy; as the *New York Times* put it, "He was a man who wasn't afraid of a dress."[58] But to put perhaps too fine a point on it, he was a man who wasn't afraid to strap on a couple of big breasts. Thus Berle took the era's mammary fixation to at least as ridiculous and, yes, as hysterical a level than anyone who had real breasts could—with the notable exception of Jayne Mansfield.

Women have tended to react badly to the era's breast fetish, and to a certain extent no one can blame them. There is a frankly repulsive element of hostile aggression directed at women and women's bodies in the 1950s. Frank Tashlin, who I tend to treat as a cultural critic, is nonetheless as fully implicated in the commercial capitalization of women's bodies as any other Hollywood director of the period. But by foregrounding the spectacular nature of these images, by defining female display in such overstated terms, Tashlin blends capitalization with ironic commentary. In this way, Tashlin might be seen as an artistic forebear of Russ Meyer. In any case, consider Tashlin's own doublespeak on the subject:

> The immaturity of the American Male—this breast fetish. You can't sell tires without breasts. Imagine a statue with breasts like Mansfield's. Imagine *that* in marble. We don't like big feet or big ears, but we make an idol of a woman because she's deformed in the breasts. There's nothin' more hysterical to me than big-breasted women—like walking leaning towers.[59]

In this passage, Tashlin reverses his usual order of business by turning critical commentary into a joke. "Deformed in the breasts"? Tashlin's contempt couldn't be more direct. But if I can drag Freud back in for a moment, the *effect* of Tashlin's on-screen breast jokes becomes not only clearer but more pleasurable. For Freud, comedy allows us "to exploit something ridiculous in our enemy which we could not, on account of obstacles in the way, bring forward openly or consciously." And much feminist film criticism to the contrary, the enemy here is not (or not only) women. The enemy is sexual repression—not just of civilization in general but of American culture in particular, the enforced clamp on sexual desire that has resulted in a nation of objectified women and infantile men, not only on screen but (I believe) in actual fact.

I hope to bring this idea out more clearly in the following chapters. But for the present, I want to note that breasts were not only the objects of comic pleasure for television and film audiences as well as the objects of masturbatory pleasure for readers of *Playboy* and the other skin mags that followed. They were also the objects of study for postwar psychoanalysts. In 1946, for instance, B. D. Lewin introduced the concept of the "dream screen." Lewin's theory holds that "every dream is said to be projected onto a blank screen, generally unperceived by the dreamer, which symbolizes the mother's breast as hallucinated by the infant during the sleep which follows feeding."[60] I hope that it is already clear that the dream screen concept is of highly suggestive value to the culture of the 1950s, a time when the silver screen was itself largely and literally filled by images of gigantic breasts.

The relationship between psychoanalysis and Hollywood cinema is especially emphatic when one considers the psychoanalytic thrust of the era's films. On-screen as well as in real analytic practice, Freud and Freudians dominated, with a consequent emphasis on Oedipal trauma as the defining passage in human psychic development. But the postwar era also spurred the continuing rise and limited popularization of object relations theory, which focused interest on infant psychology, in particular on the relation between baby and mother. Helene Deutsch, Karen Horney, and Melanie Klein had already shifted psychoanalytic thinking toward maternal dynamics. For instance, Deutsch's two-volume *The Psychology of Women* (1944–45) discusses (among other things) the sense of psychic unity that binds mother and baby as well as the alternate feelings of nurturing and hostility engendered in the breast-feeding mother. Klein and, later, D. W. Winnicott provided detailed insights into the conflicting feelings of babies toward mothers, an ambivalence that film theorist Gaylyn Studlar draws out in her provocative study of masochism and cinematic pleasure. Again, later chapters will explore Studlar's ideas as they pertain to comedies of the 1950s, but for the moment I would like only to note the similarity between this ambivalence and the conflict that fifties culture voiced, oftentimes quite shrilly, in its diametrically opposed visions of Mom.

If asked to describe how American culture depicted mothers in the 1950s, most Americans, I suspect, would respond by naming June Cleaver, the unflappable cake-baking protectress in the television series *Leave It to Beaver* (1957–1963). But June tells only half the story, if that. The decade of the fifties was a period of extraordinary, equally exaggerated hostility to mothers and motherhood, a trend that had begun earnestly a decade earlier with the publication of Philip Wylie's *Generation of Vipers* in 1942. Wylie took a dim view of American "Momism," which he decried in his wildly popular book as a vicious plot by American wives to dominate their husbands and emasculate their sons. "I give you Mom," Wylie concluded with a flourish. "I give you the destroying mother. I give you Medusa."[61]

As the postwar baby boom boomed, so did American culture's elastic ambivalence about Mom. There were emotionally constricted mothers (*The Man Who Knew Too Much*, 1956; *Peyton Place*, 1957; *Auntie Mame*, 1958); batty or oblivious mothers (a Hitchcock specialty: *Strangers on a Train*, 1951; *North by Northwest*, 1959); vicious, morally decrepit mothers (*The Goddess*, 1958; *Suddenly, Last Summer*, 1959); pathetic mothers (*Magnificent Obsession*, 1954; *Rebel Without a Cause*, 1955); incompetent and blameworthy mothers (*My Son John*, 1952; *The Bad Seed*, 1956); and even more. Norman Bates's infamous maternal introject didn't just come out of thin air in 1960.

Cultural historian Michael Rogin argues that motherhood in the 1950s found its demonic Other in communism, and vice versa, and that as a direct consequence of this demonology the lines between the two began to blur:

> American history in each countersubversive moment has constituted itself in binary opposition to the subversive force that threatened it. Demonology begins as a rigid insistence on difference. That insistence has strategic propaganda purposes, but it also derives from fears of and forbidden desires for identity with the excluded object. In counter-subversive discourse, therefore, the opposition breaks down. Its cultural and political productions register the collapse of demonological polarities in a return of the politically and psychologically repressed.[62]

I will argue throughout this book that comedy not only allowed the repressed to return during the 1950s but actively encouraged it for the express purpose of inducing an otherwise denied pleasure. From *Monkey Business* to *Will Success Spoil Rock Hunter?* the films discussed in the following chapters are therefore anything but countersubversive. It may or may not be coincidental that there are precious few mothers in these comedies. But for the time being, I would only like to note Rogin's observations on motherhood and, by logical extension, of womanhood in the era:

> Just as the free man was the polar opposite of the subversive in society, the subversive's opposite in the family was the mother. But just as the boundary between the free man and the state was a permeable one, so also the line dividing mothers from Communism proved to be no iron curtain.[63]

All of this is simply to say that sex, gender, politics, economics, and art were all stewing together on the modern electric range of the 1950s, and that certain comedies not only brought these tensions and contradictions out into the open but specifically brought them into the gratifying glare of hilarity. Rogin may be generally correct when he writes that postwar domestic ideology "attacked female sexual aggression," but this was not always the case in film comedy, where the appearance of a pair of huge breasts was itself enough to generate peals of hysterical laughter. In fact, in fifties comedies female sexual aggression (which is admittedly often couched in sexual-aggression-despite-itself terms—in other words, the "dumb blonde" phenomenon) can be openly celebrated.

In a number of fifties comedies, both men and women are invited to regress to infancy and even beyond—not only to babies but sometimes to baby monkeys. And in comedy, as in psychotherapy, regression is a good first step on the road to mental health. As Marcuse wrote in 1955: "The psychoanalytic liberation of memory explodes the rationality of the repressed individual. As cognition gives way to re-cognition, the forbidden images and impulses of childhood begin to tell the truth that reason denies. Regression assumes a progressive function."[64] Through regression, and regressive laugh riots on the dream screen, we are invited to reengage truthfully with our deepest, most solemnly buried selves. It's a fun-filled submission to the biggest, scariest, and yet most nurturing breasts you ever saw. If the decade of the fifties was a period of conflicted Momism, then Hollywood comedies must be the mother of us all.

one

HOWARD HAWKS AND THE COMEDY OF FRUSTRATION

Regressing: The World of *Monkey Business*

Bonzo and His Friends

Monkeys, babies, beautiful blondes, money, and cruelty were enormously popular subjects for humor and entertainment in the early 1950s. To the men, women, and children who found themselves embroiled in life in these United States, they crystallized the peculiar pleasures of the era. Here is how critic Erik Barnouw describes what was on television in 1952:

> Bishop Fulton J. Sheen was pitted in a weekly series against Milton Berle and his Texaco program. (Berle quipped: "We both work for the same boss, Sky Chief.") Violent roller-skating derbies were winning a vogue. The wrestler Gorgeous George, with marcelled hair, made periodic appearances. . . . Jackie Gleason had become a bus driver in *The Honeymooners*. Dr. Frances Horwich talked to pre-school children on *Ding Dong Schoolhouse*. . . . Children sat spellbound by ancient cartoons and westerns. Politicians came when they could: televised crime hearings had made a national figure out of U.S. Senator Estes Kefauver of Tennessee. The *Today* series began, partly

newscast and partly variety show; its purpose at first baffled reviewers, and it won neither audience nor sponsor until the arrival of J.
Fred Muggs, a baby chimpanzee owned by two former NBC pages.
A *Today* staff member saw him waiting for an elevator while sucking
formula from a plastic bottle.[1]

J. Fred Muggs touched a sympathetic nerve all across the country:
people related to him. Advertisers sought his endorsements. Starlets
posed for pictures with him. He christened ships and was once a guest
in a Florida hotel that refused to rent rooms to African-Americans.
Muggs received proposals of marriage from women who evidently
saw him as an ideal fifties mate. And in a triumphant appearance in
Central Park, J. Fred Muggs proclaimed himself to the country as its
model citizen as the guest of honor in a patriotic "I Am An American Day" rally.[2]

Fred wasn't alone. In *My Friend Irma Goes West* (1950), Jerry Lewis
plays a number of scenes with a chimpanzee. And as every Democrat
of the 1980s well remembers (in spirit if not in personal experience),
Ronald Reagan had a chimp child in *Bedtime for Bonzo* (1951). Bonzo
walked away with a sequel deal for *Bonzo Goes to College* (1952),
though Reagan had had enough. Here as elsewhere, it is tempting to
generalize about the psychocultural need expressed by Americans'
fascination with an adorable monkey movie star, especially when the
human star nurses the chimp, as Reagan did, from a baby bottle. But
whatever Bonzo was, he was clearly not an aberration. This was the
tenor of the times.

As a way of approaching fifties film comedies, in particular *Monkey
Business* (1952), a film about violent regression, it might be best to
begin by lurching backward—to 1949, the year of director George
Sherman's musical comedy, *Yes, Sir, That's My Baby*. Starring Donald
O'Connor, Gloria De Haven, and Charles Coburn, *Yes, Sir, That's
My Baby* provides a handy starting point for a discussion of *Monkey
Business*: both films are comedies about babies, both compare men to
infants, both take place in the world of the intellectual, and both use
Coburn as a comic representation of aging and deterioration.

While *Monkey Business* is more or less consistent in tone and coherent in structure, *Yes, Sir, That's My Baby* is quite the opposite. Its treatment of most of the questions it raises is confused, its artistic merits questionable. Unlike *Monkey Business*, *Yes, Sir, That's My Baby* is naive in content and uneven in execution, but two moments in the beginning of the film are purely horrifying as imitations of life in baby-booming postwar America. First, O'Connor mistakes an alarm clock for his own son, cuddles it, then puts the real baby on the bed and tries to smother it with a pillow. In the following scene, O'Connor picks up the innocent tyke, an infant still in his crib, and smacks him in frustration and anger. This brutal, impulsive act appalls De Haven, who counters by claiming on the authority of unnamed "psychologists" that parents should avoid physical contact with their babies altogether.

Yes, Sir, That's My Baby is the story of a group of GI Bill students attending a university presided over (thematically if not administratively) by a male biology professor (Coburn) and a female psychology professor (Barbara Brown). As Thomas M. Pryor dourly explained in the *New York Times*, the film "represents a sorry attempt to make something bright and funny out of the family problems of a group of young war veterans completing their college education," a topic apparently too grim for humor.[3] The dramatic conflict and its ideological message are both fairly blunt. Coburn tells his students, "Babies or no babies, biology must go on, if we are to have more babies." Meanwhile, the protofeminist travesty, Professor Boland (who dresses in a series of mannish tailored suits) lectures psychology students on the "eternal vigilance" necessary to keep women safe from male domination.

Yes, Sir, That's My Baby is a battle-of-the-sexes story, with baby Boopkins caught in the middle of the war breaking out on the homefront. Gender and infancy jokes abound. Coburn, through the machinations of a forced gag involving the drinking of rubbing alcohol, ends up drinking out of a baby's bottle, surely one of the most suggestive of the great postwar American cultural icons. Moreover, O'Connor's football team buddies sing a song about how they "never figured out a woman" and in the process compare and contrast a woman to more easily understood contraptions—"a washer," "a heater," and "a gadget." De Haven sings that "men are fine" but compares them nevertheless to spoiled brats, with faulty parallelism adding at least one level of unintentional irony: "They'll be like a brother if you treat them like a mother."

Yes, Sir, That's My Baby resolves itself through the intimation of a romantic attachment developing between the two professors, but it is only the female who yields her ground, ultimately being forced to admit that "the girls made me realize what a vicious, meddlesome old woman I've become." Her lovely feminine instincts return, Coburn is charmed, and tiny Boopkins acts as the procreated catalyst toward the restoration of order, which takes the form of a return to traditional gender roles.

The disruption of these roles by historical change—the GI Bill enabling working-class men with families to get a college education, a broadened awareness of a nascent women's rights movement seen here in parody form, the increasing availability of household appliances designed (at least in advertising rhetoric) to free women from tiring and time-consuming household chores—provides the focus of *Yes, Sir, That's My Baby*'s comedy. But only the first of these three retains the film's endorsement by the end. World War II had brought women into the nation's factories and offices in unprecedented ways, let alone numbers, and while the war's end caused a temporary retreat as ex-soldiers returned to work and displaced the newly skilled women, the social tensions wrought by these gender redefinitions continued. *Yes, Sir, That's My Baby*'s comedy has a clear terminus: the restoration of male supremacy. Having won the war against the Nazis and the Imperial Japanese, these ex-soldiers must fight at home—and win.

For instance, while O'Connor and his pals are able to sing and dance through an expansive, multilevel laundromat set, the film forces Professor Boland to severely restrict her ideas about the oppression of women—in other words, to denounce herself and her profession as frauds. Within the terms of the film, this denial of a woman's ideas is not only desirable; it's demanded. This film hinges on a conflict between three sets of overlapping oppositions—male versus female, biology versus psychology, "natural" drives versus "unnatural" thinking. By the end, the embodiment of the film's anxieties—a woman dressed like a man—surrenders by declaring her own monstrosity. Resolution thus means restoration, for in order for the comedy of *Yes, Sir, That's My Baby* to end, the cause of the rupture must conform to a traditional role—the benign nurturing mother figure. Sure enough, the chastened lady professor arrives at the end to babysit for little Boopkins.

Another Kind of Fun

In Howard Hawks's films, things tend to work out differently. Referring to Hollywood's ideological conventions, particularly to the heterosexually resolved and coupled heroes and heroines whose marital unions close off countless films, Robin Wood describes Hawks as offering a challenge:

> The strength and conviction of such generic resolutions, however, are everywhere undermined by the pervasive sense of impermanence that characterizes Hawks's world. This conflict sometimes produces flaws in the films' narrative coherence, a danger that even *Rio Bravo* (still in my opinion Hawks's masterpiece, the definitive elaboration of his 'world') does not escape. The final John Wayne/Angie Dickinson scene in that film is curiously redundant: the tension it appears to be resolving was resolved much earlier in the film. What the logic of the narrative demands is a further *development* of the relationship; Hawks, unable to imagine this, produces only repetition.[4]

One might argue with Wood's premises—that narrative logic means narrative *development* and that disruptions in this schema are "flaws"— but his analysis of the distinct lack of security in Hawks's world is provocative in that it locates Hawks's lack of conviction structurally in narrative reiteration. In Wood's view, *Rio Bravo* (1959) reaches a conclusion imposed by generic expectation, but it reaches it too soon. Forced to elaborate on a situation in conflict with his sense of civilization's overriding precariousness, Hawks could only spin his wheels. Whether intentionally or unconsciously (or, as is most likely, a mix of both), Hawks habitually pointed out certain impasses—narrative moments that subvert much more than the linearity of the story at hand.

In Hawks's adventure films, the sexual drama may end too early, as in *Rio Bravo*, but it may also end with a subtle but provocative qualification, as in the final moments of *To Have and Have Not* (1944) when Lauren Bacall's "Slim" does her famous wiggle *after* she has committed herself to an assumedly monogamous relationship with Bogart's Harry Morgan. It may not even end at all, as in *El Dorado* (1967): the John Wayne–Charlene Holt relationship is never really resolved.[5] Stranger still, it may end in comic confusion: having spent nearly the entire film setting up an exceptionally violent father-son conflict in *Red River* (1948), one that deals with a triple-threat complex of property inheritance, shooting skill, and sexual rivalry, Hawks is unable to resolve the conflict within the tonal terms of the western and provides what passes for a resolution only by turning Oedipal tragedy into farce. Matthew Garth (Montgomery Clift) and Tom Dunson (John Wayne) can do nothing but beat each other senseless. But even here the resolution demands a fight to the death (as Dunson has sworn earlier), so Hawks has heroine Tess Millay (Joanne Dru) commandeer a gun and thus appropriate the central symbol of male potency in the western and ridicule it through a reversal of gender and genre expectation—a neat screwball-inspired twist. With the gun in the hands of a woman, Garth and Dunson have no other choice but to laugh.

Ironically, it was also Robin Wood who originally described the narrative structure of *Monkey Business* as "organic," a strongly connotative term which film historian John Belton later picked up to elaborate on the seemingly natural and logical development of both story and character.[6] And yet Wood, Belton, and other Hawks critics have hesitated to appreciate what I see as a glaring *lack* of development in both *Monkey Business* and *Gentlemen Prefer Blondes* (1953), a pronounced disruption of linearity which sets these particular comedies somewhat apart from other Hawks films.

In the world of academic film criticism, *Monkey Business* and *Gentlemen Prefer Blondes* have been lost in the shuffle of conscious polemics and unconscious ideologies, and this chapter offers an alternative reading of Hawks's fifties humor. But the greater object of this study is to demonstrate that Hawks's comedies in the 1950s articulate the contradictions that in retrospect seemed to be plaguing society at large, and that these contradictions are what gives the films their comic coherence. The collision of genre expectation and Hawks's point of view (the kind that led Tess Millay to disrupt the end of *Red River*) is, in *Monkey Business* and *Gentlemen Prefer Blondes*, taken as such a given that Hawks cannot *develop*. He can only reiterate, and such arrested development makes the comedy of *Monkey Business* a matter of reverses, inverses, and confrontations.

Normative Subversion: Howard Hawks and His Era

Film historians have typically described Hawks as a normative Hollywood director—perhaps *the* normative Hollywood director, the apotheosis of the so-called invisible Hollywood style. Andrew Sarris's take on Hawks ("This is good, clean, direct, functional cinema, perhaps the most distinctively American cinema of all") is as essentially accurate today as it was when Sarris first described it in the late 1960s.[7] At the same time, Hawks's work remains fascinating precisely because of the sexual tensions and dark moral questions that erupt within his normative world: the anarchy of *Bringing Up Baby* (1938), the appealing homoeroticism of *Only Angels Have Wings* (1939) and *The Big Sky* (1952), the delight in cool competent women and their simultaneous and disturbing subjugation in *His Girl Friday* (1940) and *Ball of Fire* (1941). For Hawks, as for any modern classicist, *normative* does not mean a lack of neurosis. It doesn't even mean the absence of outright subversion. And yet, to call an artist or an artwork normative is to describe a kind of containment of disruption, with the goal (however tentative) of maintaining artistic as well as social and cultural conventions. In other words, the expression of trouble in Hawks's work stops short of revolution. But look at the trouble.

The intimate bond between comedy and sexual anxiety that forms the basis of other Hawks comedies like *Bringing Up Baby*, *His Girl Friday*, *Ball of Fire*, and *I Was a Male War Bride* (1949) finds clear expression in *Monkey Business* in the manic energy that goes hand in hand with cross-dressing, male humiliation, and physical pain. For Hawks, cross-dressing is a fine form of trouble. *Transvestism*, a word often employed to mean any kind of cross-dressing, seems to me inappropriate to use to describe Cary Grant's farcical appearance in a ritzy Persian lamb jacket in *Monkey Business*. It is at least as inappropriate here as it is to describe the modus operandi of *Some Like It Hot*. The two films may share the same coscreenwriter (I.A.L. Diamond), but their uses of cross-dressing point in very different directions. Still, both cases call to mind the hearing room at the end of *Psycho*, when a psychiatrist answers the charge that Norman Bates is "a transvestite" because he dresses in his mother's clothes with a dramatic physical gesture and the words, "Not exactly." The reason for Norman's condition being "not exactly" transvestism is rather like that of Hawks's cross-dressed characters: "sexual" satisfaction is not exactly the goal. Hawks tends to use women's clothes as a way of humiliating the men who wear them, not as a way of gratifying them. And yet the recurrence of cross-dressing in Hawks's comedies, the delight he takes in getting Grant into women's clothes throughout their joint career (a frilly dressing gown in *Bringing Up Baby*, a no-nonsense WAC uniform in *War Bride*, and the lovely fur jacket in 1952) does indeed suggest pleasurable gratification—Hawks's and Grant's on an underlying level, the audience's on an overt one.

Sexual pleasure lies at the heart of cross-dressing, but not in a simple way. Today's dictionary definition of transvestism keeps the word a simple Latin-to-English cognate, but as Marjorie Garber points out in *Vested Interests*, the term is blurrier and thus more interesting. It seems to me impossible to use the same word to describe, say, a gay drag queen lip-synching Nancy Sinatra songs, Cary Grant in *Monkey Business*, and a straight truck driver putting on black lingerie specifi-

cally to give himself an erection. To me, the truck driver is the transvestite, the drag queen is, yes, a drag queen, and Cary Grant in *Monkey Business* is a cross-dresser. All transvestites and drag queens are
cross-dressers, but not necessarily vice versa.

In any case, *Monkey Business* is a late screwball comedy in which
male humiliation stops short of female triumph. In this regard, *Gentlemen Prefer Blondes* is the next logical step. If a man is peculiarly
empowered by wearing women's clothes (and in *Monkey Business* this
power is all too short-lived), the women in *Gentlemen Prefer Blondes*
take their costumes and run with them.

Monkey Business, which takes the idea of a fountain-of-youth drug
as its comic premise, and *Gentlemen Prefer Blondes*, which Hawks
adapted from the stage musical based on Anita Loos' novel, are visually and thematically quite different. *Monkey Business* is in black and
white; *Blondes* is in Technicolor. *Monkey Business* stars two actors who
had become very familiar to audiences as early as the 1930s; *Blondes*
features Jane Russell, whose first starring role was in 1942, and Marilyn Monroe, who, at the time the film was made, was just rising to
star status. *Monkey Business* concerns characters who are firmly established in a stable marriage; *Blondes* details characters' courtships and
culminates in marriage. And finally, *Monkey Business* was written for
the screen; *Blondes* is an adaptation.

At the same time, a certain comic vision oversees the two films,
and it is a vision that brings Hawks's normative tensions squarely
within the neurotic culture of the 1950s. Hawks imprinted his authorial voice so strongly on these comedies that their otherwise disparate
messages merge together into a coherent if not completely unified
whole. While *Monkey Business* is self-evidently a Howard Hawks film
in comic tone, casting, form, and theme, *Gentlemen Prefer Blondes*
might well have become a project for George Cukor, a director
known for his talent for directing women, or Vincente Minnelli, who
had already directed several big splashy musicals. But Hawks found
something about the concept personally appealing: the film's central
characters are women whose relationship to each other is much
stronger than their relationships with any other characters, including
the men they eventually marry. These are comedies of the zeitgeist;

Hawks's normative fifties world had become quite troubled. And these troubles played right into his worldview.

Buddyism, less a theme than an ethos in Hawks's other works, was ready for inversion in 1953. Speaking of *Gentlemen Prefer Blondes*, Hawks said: "That was just fun. In the other films, you have two men who go and try to find some pretty girls to have some fun with. We thought of the opposite and took two girls who go and find some men to have some fun with—a perfectly modern story."[8] But as Peter Wollen describes it, "just fun" for Hawks can be hideously painful: "In *Sergeant York* it is 'fun' to shoot Germans 'like turkeys'; in *Air Force* it is 'fun' to blow up the Japanese fleet. In *Rio Bravo* the geligniting of the badmen 'was very funny.'"[9]

In keeping with the war films and the westerns, the heroines' fun in *Gentlemen Prefer Blondes* demeans and demoralizes the hapless men they attack. Likewise, the fun of *Monkey Business* has a bracingly vicious undercurrent. When Barnaby and Edwina Fulton splatter paint all over each other under the influence of the drug, "B-4," they make the brushes function as small clubs rather than simply as painting tools. When sexual and marital expectations break down, things get ugly.

While *Gentlemen Prefer Blondes* takes a reversal as its premise, *Monkey Business* begins with an ordinary man and woman from the suburbs, people who routinely follow an accepted pattern of behavior only to revert wildly to anarchic children in the course of the film. The reversal that characterizes *Monkey Business* leads characters from an initial position of stability to one of chaos by systematically undercutting the foundations of their adult lives. It is, I think, the progressiveness of this reversion, its backwards logic, that Wood and Belton believe to be "organic." But if character development is a process of fictional maturation, Hawks in fact works against the Fultons' development not only in terms of plot (their reduction to infantilism) but in narrative structure as well. In the final analysis, both *Monkey Business* and *Gentlemen Prefer Blondes* may be among the *least* developed films of Hawks's career. Reiterating tension rather than resolving it, both films have a kind of contemporary musical quality: "Crazy man crazy / crazy man crazy / crazy man crazy / Oh man that music's gone,

gone, gone, gone. . . ." Or, on a more regressive note, "Be-bop-a-lula she's my baby / Be-bop-a-lula I don't mean maybe / Be-bop-a-lula she she she's my baby now / my baby now / my baby now / my baby now . . ."

Personal Grotesquerie

The regressive *Yes, Sir, That's My Baby* takes great pains to cover over the conflicts it presents, but *Monkey Business* just as vigorously exposes them. As critic Raymond Durgnat described it, *Monkey Business* is one of the first films that took "personal grotesquerie" as the central source of comic delight.[10] As Durgnat puts it, Hawks paired "the suavest of 30's comedy stars, Cary Grant, and the most earthily commonsensical, Ginger Rogers, and made something rather sillier than monkeys out of the pair of them."[11] While *Yes, Sir, That's My Baby* begins with disruption only to eliminate whatever humorous and discomfiting developments get in its characters' way, *Monkey Business* takes the solid, familiar images of well-known stars and progressively strips them of their respectability by exposing not only the underpinnings of their screen personas but also the foundations of the limited and marriage-centered world of their era.

The accuracy of his comment notwithstanding, Durgnat still underestimates Cary Grant, who had already suffered (and embraced) humiliation in the middle-screwball period, especially in *Bringing Up Baby* and *My Favorite Wife* (1940), not to mention the painful, emasculating assault of Hawks's late-screwball *I Was a Male War Bride*. This breathtakingly good-looking actor was consistently able to undercut his own masculine appeal for comic effect, perhaps more than any other major star. In comedies, particularly Hawks's, Grant's image lends itself to its own ridicule. The extent of Grant's built-in breakdown is all the clearer when contrasting him with Ginger Rogers. Self-reflection and irony were virtually eliminated from Rogers' screen image upon the imposition of the Production Code. Before the Code, Rogers could make fun of her working girls' go-get-'em zeal. In *Golddiggers of 1933*, for instance, she's obviously playing a fun-loving whore. Once the censors' lid came down, however, Rogers reinvented herself, and her new persona tended to be so rigidly virtuous that it allowed little in the way of ironic self-awareness.

Grant's and Rogers' personae are nevertheless linked by the mandated suppression of a kind of inner chaos, the incessant putting down of a freewheeling nature in the name of the stars' public images. For Hawks, stripping away this surface dignity is a central comic task, and on this point Durgnat's comment is exceedingly accurate. The 1950s demanded exposure as well as suppression, and for Cary Grant and Ginger Rogers the result was personal grotesquerie. For Hawks, a crucial scene in this project of timely comic disruption takes place inside Barnaby Fulton's laboratory. It's not one of the film's most openly comic scenes, serving more as an expository prelude to the high-pitched infantile behavior and physical action that follows. The scene in question concerns Edwina's seemingly casual yen for a cup of coffee. Although she herself is a trained ichthyologist and has, presumably, some familiarity with standard laboratory procedures, she absent-mindedly reaches for the lab water spigot. Barnaby's reaction to this minor gaffe is extraordinary, however, considering just how minor it is. He snaps at her as if she was a stupid child, "Don't use this water! Can't you see the sign? Use the bottled water!"

Robin Wood describes Barnaby at this point as being "slightly on edge" as he directs Edwina to the water cooler in which the monkey has hidden the drug, B-4, but Barnaby's reaction is much more extreme.[12] His hostility is not explained by the effects of B-4, since he hasn't ingested any at that point. And it appears that his harsh, abrasive tone is a normal part of their marriage, as Edwina demonstrates by not responding to it as being out of the ordinary. She simply takes it as a given that her husband would bark at her over something as insignificant as a glass of water.

If this scene occurred in isolation, it would still be a subtle but no less powerful revelation about the dissolute state of the Fultons' marriage, its unnervingly rote hostility. But Hawks has already demonstrated the less-than-vibrant nature of the Fultons' everyday lives, and it is particularly amusing that Barnaby's snapping turns out to be an unwitting appeal to Edwina to take a powerful drug—to leave, thanks to chemicals, the drab world of bickering, boredom, and mindless prosaic routines and to enter into a state of bliss. To put it tersely, Barnaby invites Edwina to get herself out of their marriage, and she accepts the offer instantly. This is evidently a wish that has teetered on the edge of consciousness for some time, a desire itching for any excuse, however pathetic and minor, to be gratified. All the while, Hawks is presenting his audience with a prickly, peevish, and decidedly unromantic Cary Grant and a Ginger Rogers who can't wait to burst out of her shell of conformity. The comic pleasure comes from seeing with take-it-for-granted clarity what one had suspected all along.

Within the terms of the film, the extent of the boredom and regularity of this snappish little interchange is further underscored by the fact that this one occurs *immediately* after Edwina tells Barnaby, "We shouldn't be fighting—having doubts about our marriage. That isn't right." Edwina has accused Barnaby of harboring "buried resentment that [he does not] consciously realize," and Barnaby has retorted by citing Edwina's near obsession with a former suitor: "What about the way you kept bringing up Hank Entwhistle?" "Are you in love with Miss Whosiwhats?" Edwina immediately demands. No sooner does the fight reach its zenith than Barnaby snaps at her about which water to use to make coffee. Instead of hastening them back to sobriety, the coffee ends up hurtling them into chaotic and violent episodes of regression, puerile behavior, and alarmingly painful slapstick.

In its comic structure and the ideas such a structure implies, this sequence moves from ironic detachment to active participation through physical comedy. Barnaby, describing youth in the beginning of the scene as "a series of low comedy disasters," coolly expresses one of the film's central concerns—namely, that comedy, youth, sexual energy, and freedom from repression pose a marked danger to the everyday fifties world in which the Fultons have a deeply personal stake. It is important to see that while the Fultons do not become the teenagers and children they actually would have been (according to what we learn of their lives), neither do they turn into different people under the influence of B-4.[13] What B-4 releases instead is a comic mirror image of themselves as adults. Part parody, part low farce, their comic doubles are invested with the power to express what their constrained selves cannot.

Still, the transformations they undergo are not simply related to the release of suppressed emotions. While suppression and its sudden, unexpected breakdown do constitute a great part of the humor of *Monkey Business*, both Barnaby and Edwina Fulton find the *consistency* of their personalities coming under attack under B-4's spell. If youth is a disaster and subconscious desire a terrifying threat, the underlying foundation of character unity—the coherence of the individual—is what the comedy of *Monkey Business* ultimately destroys. When Barnaby instructs Edwina to use the tainted water to make a pot of coffee, their joint action turns out to be a means toward mutual dissolution. This destruction of his characters' integrity stands in stark contrast to the deep-seated coherence of character in other Hawks films. Think of Gary Cooper in *Sergeant York* (1941), or Humphrey Bogart in *To Have and Have Not* and *The Big Sleep* (1946), or Cary Grant himself in *Only Angels Have Wings*. These men are strained by dark circumstance, but they never break down. And it's not entirely a distinction between drama and comedy. Think even of Cary Grant in *Bringing Up Baby*. Grant's David Huxley becomes increasingly desperate under the onslaught of Katharine Hepburn's Susan Vance, but he never falls apart. It's the dinosaur skeleton that crumbles at the end, not Cary Grant. The closest a Hawks hero comes to disintegration is John Wayne's Tom Dunson in *Red River*, three years earlier. But then, at the moment of the dramatic climax in that film, what Hawks sees is comedy.

Anti-Maturity: Childishness as Liberation

Given that their relationship is constituted both by its normality and its crumminess, the Fultons are in dire need of a brutal remaking. And Hawks clearly delights in B-4 and the liberation it engenders. But as routinized and prone to disturbance as the Fultons' marriage is, Hawks's critical fans have felt the need to defend it against what the film itself insists upon. Gerald Mast describes the Fultons' home as harboring "something dead," yet he characterizes the rejuvenated world of B-4 as follows:

> It is a world of feeling without thought, passion without reflection, simple doing without complex making. It is a world, in short, which nullifies all the complex accomplishments of human history and human civilization, all sciences and arts, not the least of which is this very movie, a complex evolutionary synthesis of both science and art.[14]

Although, as Mast himself points out, *Monkey Business*'s script describes the drug's effects as leading to a world with "no philosophy, no science, no statesmen, nothing," it goes on to add one crucial attribute: "There'd only be poetry."[15] Mast's elaboration distorts the script's distinctions by making "poetry" seem thoughtless, empty, and antihuman. This is a real discomfort with the anarchic bodily *healthiness* of comedy, and it's typical. The comic world opened up by B-4 doesn't have to be belittled in order to bolster and defend a world called "dead."

"Low comedy"—the term itself is hardly free from ideology—is neither as programmatic nor as piously allegorical as Mast and others suggest. For example, when Barnaby begins to notice the effects of the drug in his initial experiment, he decides to check to see if his bursitis has improved. Seen in a two shot with the assistant hovering over his right shoulder, Barnaby swings his right arm around and promptly raps his assistant squarely in the mouth. This bit of slapstick humor, the first visual rendering of B-4's marvelous medicinal value, is only marginally related to the effects of the drug, however, since Barnaby himself doesn't see it as being particularly funny. If Hawks had treated slapstick comedy as something to be grown out of, logic would demand that Barnaby, now transported to a "lower" level, would laugh uproariously at the cruelty he has just inflicted on his colleague. In fact, however, he doesn't even notice it. In marked contrast to scenes in which raucous, childish jokes are played on the film's characters *by* those characters, this comic business is played by the director for the amusement of his audience. Unless one is willing to assign comedy a solemn, didactic function, Mast's conclusion—that the ending of *Monkey Business* "represents a rediscovery of [Barnaby's] human feelings, and a resynthesis of thought and feeling"—radically misinterprets everything the film promotes and the receptive audience experiences. Like many other critics, Mast makes slapstick comedy acceptable only insofar as it teaches both participants and spectators to rise above it.

Mast is hardly alone in his sober moral reading. Other critics have rationalized the low comedy of *Monkey Business* by tying it into a form of marriage counseling for the Fultons. Leland Poague applauds "the distance the film has traveled" between its opening and closing scenes, approving wholeheartedly of what he sees as its positive, marriage-affirming resolution.[16] John Belton, in a more complex treatment of *Monkey Business*, writes of Hawks: "It is his ordered structuring of his characters' chaotic experiences that leads them to an understanding of their own actions, to a confrontation with their own insanity, and to a final recognition of nature and accord with the world around them."[17]

In varying degrees, these critics feel compelled to apologize for comedy by finding a conventional moral purpose to justify it. And in each case, the apology conforms to both genre convention and ideological imperative: the restoration of a marriage. Of the three, only Belton incorporates the "insanity" of the Fultons' lives into the resolution; both Poague and Mast see the ending of the film as being secure in its projection of a stable marriage and unqualified in its presentation of character consistency. As ideology, these readings rest on the premise and actively work toward the goal of setting up *Monkey Business* as an aesthetically superior work of art because of the reestablishment of a happy heterosexual union at its end.

In the Chute

Monkey Business is less palliative. In terms of structure, the film begins *and ends* with the following conflicts intact: mobility against immobility, music overcoming silence, monkeys exulting over humanity, and youth reigning impossibly over the world of adults. Every film necessarily harbors tension between movement and stasis, but Hawks invests this ongoing war with a specific and more or less unified thematic meaning by using tracking shots to express the fluidity of characters' constitutions in the presence of B-4. Throughout *Monkey Business*, Hawks contrasts the staidness of the Fultons' quotidian lives with the freedom of movement they experience under the drug's influence. This sudden sense of flight is generally strongest on a character after he or she has consumed the drug: Barnaby skates and high-dives, and Edwina dances as if reverting more to her creator's earlier screen persona than to the character's own youth. But sometimes its power to move a character extends beyond the drugged individual. While the opening shot of the film—the Fultons' doorway taken from a static camera in medium distance—connotes an unchanging facade (and specifically *denotes* Barnaby's inability to get out of the house), the bizarre shot of Barnaby flying down the laundry chute, propelled as much by his own frustration as by his wife's childish and drug-induced behavior, reveals a world literally destabilized and in flux. B-4 affects Barnaby by literally hurling him into an abyss, even though he himself hasn't been dosed. And Hawks's aim is to please his audience by putting us in the flying man's place.

What happens to Barnaby at that moment is telling. For Barnaby, dull stability gives way to comic liberation, an untrammeled sexuality that crosses not only genders but species. Barnaby loses two important items when Edwina banishes him from the hotel room: his glasses and the belt that holds up his pajama bottoms. Plunged into a hazy world in which what had once been clear is now a blur, Barnaby is simultaneously threatened with an especially graphic form of sexual liberation from his pants. And the laundry chute into which he almost immediately flies isn't the typical rectangular model. It has a round, tunnel-like shape, and in an unusual process shot (which prefigures Hitchcock's simultaneous track/zoom in 1958's *Vertigo*) Barnaby flies forward while the camera pulls back, thereby elongating the tubular shape. Bluntly put, Barnaby is denied sex by his wife, so he gets it in nightmare form in this chute. He is then deposited into a large wheeled laundry bin which is propelled forward by Barnaby's momentum until it rams against the wall, with Barnaby's head acting as its bumper. If the sexual nature of this tumble is still in doubt, the dialogue offers some fairly convincing proof: "Let me in, Edwina," Barnaby moans in a concussive stupor, "let me in."

In the following scene, Edwina, now returned to her usual maternal/spousal self, offers Barnaby her fur jacket to keep him warm. He puts it on willingly, seemingly oblivious to the way it further undermines his masculinity. But the newspaper reporter and photographer who catch him wearing it are not as unaware. They immediately snap his picture and ask him about his crumbling marriage and the tantalizing possibility of adultery. But Barnaby responds, no less accurately, by talking about another form of experimentation—with the drug B-4. Since he is wearing fur at that moment, his cross-species double entendre makes a very different kind of comic sense: "My wife has been my only victim so far," he notes. "I'll have a much better story for you when I've experimented with ten or twenty others. I'm not going to try it with human beings for a while. I'll stick to chimpanzees."

With J. Fred Muggs, Bonzo, and Pierre (Jerry Lewis's simian friend in the *Irma* film), America in the early 1950s liked to think of monkeys simply as ersatz human babies. On screen, they were children for the childless; Bonzo, Pierre, and Barnaby's lab monkeys all thrive in child-free environments, and J. Fred Muggs served in the domestic early fifties to make the *Today* team a familiar family. These chimps were all riotous commentaries on the baby boom, hairy parodies of human procreation. And like the millions of real-life postwar kids who were already revolutionizing American culture by transforming it into a youth-oriented fantasy marketplace that continues, nearly a half century later, to drive the economics of today's entertainment industry, these chimps had a disturbing but profoundly comical tendency to *take over.*

This chimp-child fixation aside, Barnaby's extended double entendre about sticking with chimpanzees instead of his wife is one of the rare moments where chimps become the (significantly) displaced objects of sexual fantasy. In *Son of Paleface*, also from 1952, Frank

Tashlin gets reluctant cowboy Bob Hope in bed with Trigger, a cozy bestial pleasure informed by both regression and repression—by the early 1950s, the conventional screen cowboy's apparent preference for horse over woman was ripe for conscious send-up. Hawks, a less obvious comedian than Tashlin, is more interested in his character's interior psychology and the logic of its unraveling. Perhaps Robin Wood and John Belton do have a point about the film's "organic" nature: for Barnaby, what happens in the morning follows precisely as a perverse consequence of the night before. If Barnaby's trip down the laundry chute is an eroticized return to the womb, his unintentionally voiced desire for sex with a chimp points his regressive urges back before the dawn of humanity. B-4 is potent stuff.

Primates and Secondaries

As the title implies, this is a story about the genesis of modern mankind. The aged male monkey, Rudolph, is the object of fountain-of-youth drug experiments because he's sufficiently close to human beings in his physical and mental makeup. Hawks then takes this Darwinian link and makes him a simian parody of Mr. Oxly (Charles Coburn), the industrialist buffoon who openly and shamelessly identifies with a monkey, perhaps on the basis of the old man's already beast-based name. And while monkey and corporation boss share a tired masculinity, the young female monkey, Esther, seizes the reins and becomes the film's most creative character. It is Esther who actually invents B-4 by successfully mimicking the advanced scientist, Barnaby, in the physical action of mixing the formula. But Esther triumphs over Barnaby by overcoming the obstacles of human logic and gender expectation, and thus she succeeds where Barnaby fails: *her formula works.*

The opposing categories of youth and age, a crucial concern of the baby boom years, form the film's central conflict, and all other oppositions fall under them. If adulthood is the world of the static home, youth is the world of change. If adulthood means being too tired to dance, youth means boundless energy. If aging equals consistency as an adult human being, youth gives one the ability to play, to assume other identities at will. Every moment in the film relates to this opposition. Several instances are: the contrast between Edwina and Miss Laurel (the middle-aged wife, played by an established star, versus the youthful bombshell played by a virtual unknown); Barnaby's disturbing relationship with a group of children playing Indians (with George Winslow playing a little boy who is grotesquely more adult-like and stolid than Barnaby); and the film's climactic scenes in which Edwina, the world having been reduced to chaos around her, confronts a tiny infant dressed in a diaper and assumes—naturally!—that he is her husband.

Monkey Business features four secondary characters who in varying degrees represent variations on the themes of aging and sexuality: Miss Laurel, the secretary who can't type; Hank Entwhistle, Edwina's old suitor and now the Fultons' friend and lawyer; Edwina's mother, who appears briefly, but whose maternal authority dramatically reasserts itself on-screen and off when Edwina relives her wedding night under B-4; and Mr. Oxly, Barnaby's decrepit boss.

At the time *Monkey Business* was made, Marilyn Monroe's career was just beginning. She had already appeared briefly in *All About Eve* (1950) in a comic role, and in *Monkey Business*, as Miss Laurel, she expanded upon the kind of wordplay that characterized her part in the earlier film, in which the following interchange between Monroe and George Sanders occurs:

Miss Caswell: Oh, waiter!
Addison DeWitt: That isn't a waiter, my dear. That's a butler.
Miss Caswell: Well I can't yell, "Oh, butler!" can I? Maybe
somebody's *name* is Butler!

There, as in *Monkey Business*, Monroe's sexual authority combines with her character's apparent underintelligence to produce linguistic problems, verbal slips that end up meaning more than the sum total of the words she utters. Just as her appearance tends to exceed itself in terms of the specific sexual object she represents, her utterances exceed themselves in meaning. As a star, Monroe always radiates more meaning than she specifically represents, and what she says expands accordingly. (As critic Richard Dyer puts it, "She seemed to 'be' the very tensions that ran through the ideological life of fifties America.")[18]

Monroe's introductory scene in *Monkey Business* contains the following line: "Mr. Oxly told me to be careful about my punctuation, so I try to get here before nine." While Monroe's physicality may be the most definitive aspect of her character, the comedy she generates is often verbal, and it's so powerful that it even causes the humorless Barnaby to make an unintentional pun. When Miss Laurel exhibits her leg to him, Barnaby regards it clinically, distantly, even confusedly, and he only takes an interest when she tells him that it's the material he developed in the lab. Barnaby then explains himself to the jealous Mr. Oxly: "Miss Laurel was just showing me her acetates." Later, Oxly tells Miss Laurel, "Go to every Ford agency in town and find Dr. Fulton." "Which shall I do first?" she asks. While the double meaning of Barnaby's pun remains beyond his immediate consciousness, Miss Laurel actually makes Oxly's command more complex than Oxly had intended.

Combined with what Barnaby calls her "half-infant" quality (aside from her childlike innocence, which survives even in the face of Oxly's leers, even her name suggests childhood in that it's unclear whether "Laurel" is her first or last name), her overt sexuality makes her immune to the constricted boredom of Barnaby and Edwina. This lack of constitutional adulthood is also related to linguistic slippage in that she hasn't mastered the language well enough to make meaning rigid. In all cases, Miss Laurel generates comedy ignorantly; she makes jokes despite herself; she doesn't get them. This is, one might add, in marked contrast to the male lab janitor, Gus, who responds to the question, "Did the monkeys take a bath this morning?" by asking, "Why? Is one missing?" and laughing loudly. Needless to say, he's the only one who finds the joke funny.

To a certain extent, Miss Laurel's powerlessness, stemming from gender, leads to an inability to make jokes on a conscious level. In contrast to Lorelei Lee in *Gentlemen Prefer Blondes*, Monroe's character in this film is always the brunt of her own jokes and never their calculating creator. But then jokes would serve no real purpose for her, since she has no need for what Freud called the pleasurable "economy of expenditure" of psychic energy in joke-making.[19] Comedy provides a momentary skirting of psychic pathways, but Miss Laurel's world is *already* the world of pleasure as Freud described it:

> the mood of a period of life in which we were accustomed to deal with our psychical work in general with a small expenditure of energy—the mood of our childhood, when we were ignorant of the comic, when we were incapable of jokes and when we had no need of humor to make us feel happy in our life.[20]

Hank Entwhistle's humor, in contrast, arises from his role as rejected suitor, one who expends a great deal of energy toward an unreachable goal. Hawks inflicts great cruelty on this character, making him act first as outside witness to the Fultons' domestic life—a life from which he has been excluded; then as Edwina's eager legal and emotional savior after the disastrous wedding-night replay, after which she casually rejects him once again; and finally as the physically disfigured victim of Barnaby's jealous rage after Barnaby gives him a Mohawk.

In the first two instances, Entwhistle's "physical" humor is nothing more than his necessarily humiliating physical presence. That he should continue to be available to act as Edwina's friend, confidant, and lawyer—to watch impotently as she directs all her energies toward Barnaby—makes him the embodiment of unfulfillment, an unmarried heterosexual buffoon in a decade of fetishized marriage. Since the Fultons' marital union exists at his expense, he is a man whose sexual goal lies only in the past or in fantasy. He evokes an adolescent period, and a particularly dull one at that; like Miss Laurel, he is an adult caught in a distorted sexual time-warp, only his is boring. He appears—and reappears, and reappears again—as a comic refrain of frustration.

Edwina's mother, on the other hand, reigns as a terrifying social power. She's a classical type: the mother-in-law, invoked in curious terms by Edwina in the context of Edwina's loss of virginity:

Edwina: Oh Barney, I'm so happy! (*she bursts into tears*)
Barnaby: Why are you crying?
Edwina: I can't help it. I was just thinking.
Barnaby: What about?
Edwina: Mother . . .
Barnaby: Oh, now I understand.
Edwina: . . . what she must be feeling tonight.

Edwina weeps at the idea that her mother is thinking about her sex life. Sexual union, the archetypical comic ending, turns into tragedy in the social order presided over by Mom.

The film's most thorough example of "personal grotesquerie" comes in the form of Mr. Oxly, since his material, spiritual, and sexual drives come together in the development of a drug that reverses biology itself. As in *Yes, Sir, That's My Baby*, Charles Coburn's physical type lends itself to this kind of biological humor. With his walrussy jowls and portly build, Coburn's physique suggests plenitude and authority. In Douglas Sirk's 1952 comedy, *Has Anybody Seen My Gal?*, Coburn plays a multimillionaire Santa Claus; in *Yes, Sir, That's My Baby* he plays a professor; in *Monkey Business* he owns a company; in *Gentlemen Prefer Blondes* he's a multimillionaire diamond dealer. But each of these vocations merely plays upon what is evident in his appearance—that of the aging white male, and his characters necessarily reflect that maturity financially and spiritually as well as physically.

In this light, it is notable that all four films use Coburn's character as a springboard for intense dissatisfaction. Sirk has Coburn remain a lonely old man even at the end of *Has Anybody Seen My Gal?*, with the character's great gratification lying in seeing to it that none of his would-be beneficiaries will turn out like him. In *Yes, Sir, That's My Baby*, it is loneliness and stodginess once again; in *Gentle-*

men Prefer Blondes, it is the restlessness and egocentrism of a man who can buy anything. In *Monkey Business* Hawks pushes these distressing by-products of maturity to an extreme by creating a character whose desperate drive to regain his primal vigor leads him to the point of identifying with a primate. Encroaching senility and incipient despair were not, one imagines, the industrialist character traits Ayn Rand had in mind to replace cheating and exploitation. Maybe the fact that they keep reappearing in American comedies of this period suggests that capitalists rather than communists were to blame after all.

A fifth character, an intensely stolid child played by George Winslow, brings the skewed sexuality of *Monkey Business* full circle. Hawks's use of Winslow as a parody of adult masculinity becomes much more extreme in *Gentlemen Prefer Blondes*, but even here Hawks poses him as an asexual (rather than presexual) boy in a game of cowboys and Indians by having him interested only in rules and unable to play. As in *Gentlemen Prefer Blondes*, Winslow's character in *Monkey Business* makes sense only insofar as it modifies and comments upon the actions of the adults. With the three supporting males—the frustrated Hank Entwhistle, the desperate Mr. Oxly, and this grotesquely methodical child—Hawks surrounds Barnaby with a set of specialized and condensed representations of his own emotional and sexual makeup. The fact that Barnaby is also Cary Grant, as the opening sequence playfully announces, only amplifies Hawks's case against the American male, since Grant is on the one hand one of Hollywood's most popular romantic leads and, on the other hand, the man who is compared to a horse's ass—literally—in *I Was a Male War Bride*.

As for the women, Miss Laurel and Mother provide Edwina with similarly condensed representations. Caught between a ridiculously potent image of sexual energy rendered neutral by its reduction to childlike innocence on the one hand, and a domineering matriarch who turns sex into a cause for tears on the other, Edwina is scarcely able to construct a reasonable alternative for herself on the basis of what this particular world offers. In short, the impossible sexual bind that Hawks describes in *Monkey Business* pervades the society he represents, and the film's comedy means little if it isn't an attempt blow it all apart. Marriage, capital, the law, parents, even a game of cowboys and Indians—every facet of this world cries out frantically for release.

Baa Baa Baa

Comedy presents just such a mechanism. But it doesn't merely serve a regulatory function, the position taken by those who argue that the end of *Monkey Business* provides a restoration of order and stability. *Monkey Business* doesn't promote an acceptance of the same social institutions that engendered such fierce anxieties to begin with. The film's ending is more ambiguous, if not overtly contrary. In the final scene of the film, Barnaby and Edwina decide not to go out but rather to stay at home and, presumably, make love. What happens in the scene is this:

Edwina, in a black dress, and Barnaby, with his suspenders unhooked and hanging ridiculously around his butt, are dressing for dinner. Their casual, methodical actions are still those of a couple who have been together for quite some time, but now they act as if they have been through an ordeal, as indeed they have. Barnaby, with recent disasters still fresh in his mind, remarks that he has found a "new formula," and suddenly music is heard on the soundtrack. It is "The Whiffenpoof Song," a song about sheep. ("We're poor little lambs who have lost our way, baa baa baa.") Except for the title sequence, this is the first time any asynchronous music has been sounded without B-4 being present. Barnaby then describes his new formula, with Grant delivering his lines in an unusually sing-song fashion: "It's a word you keep in your heart, someone you hold in your arms." Barnaby and Edwina embrace, and Barnaby asks, "You like my formula?" Edwina responds, "Makes you think, doesn't it?" (This is itself rather ominous, considering where thinking has taken them.) "What time did you order the table?" asks Barnaby, and they kiss.

The final question may mean that, having thought about it, this couple has decided to go out and eat after all; at best, it's ambiguous. In any case, the abrupt inclusion of soundtrack music—reversing a pattern that has been absolutely consistent until that point—suggests that B-4 has presented them with more than a vague clue about why their marriage has become so dull. With chaos as a corrective and childishness as a tonic, B-4 has taught the Fultons that *less* stability can be beneficial and even crucial in a world of rigid despair. Music, having been used thus far as a prelude to rampant inanity, now signals the second phase of this marriage. And Barnaby's uncharacteristically whimsical way of describing his "formula" brings his character back to the rejuvenated persona he adopted under B-4. Since *Monkey Business* is a film about healthy irresolution, it's appropriate that it ends with three questions.

The final scene of *Monkey Business* incorporates the "poetry" of the world of B-4 into the staid confines of a 1952 suburban home. Their personalities liberated by the "low comedy disasters" of youth, Barnaby and Edwina Fulton reject what the heroes and heroines of *Yes, Sir, That's My Baby* wind up defending—namely, the rhetoric of ongoing and changeless normality that characterized the reactionary side of the period. Marriage, commerce, education, even Homo sapiens himself—each of these categories finds itself the brunt of *Monkey Business*'s jokes, and while Hawks provides no radical alternative in terms of a demonstrable situation, his goal here is to ridicule society, not to re-create it in a serious vein.

Like the rest of society, Hawks was caught between expectation and desire: genre expectation and his own sensibility, marital conformity and an urge to rebel. Irresolution was evidently the only way out. But this lack of finality is the key to the film's comedy, for humor (in this case) is the pleasure to be gained by confronting interior tensions. The final joke of *Monkey Business* is the liberating sense of characters and genres coming apart at the seams, and contradiction rather than reaffirmation is its happy ending. The means by which Hawks turns stability into chaos, respectability into silliness, continue in *Gentlemen Prefer Blondes*, only there the destruction of male security is even more extreme and the conclusive marital response even more ambiguous.

Turning the Tables: *Gentlemen Prefer Blondes*

"Jane Russell was supposed to represent sanity"[21]

Hawks wasn't thrilled with *Gentlemen Prefer Blondes*, but his self-critical chagrin also has something of a comic edge since it contains an ironic contradiction about sex and brains. Hawks is describing the sexual reversals of *Gentlemen Prefer Blondes*, the near evacuation of romantic charm from men and its compensation, in women, by less subtle aspects of romance—golddigging and lust. As Hawks implies in his remark about Jane Russell, the problem with *Gentlemen Prefer Blondes* is that a bosomy woman couldn't succeed as a representation of sanity except in a film conceived as "fun." Her body would somehow preclude it.

On the surface, Hawks's remark about Jane Russell's implausible sanity is just sarcasm, the perceived contradiction between body and brain a myth. It's a potent myth, though, and it invades and defines not only the garish world Hawks depicts but also creeps into attacks leveled against *Gentlemen Prefer Blondes* and Russell herself. According to Robin Wood, Russell, as Dorothy, "devours men for sex."[22] Maureen Turim claims in a particularly bitter attack on the film that "it is the hourglass figure . . . which sells the film" and that *any* such figure—not simply Russell's—has but two functions in American culture: "The female body is not only a sex-object, but also an object of exchange."[23] Turim's view of the literal role the female body plays in American culture may be tunnel vision, but when one reads reviews of Jane Russell's performances one sees precisely what Turim is responding to. The *New York Times*'s Bosley Crowther, for instance, rarely missed an opportunity to comment crudely on Russell's body. Crowther had hated *The Las Vegas Story* (1952) and had no qualms about extending his contempt for the film's "obsession" with Russell's breasts to Russell's breasts themselves. Only nine months later, Crowther's perception of Russell underwent a remarkable change when he enjoyed Frank Tashlin's *Son of Paleface* (1952); there, she played "a saloon singer on the surface—and what a surface, she being

Miss Russell!" By the following July, Crowther was again using Russell's body as a weapon against a film he disliked, noting that *Gentlemen Prefer Blondes* had "bumped and gyrated broadly into the Roxy" and making the film's only breast-related joke ("Those girls couldn't drown") the central metaphor of his review by harping on the film's "buoyancy."[24] As for other representative critics, Pauline Kael once summed up one of Russell's performances as "Russell swings her bosom around," and Peter Biskind, discussing Russell's character in Joseph Pevney's *Foxfire* (1955), describes her as "a handful, decked out in '50s proto-punk tight black pants, bright pink blouse, and butch haircut, not to mention Jane Russell's Big Bertha breasts."[25]

Whatever one's response to Jane Russell may be, one thing is certain: her breasts have made a striking impression on a wide variety of people. Each of these critics, Turim included, consigns the star to a set of meanings that overrides anything either she or her character might do or say. The breasts, perceived as being so large that they overwhelm everything else, take on a paradoxically greater and more limiting function than society has already forced upon them, if such a thing is possible. Biskind even disembodies them from the rest of Russell's corpus and treats them instead as a fashion accessory.

What's surprising is the extent to which retrospective critiques of the breast-obsessed fifties fail to distance themselves from that decade's hysterical fixation on what Molly Haskell calls "bosom power" and, in fact, often incorporate the fixation into the analyses.[26] Sometimes, the fixation can be subtle. Robin Wood's comment about Dorothy "devouring men" strikes a clinical note in its suggestion of a carnivorous, enveloping woman, but on a factual level it's simply wrong. Dorothy has only one beau in the course of the film and he is just as mercenary as she is, if much less authoritative. Moreover, Dorothy fails to retain the attention of even one member of the male Olympic team during the celebrated musical number they share (a point Wood himself acknowledges). Cruder in their treatment of Jane Russell—an unusually good-natured star who always deserved better notices than she got—other critics tend to punish her for her body, all the while purporting to scorn the period's breast fetish. As it happened, Hawks fell into the same dismissive trap. Still, his on-screen depiction of her—and of Monroe, and, by extension, of women in general—is more complex, less patronizing, and eminently more liberating than the attacks of his critics.

Breasts, Threat, and Pleasure

What's going on with the breasts, anyway? Even when Maureen Turim castigates Hawks for reducing women to objects, an underlying cultural correlative springs into action and forces Turim to push women's bodies further into objectivity by denying them any other possible function. Thus she reassures the dominant culture of its dominance. In her discussion of the female body as a commodity, Turim doesn't see the central point of this most unreassuring comedy—namely, that "showgirls," by way of theater, seize at least some measure of control over the way their bodies appear. This power enables them to distinguish between their interior lives and the theatrical representations they ply to their own advantage. These female performers (Dorothy and Lorelei on the narrative level, Russell and Monroe on the cultural plane) construct stage and screen personalities out of the materials and presuppositions available to them as women in a male-dominated culture, and they manipulate these images, insofar as they are able, to their own economic benefit. Such a split between two aspects of a single body becomes increasingly extreme in *Gentlemen Prefer Blondes* as both Lorelei and Dorothy insist on treating men with an acute ironic distance, a tension that reaches its apex when Dorothy, dressed as Lorelei, does an impression of Lorelei acting *not* as Lorelei does when she's with Dorothy, but as Lorelei acts on stage and in the presence of men.[27] And throughout all of this, four prominent breasts achieve a meaning that remains all the more profound because it is almost entirely unspoken.

Turim isn't an anomaly. Oddly, many feminist film critics disregard the commanding power of the image of woman on screen. Psychoanalytic film theory is only recently beginning to see beyond—and behind—the father, Oedipus, and sexual difference, and to appreciate the magnitude of object relations psychology and the centrality of the mother both in individual psychic development and in the culture at large. Looking at women like Marilyn Monroe and Jane Russell, critics have tended to see only two bosomy women whose images remain oddly devoid of the very maternal authority their breasts so emphatically represent. For this reason, the reading of *Gentlemen Prefer Blondes* offered by Lucie Arbuthnot and Gail Seneca is particularly refreshing:

> Through look, stance, and use of space, Monroe and Russell subvert male objectification. By becoming active themselves, they make it impossible for men to act upon them. . . . It is the clear and celebrated connection between Marilyn Monroe and Jane Russell which, for us, transforms *Gentlemen Prefer Blondes* into a profoundly feminist text.[28]

In contemporary dress styles, in Hollywood's selection of actresses, and in the profusion of mammary humor, heterosexual male desire certainly attempted to govern female appearance throughout the 1950s, just as it had done earlier. Now, however, it had a new, shriller tone, an intensity that brought the image of woman to the level of imminent criticism. Physically shaped, narratively structured, and ideologically manipulated, the idealized representations of women in fashion and on screen in the fifties struggled for heterosexual male gratification, at least on the most obvious level.[29] Tightly fitting dresses accented the breasts and waists, stars like Monroe and Mansfield posed however self-consciously as sex kittens, and writers and directors often aimed comedy *at* women's physiques rather than away from them. The extremity of each of these aspects of the decade, the violence they commit against women, can't be denied. And yet films like *Gentlemen Prefer Blondes* and *The Girl Can't Help It* (1956) take the representational excesses of their era as premises and proceed to open some interesting cultural fissures by way of comedy. These films offer a substantially more disruptive reading of the culture in which they were produced than Turim, Wood, and others have cared to admit.

Gentlemen Prefer Blondes opens with one of the cinema's most zealous uses of Technicolor. A screaming blue-sequined curtain bursts open as Russell and Monroe, packed into tight and brilliant red-sequined dresses, storm onto the stage to the brassy opening chords of "Two Little Girls from Little Rock." No opening credits, not even a title—nothing appears on screen to distract the audience from these two aggressive women. As Jonathan Rosenbaum puts it in a brilliant analysis of the film, the sequence is "as awesome a demonstration of kino-fist strategies as anything in *Potemkin*."[30]

As the sequence develops, Hawks makes it clear that the audience is in two parts, the assault on two different but related fronts. The first, incorporated into the film itself, centers on the meek Mr. Esmond (Tommy Noonan), Lorelei's latest catch, who watches from a table as Lorelei and Dorothy perform for him and for other paying customers at a nightclub. The second audience, of course, is in the movie theater, where customers have also paid to watch but remain at a safe (or at least safer) distance from the performance. As Rosenbaum puts it, Esmond is "the viewer's uninvited surrogate . . . a neuter/neutral surface off which the dynamism of Monroe is allowed to ricochet." For Rosenbaum, Monroe, on stage, and Noonan, in the audience, define "the dialectical limits of this film's cartoon universe, and the only equals to be seen anywhere will be the two stars themselves," by which of course he means Monroe *and Russell*, not Monroe and the distinctly second-tier character actor Hawks chose to play the male lead.[31] Nevertheless, Rosenbaum misses one subtlety of the sequence: because Hawks places the camera at the height of the performers, the second audience is granted a privileged position. Through camera height, Hawks gives the filmgoer a more or less eye-level view, one that Esmond cannot have; by shifting the audience upward toward the emotional plane of the performer, Hawks puts us at an ironic remove from the affective level of the pathetic suitor/spectator—the better to view him clearly for what he is when the camera momentarily squats down to his level.

Seen in medium shot waving meekly to Lorelei, Esmond is the most obviously and readily damaged victim of the women's attack on the senses. Possessive but frightened, wealthy but impotent against his lover's performance, Esmond embodies the masculine side of Hawks's gender reversal and provides an immediate and comically self-evident contrast to the confident, talented, physically attractive, and deliriously attired women whose traits clearly both intimidate and arouse the little man. Further, Hawks never frames the women and Esmond together in this sequence. They remain in two different spheres: one, the lurid realm of female theater characterized by the two shot, and the other the timorous, rather haunted world of the male spectator, who sits alone.

In her book *In the Realm of Pleasure*, film historian and theorist Gaylyn Studlar offers a radical theory of cinematic pleasure and spectatorship, using the psychoanalytic and aesthetic structures of masochism to explain the subjective positions of male and female viewers. Studlar's argument, the most actively liberating in contemporary film theory, is complex and multivalent, and to rehearse it in capsule form is to do it a disservice. Nevertheless, its application to the opening sequence of *Gentlemen Prefer Blondes* is so magnetic that a brief restatement is necessary. According to Studlar, who derives her argument from the work of Gilles Deleuze, contemporary psychoanalytic and feminist film theory has misapprehended the nature of cinematic viewing pleasure. For Studlar, the dominant theory's restrictive description of the spectator's pleasurable position relies on a false conception of sadism and castration anxiety in which the spectator experiences viewed images—particularly those of women—in a sadistic and controlling manner. The idea that visual pleasure and sadism are inextricably bound was developed by Laura Mulvey from the work of Freud, Jacques Lacan, and Christian Metz, and it has wielded enormous influence in feminist cultural theory. One can easily see the appeal of Mulvey's argument; given a world so thoroughly defined by males, it isn't too much of a stretch to brand the cinematic apparatus itself as male-dominated, not only in terms of narrative structure (not to mention the economics of the workplace) but in the very nature of seeing, the basic vision it utilizes and promotes.

But as Studlar demonstrates, the theory is wrong. Studlar deftly explains that cinematic pleasure returns the spectator regressively not to an Oedipal moment wherein sexual difference is defined but rather to a *pre*-Oedipal state in which the image of woman, a maternal imago, retains a primal dominating power. In the cinema as in infancy, the spectator is held fast by this image, rapt in a pleasurable masochism, a little light bondage, the audiovisual and narrative equivalent of leather restraints. The baby is held and nursed; the audience stays in its seat and is entertained.

The consequences of Studlar's extraordinary thesis are profound. Cinematic pleasure, traced etiologically to a pre-Oedipal period in childhood, becomes neither constitutionally masculine nor feminine but rather—like the child's psychic constitution in that period—polymorphous and bisexual. In this way, visual pleasure is open to everyone, male and female, gay and heterosexual. And as an added benefit, Studlar's theory overturns the perversely conflicted puritanism of a film studies curriculum that purports to despise the very object of study. Under Studlar's revisionism, we get to like what we watch, with no concomitant lapse in intellectual rigor. To their credit, Arbuthnot and Seneca reach toward a similar pleasure principle as far as watching films is concerned, but they remain deeply invested in archconservative notions of "male" and "female," albeit with a modern flair. In other words, "male" pleasure is bad while "women's pleasure" is good. The idea that men—even those great villains of contemporary cultural studies, white straight guys—may find pleasure in a return to pre-Oedipal bisexuality is an idea that remains largely unexamined, not only by Arbuthnot and Seneca but by film theorists in general. Gaylyn Studlar's theory is a relief.

Submission as Pleasure

Using a sequence such as the "Little Rock" number in *Gentlemen Prefer Blondes* to demonstrate a theoretical proposition is, as always, dangerous, since the application of theory to practice becomes rather like applying a salve to a wound: the presumedly offensive and disturbing thing is thought to be somehow healed by way of a carefully nursed explanation. Moreover, Studlar grounds her thesis in general psychological principles, and therefore it applies to every instance of narrative cinema, not merely to those moments in which male characters are held in submission by dominating women. And yet the opening sequence of this particular film—not to mention the many big-breast-oriented moments throughout films of the 1950s—is an almost literal rendering of her case. Consider, in the reflected light of the women's blazing red sequins, Studlar's remarks about Deleuze's vision of women in (heterosexual) male masochism:

> Deleuze regards the female in the male's masochistic fantasy as the loving inflictor of punishment, not the substitute for a hidden father. The mother, simultaneously love object and controlling agent, is the object of the child's ambivalence. . . . (M)asochistic desire merges the plenitude of the mother with the subject's need for suffering.[32]

Look at meek Mr. Esmond and see, as Sacher-Masoch himself described in his novel *Venus in Furs*, "the blissful torment of worshipping a woman who treats him as a plaything."[33] And as Studlar points out, "Pleasure does not involve the mastery of the female but submission to her body and her gaze. This pleasure applies to the infant, the masochist, and the film spectator," who is more or less accurately satirized by the tremulous figure of Mr. Esmond, with Hawks's cutting and camera placement serving to encourage irony as well as identification.[34]

A bit of costuming history further explains the opening number. According to historian David Chierichetti, executives at Twentieth Century-Fox worried about showing any of the stars' cleavage. In a strangely literal way, large breasts were one thing, cleavage something else again; instead of two breasts, costuming made them a unified whole. There's also a tease here, as a tapered strip of flesh-colored material divides the breasts in simulated cleavage without actually revealing anything. In addition, costume designer William Travilla wired the stars' dresses to keep their breasts from bouncing, shaking, or otherwise acting as real parts of women's bodies.[35] In effect, these design mandates served to contain the women's bodies even while encouraging the spectator to view their expansiveness. Neither successfully exposed nor successfully repressed, Monroe's and Russell's fetishized breasts function in—and as—a kind of *suspense*, a formal figure which Studlar describes as being essential to masochistic pleasure: "Masochism tells its story through very precisely delimited means: fantasy, disavowal, fetishism, and suspense are its formal and psychoanalytic foundations."[36]

The physical and visual suspension of women's breasts, literalized earlier in Jane Russell's career by Howard Hughes's heavily publicized invention of the cantilever bra in 1943, is only the practical formal result of a much more pervasive cultural phenomenon of the World War II and postwar periods. (And by the way, Russell reports in her autobiography that she never wore the bra: "Believe me, he could design planes, but a Mr. Playtex he wasn't.")[37] Begun on a mass level with GIs' pinups, images of large-breasted women assumed a seemingly inordinate influence on American culture, a power that only seemed to increase through the 1950s. Displayed in Hollywood films but *never* revealed, the idealized imago's breasts held the gaze of a mass audience all too eager to be fixated and even dominated by them. In the cinema the authority assumed by the female breast throughout the 1950s is, I believe, almost clinically hysterical—a pure malady through wild representation, as the enforced domesticity of postwar America manifested itself through a riotous interest in nurturing/threatening breasts. In essence, big fifties film breasts are the psychoanalytic dream screen literalized with a conviction so absolute that it required its own repression. The result was the middle ground of subconsciousness; as Arbuthnot and Seneca describe Monroe and Russell's costumes, "Even their most revealing costumes are cocktail dresses which neither expose nor reveal their breasts."[38]

What makes the two women in *Gentlemen Prefer Blondes* so admirable is that, unlike their sisters in most other films of the period (let alone those in the era's burgeoning "girlie" magazine trade), they immediately appreciate and exploit the authority their very bodies have granted them. In gesture, music, lyrics, and costume, Lorelei and Dorothy go on the offensive from the very first moments of the film: "And one of these days in my fancy clothes I'm a'goin' back home and punch the nose of the one who broke my heart—the one who broke my heart!—the one who broke my heart in Little Rock, Little Rock, Little Rock, Little Rock!" With synchronized movements, the women gracefully and seemingly effortlessly (especially so considering the constrictions of the dresses) sing and dance across the stage, emphasizing one of their movements in a particularly proud and belligerent way. The song contains a repetitive rhythm that occurs at the end of certain musical phrases: two beats, heightened by horns and woodwinds—a kind of "boom-boom" that precedes a new stanza. At the "boom-boom," Dorothy and Lorelei swing their hips out to the side twice in time to the rhythm, making their bodies function metaphorically as drum mallets in an audiovisual link that accents their pagan, warlike quality.

At one point in particular, Lorelei uses this gesture specifically against Mr. Esmond: "Find a gentleman who is shy or bold," she coos in medium shot as Hawks cuts to Esmond blushing and coyly waving his hand, "Or short or tall or young or old . . ." Just then, she and Dorothy, who has reentered the frame, clap their hands twice in triumph and then deliver the brutal punchline: "as long as the guy's a millionaire!" The two women close the stanza with their hips— boom-boom!—summarily defeating the poor schnook by openly championing their economic motives. But don't forget: this a masochistic humiliation which the male expressly seeks and enjoys. He nurtures his suffering throughout the film, faltering only once when he asserts his only available power by cutting off Lorelei's letter of credit, a mistake for which he is ultimately delighted to pay.

The Female Two Shot: A Controlling Image

Throughout *Gentlemen Prefer Blondes*, Hawks consistently films Lorelei and Dorothy as a pair, a union. In the opening sequence, Hawks frames them in a persistent two shot, a composition which in this case leaves little space on either side of them. This visual figure not only sets up an enduring bond between the two women, but it also secures their command of the image by eliminating all extraneous space around them. The two shot gives way only twice during the song—first, when Dorothy exists screen right to allow Lorelei to sing that "someone broke my heart in Little Rock" and, second, when Dorothy again leaves Lorelei alone to give her advice about finding a "gentleman who is shy or bold." In both cases, Dorothy reenters the frame when the lyrics suggest feminine strategies: "I came to New York and I found out that men are the same way everywhere," and "as long as the guy's a millionaire!"

Contrary to Maureen Turim's claim, this film is not in Cinema-Scope. If *Gentlemen Prefer Blondes* had been "an elaborate Cinema-Scope Technicolor production," the spatial relationship Hawks develops between Lorelei and Dorothy would have been quite different. The same sequence filmed in CinemaScope—with the same camera setups and cutting pattern—would have yielded an image of two women engulfed by a great deal of empty blue-sequined space on both sides of the screen and a view of Mr. Esmond that would not have suggested his isolation from the other spectators with nearly as much force, since many more of them would be seen surrounding him. In any event, the meaning and ideology of the sequence—and the film as a whole—derives *from* and not despite its expressive form.*

Hawks develops the strategy of teaming the women against a potentially hostile world by tracking with them as they move through crowds of passengers at dockside, in the staging of the song "When Love Goes Wrong," and finally and most importantly in the closing wedding ceremony. In all three scenes, the women are a spectacle: first for the Olympic team, then for Parisians (featuring two young Algerian boys who both watch the song and participate in it by dancing, their race and age setting them apart from traditional centers of power and uniting them with the women), and finally for the ship's passengers, who act as wedding guests. At the same time, these female spectacles are also the camera's driving force; following Studlar's argument, the camera is subject to their controlling image. The moving camera defines the women separately from the crowds around them

---

*According to John Belton, the "Diamonds" number was reshot in CinemaScope promotion in the winter of 1953; this CinemaScope sequence was never part of the film.

and delineates their apparently paradoxical position as the object of a crowd's gaze and the motivating energy governing the camera.

Yet the paradox is only apparent. In fact, Hawks links the two aspects together as the film's central thematic preoccupation. These women have joined together to parlay their looks and talents into economic gain. Prevented by their gender from participating in a world order dominated by weaklings like Mr. Esmond, scoundrels like Sir Francis "Piggie" Beekman (Charles Coburn), and nondescript pseudomanipulators like detective Malone (Elliot Reid), Dorothy and Lorelei seize whatever power they can from their showgirl roles and become motivators in their own right. The power to attract the gaze is theirs, the fact of which they never lose sight.

Such a project drives a wedge between men and their money: "For a kid from a small street I did very well on Wall Street, though I never owned a share of stock." As lumpen as they are talented, Dorothy and Lorelei are able to move between classes—from "the wrong side of the tracks" to the first-class deck on the oceanliner—without ever belonging to either one. Lorelei in particular is painfully direct about her motives, and Esmond, though he knows that Lorelei wants his money, cannot help but succumb. Even his father, late in the film, submits to Lorelei's overt golddigging, noting with surprise that "they told me you were stupid. You don't sound stupid to me."

One of Douglas Sirk's early fifties comedies is called *No Room for the Groom* (1952). In *Gentlemen Prefer Blondes*, the groom's absence is literal in—of all places—the concluding wedding sequence. In the final analysis, the two women in *Gentlemen Prefer Blondes* seem to have achieved as much control over the camera as they do over their lovers. At the wedding sequence's finale, Hawks begins with a two shot of Malone and Dorothy at the altar, pans right to an identically framed shot of Lorelei and Gus, then pans back left to another two shot of Dorothy and Lorelei. In this single shot are three different couples, the first two being traditionally united in marriage, the third and final being the women who continue as a unit *despite* the wedding. As if this were not enough of an indication of Hawks's need to express the women's centrality by banishing the men from the frame, he then cuts to a long shot of the foursome only to track forward again to a two shot of the women, *again* cutting the men out. If marriage is the classical comic resolution, Hawks's variation/repetition skews the terms of such a resolution by reiterating the strength of the female unit to the point of repeatedly dismissing both grooms.

Imagine the same sequence in CinemaScope. There would likely be no need to move the camera, since the four characters could be stretched out across the image while keeping the camera relatively close. The ending of the film would thus be utterly conventional: a nice double wedding with all the characters on-screen at the end. Jonathan Rosenbaum generously attempts to lift Turim off the hook by describing the film as having "the overall effect of the process [CinemaScope] without actually using it," and he even goes so far as to use the final sequence as an example. In fact, however, Hawks's repeated use of the two shot to frame the women as a unit separate and distinct from the men they marry would be next to impossible in CinemaScope without Hawks driving a spatial wedge between the women themselves, which of course would run counter to his comic worldview.

Diamonds

Despite the insistence with which Hawks reiterates the bond between the two women, as well as their absolute superiority over every male in the film, it would be difficult to argue that Dorothy and Lorelei represent radical feminism, even if such an anachronistic reading was somehow desirable. They *subvert* patriarchy—they don't overturn it. One of the clearest and most concise instances of this distinction occurs when Lorelei looks at Piggie and turns his head fantastically into a gigantic and luminescent diamond. Hawks rarely uses process shots that call attention to themselves as cinematic devices, the laundry-chute shot in *Monkey Business* to the contrary notwithstanding. And the isolated subjectivity of point-of-view shots goes against the grain of Hawks's normative, eye-level simulation of objective vision. His resistance to both process shots and POV shots makes this particular superimposition/matte POV even more striking as an anomaly. The shot occurs immediately after Lorelei, who (from the second scene of the film) has been characterized by her obsession with diamonds, meets Piggie, the film's most physically unattractive male. Piggie has been seated at the bar with a man who introduces him to Dorothy, telling her about his diamond mine as well as pointing out his "blood red ruby eyes." No sooner does Dorothy warn Piggie that her friend is diamond mad than Lorelei arrives: "Did I hear someone say something about diamonds?"

If Lorelei is the definitive golddigger, Piggie is patriarchy incarnate. A wealthy English nobleman as swinish as his nickname, Piggie will turn out to be even more morally decrepit than he appears at this point in the film. Hawks uses Charles Coburn once again to convey a sense of comic despair regarding aging, and Technicolor only serves to intensify one's sense of the character's physical degeneration. His skin is very mottled, and costumer Travilla exaggerates this further by dressing him with a red paisley scarf around his neck. Lorelei and Piggie are a study in opposites: an extraordinarily attractive woman who has no money of her own, but who knows how to dress, opposes a very rich man who can buy whatever he wants but who cannot ever hope to make himself physically appealing. Hawks has the two characters stare wide-eyed at each other while Dorothy makes the introductions. Piggie ogles Lorelei, and Lorelei ogles Piggie. But while the medium close-up of Lorelei emphasizes her beauty from a closer point of view, the corresponding shot of Piggie, his mouth half open and his eyes popping out, yields exactly the opposite impression—to everyone, that is, except Lorelei, who promptly replaces his grotesque head with an enormous gemstone, a thing of spectacular beauty.

This diamond, larger than life, reflects a particularly ornate set of meanings and nuances, the first and most character-oriented being a sense of Lorelei's creativity. Whereas the rest of the world looks at Piggie and sees ugliness masquerading as desire, wealth countermanding decrepitude, Lorelei has the cognitive ability to transform brute fact to suit her own imagination. What she creates is an object more glittering than herself. More crucial to the film's ideological project, Lorelei's reduction of Piggie's head to the status of a rock makes Piggie even more of an object than she is. A solid stone perched on a man's shoulders, Piggie is so objectified that he becomes a walking contradiction between the animate and the inanimate: half animal, half mineral, Piggie becomes a visual joke that shifts the power imbalance over to Lorelei, at least temporarily. Finally, Lorelei's creative act condenses Piggie's wealth, gender, and occupation into a single term: Piggie *is* a diamond. One image literally imposed upon another, the diamond and Piggie's head are morphologically if not visually identical. Just as Freud describes a certain kind of pun as the collision of two words that takes the form of a newly created composite, the Piggie-diamond is an amalgam of two related ideas which Lorelei condenses into a single unit.[39]

It isn't that men are money. Being economically tangential—neither Lorelei nor Dorothy ever deals in cash—Lorelei has no interest in currency. Lorelei lives in a material world, and what she wants is a material object. In Piggie's case, she simply creates it. It must be said, though, that she is only speeding up a warped version of biology, wherein she rapidly compresses a decaying organism into a much more solid and shiningly indestructible product of nature. As a commodity capitalist, Lorelei is swifter than Piggie himself: turning the tables, she objectifies and defines him in a flash. It is an act of subversion rather than revolution.

Literalizing her motives in such a sophisticated fashion, Lorelei is at this moment the antithesis of Anita Loos' daffy heroine, who is ceaselessly made to be the brunt of jokes and never their creator. Hawks's *Gentlemen Prefer Blondes* isn't much like its source. Anita Loos originally wrote *Gentlemen Prefer Blondes* as a novel in 1925; it was then adapted by Loos and John Emerson into a play, which opened on Broadway in 1926, and further adapted by Loos and Joseph Fields into a Broadway musical in 1949. Hawks and Charles Lederer kept little of the musical's script, eliminating the prominent character of Mrs. Spofford entirely and turning Henry Spofford from the moralistic mama's boy who eventually marries Dorothy into (literally) a little boy. Consider, too, the difference between Hawks's introduction of Piggie and the corresponding passage from Loos' novel, written in 1925 and set contemporaneously in the Jazz Age:

So then I looked around the room and I noticed a gentleman who seemed to be quite well groomed. So I asked Major Falcon who he was and he said he was called Sir Francis Beekman and it seems he is very, very, wealthy. So then I asked Major Falcon to give us an introduction to one another and we met one another and I asked Sir Francis Beekman if he would hold my hat while I could try on the diamond tiara because I could wear it backwards with a ribbon, on account of my hair being hobbled, and I told Sir Francis Beekman that I really thought it looked quite cute. So he thought it did to, but he seemed to have another engagement. So the Countess came up to me and she is really very unrefined because she said to me "Do not waste your time on him' because she said that whenever Sir Francis Beekman spent a haypenny the statue of a gentleman called Mr Nelson took off his hat and bowed. I mean some people are so unrefined they seem to have unrefined thoughts about everything.[40]

Throughout the book, Loos is intent on humiliating Lorelei; as an author, she is a prime example of a woman who achieved power by adopting male strategies against women. Stupid and semiliterate, Loos' Lorelei errs on every level—her morals are as wrong as her grammar. One could not argue that Loos' heroine is cynical. She's simply too brainless to master the sense of irony that cynicism requires. More damaging still is Loos' first-person strategy, which filters everything through her Lorelei's contemptible point of view. Loos' relentless language—beginning sentences with "So," repeating the word "unrefined" three times—lends an annoyingly tedious quality to the character and to the work itself, a monotony that is quite contrary to Hawks's treatment. Indeed, Hawks's Lorelei serves as a delightful relief from tedium as wacky logic becomes a comic means of escape from oppressive normality. Moreover, in terms of cultural development, Hawks's updating of the story necessarily entailed raising Lorelei's IQ. Even Monroe, the era's quintessential dumb blonde, couldn't have gotten away with being as dumb as Loos's twenties version.

Lorelei's vibrant sexuality may be the most obvious reason for Piggie's interest, but her mixture of clever wit and infantile charm is no less crucial to her strategy of entrapment. In marked contrast to Lady Beekman, the industrialist's wife who shares but one short scene with Piggie in the course of film, Lorelei manipulates Piggie verbally, as in the following sequence:

Malone, in long shot, is taking pictures through a porthole. Not a good detective, he suddenly tries to cover up his activities and only succeeds in looking guiltier. Dorothy, in medium shot, is surprised to see her beau spying on her best friend; she walks toward the porthole and looks in to see what captured Malone's interest. Cut to Piggie and Lorelei standing together in the stateroom:

Piggie:	Ug ug oog ugh oog oog ug ug basha!
Lorelei:	Aren't you clever, Piggie!
Piggie:	You see, that means, "Come to my basha and I'll give you my old coconut shells." Now you see, the natives believe that coconutshells ward off the snakes. Terror, wot!
Lorelei:	(*brightly*) Africa must be fascinating. (*pouting*) Gee, a girl like I almost never gets to meet really interesting men. Sometimes my brain gets *real starved*!

In three shots, Hawks efficiently moves from Malone's spying and a dramatic example of his questionable competence to Dorothy's reaction and finally into the stateroom to see what Dorothy sees. For the audience, Piggie's noises are gibberish, and Lorelei's enthusiasm for his intelligence becomes the most extreme example yet of her ability to flatter any man for any reason. Yet their conversation isn't over, and Hawks uses the rest of it to set up Lorelei's acquisition of Lady Beekman's tiara by showing her genuine wiles. Her tactics may be transparent, but they work beautifully on Piggie. The specifics of their conversation, however, turn out to be a setup for an elaborate joke in which Lorelei reveals an acute self-awareness. Dorothy enters, Piggie departs, and the two women (in a long-take two shot) discuss Lorelei's being "in a jam":

Dorothy: What were you and Piggie doing in here before he started barking like a seal?

Lorelei: He wasn't barking—that's Swahili.

Dorothy: No, no, before that. Now think hard. Was there anything that would look incriminating in a photograph? Something you wouldn't want Mr. Esmond to see?

Lorelei: Why no. (*shocked*) My goodness, yes!

Dorothy: What?

Lorelei: Piggie was telling me about South Africa. It's very dangerous there. Practically full of snakes called pythons. And it seems a python can *grab a goat* (*she gestures dramatically with her hands*) and *kill it* by just *squeeeeeezing* it to death!

Dorothy: Well, get to the point.

Lorelei: That's all.

Dorothy: Well, what's incriminating about that?

Lorelei: Well, Piggie was being a python, and I was a goat.

Just as she literalized her equation of Piggie with diamonds, Lorelei now fails to distinguish between Piggie and the reptile she describes. Her vivid description of a python crushing a goat to death ought to be enough of an explanation of what went on in the stateroom; it is Dorothy, the representation of sanity, who asks for clarification. Even when Lorelei provides it, she does so in terms of accurate similes: Piggie was a python, and therefore she was a goat.

Male and Female Spectacle

Romance is cast in a particularly abrasive light throughout this film. Fox commissioned Hoagy Carmichael and Harold Adamson to write two new songs for the film, and both share the same despair: "Anyone Here for Love?" and "When Love Goes Wrong." Carmichael's and Adamson's musical style is different than that of the composers of the original musical, Jule Styne and Leo Robin, and the addition of the songs suggests that Hawks wanted to amplify certain moments musically. These moments are critical to the development of the sexual design of the film. Critics frequently cite the first of the numbers, "Anyone Here For Love?" as exemplary of the dehumanization of men and women in the world order presided over by Lorelei's acquisitiveness and Dorothy's lust. From Robin Wood:

> [The film exalts] a grotesque modern morality, a *reductio ad absurdum* of the contemporary values of money and erotic experience pursued as ends in themselves. The best sequence in the film is the staging of "Ain't there Anyone Here for Love?" in the ship's gymnasium, with Jane Russell surrounded by the Olympics team too self-absorbed in body-building exercises to notice her. Blank faces and mechanical movements suggest men become machines: the sequence parallels the 'Diamonds' number.[41]

From Andrew Sarris:

> Jane Russell's song number with an array of sexless musclemen is Hawks's ultimate comment on male narcissism and homosexuality.[42]

And from Gerald Mast:

> Given Hawks's deliberate sexual reversals in this film and elsewhere, the parody of [Busby] Berkeley's sexlessly smiling female faces and sexlessly geometricized female limbs may even be intentional. But there is something disturbingly "Hollywood-sterile" about these male bodies, this plethora of well-muscled flesh which is also completely (and repulsively) inhuman.[43]

For Wood, the men's failure to drop their training and go after Jane Russell is an expression of Hawks's moralism, though it's unclear whether athletics is part of the money fixation or the erotic fixation of contemporary life. For Sarris, the sequence is flatly a comment (and it isn't positive) on homosexuality, even though at the end of the song the men hoist Dorothy on their shoulders and they all drink a toast. For Mast, in an extraordinarily naked self-contradiction, the sequence represents a mechanized spectacle à la Busby Berkeley, but it is so successful in its execution that it isn't any good. Hawks's treatment of men in *Gentlemen Prefer Blondes* is particularly upsetting to Mast. Aside from his remarks about sterility and sexlessness, Mast refers elsewhere in another compact self-contradiction to "the repulsively old Sir Francis Beekman (Charles Coburn—just a bit too old and repulsive for this role)." As with Hawks's treatment of half-naked men, Mast condemns Coburn for doing too good a job.

In point of fact, the muscleboys are not an excuse for moralizing, not a comment on gays in the Olympics, and, most of all, not sexless. The fact that the men are clearly on display in the same way that Dorothy and Lorelei are doesn't mean that they lose their virility in the process. Spectacle in this film is not limited to women; it takes the form of athleticism in these men, and to this critic at least they're lots of fun to watch. Just as Lorelei and Dorothy are not personally available to all the men who pay to watch them perform on stage, the Olympic team remains at one remove from those spectators of either gender who gaze upon them. Their actions, too, are far from being "sexless." The fact that a number of male critics don't want to appear to find pleasure in men's bodies is ridiculously beside the point, especially since Hawks *invites* the pleasure by having the shirtless studs flex, perform difficult gymnastic maneuvers as coordinated in physical gestures as the ones Lorelei and Dorothy perform on stage, and finally go so far as to pump their butts in the air as Dorothy passes and vaguely swats at them with squash racquets. In fairness to Robin Wood, I must note not only that Wood has been "out" in print for many years but, more important, has insisted on incorporating his gay identity into his criticism. For this reason, Wood's position on *Gentlemen Prefer Blondes* is particularly mystifying to me and, given the revisions he made to his book on Hawks, is not entirely explained by the fact that he first wrote about *Gentlemen Prefer Blondes* before coming out in print.

The men do ignore Dorothy—that is, until the end of the song, at which point one of them literally kicks her into the water. If anything, it is this finale that remains the most disturbing moment in the film, for only after the athletes' spectacular self-absorption results in violence do the two genders make peace. Jane Russell reports in her autobiography that her dunking was actually a mistake that turned out to be fortuitous—from Hawks's idiosyncratically fun-oriented point of view. As she describes it, "One poor cluck didn't clear me, and I went head first into the pool and came up like a drowned rat. The scene had to be reshot . . . but in the final cut the first take was used."[44] The raising of Dorothy onto the shoulders of the men and the sudden appearance of a waiter with a tray of drinks may be Hawks's attempt to recuperate the nagging sexual tension that motivates the song, but it also works to resolve the tension by setting up an uneasy truce. Once they toast, the team virtually departs the film, and Dorothy never mentions them again. The performers remain in their separate sexual realms, and separation becomes the resolution that interaction had prevented.

Less disturbing by far is the (in)famous "Diamonds Are a Girl's Best Friend" number, which is often cited with revulsion by film critics but which was used to appreciative referential advantage in the late 1980s by Madonna in her "Material Girl" music video. Madonna, in characteristic postmodern style, lifts Monroe's costuming and choreography, though in decidedly toned-down versions, while simultaneously blocking any coherent, fixed meaning of her own. She claims she's "living in a material world and I am a material girl," yet she ends up in a pickup truck with a plain, seemingly working-class guy (who, in a deliberate inconsistency, is actually a wealthy film director putting on an act). Uncharacteristically, however, Madonna does not pick up on the most sexually charged aspect of the "Diamonds" number—namely, the human chandelier and *torchères* composed entirely of women suspended by black ropes and dressed in what appears to be black leather and satin. In Madonna's late-eighties rendition, the stage is bare, but in 1953 Monroe performed her paean to mercenary self-protection surrounded by living examples of what befalls women who fail to take charge. Beginning the song with as emphatic a rejection of men and male values as could be imagined ("No! No! No no no no no no no! No no no no no no no. . . . No! No! No! No! No!—NO!"), Lorelei demonstrates her authority over a pack of indistinguishable chorus boys who are in their own way as mechanical as the women in the chandelier, with one key exception: because they are bound and suspended, the women retain a quality of sexual temptation, whereas the guys aren't worth a second glance. Bondage accurately explains women's economic position here, but it also confers a kind of tantalizing power. In fact, these bound chandelier/women are, like the movie screen itself, literally the source of light: you can look, but you can't touch. And that frustration is the source of an exquisite kind of pleasure.

The social visions Hawks presents in *Monkey Business* and *Gentlemen Prefer Blondes* are suffused with the irresolution and anxiety of their era. Superficially, an existing marriage is resolved and two new marriages begin, but under the veneer of genre expectation is a dissatisfied undercurrent that erupts time and again through Hawks's expressive formal choices. Hawks's characters are themselves frustrated, particularly the men, but a broader form of frustration suffuses both comedies. For a period that mandated marriage as the ultimate social resolution, happy endings ought to have been happier. In each film, Hawks supplies the expected resolution, but he supplies it in a way that preserves tension rather than suppresses it. In *Monkey Business*, he "resolves" the Fultons' marriage too early by having them decide not to go to a party with Hank Entwhistle but to stay home instead; playing out the consequences, he then forces the couple to regress even further the next time they take B-4. In *Gentlemen Prefer Blondes*, two couples unite in holy matrimony, but the men are so tangential to the *real* union between two women that they cease to be visible.

In this way, frustration exists not only on the level of individual characters but also on the level of genre, which is to say in the culture at large. Hawks, being normative, wasn't alone in perceiving generic upheavals as well as the frazzled nerves and pounding brains of his society. Billy Wilder saw them as well, and through his eyes the world of comedy took on such levels of morbidity that death itself began to seem preferable to living. In death, at least, one could achieve a certain gratification, the sense of genuine security that fifties propriety otherwise denied.

two

BILLY WILDER AND
THE AMERICAN DREAM

Straight from the Corpse's Mouth:
The Comedy of *Sunset Boulevard*

The Devil's Laughter

In November 1950, James Agee wrote a passionate, vividly argued defense of *Sunset Boulevard* and of Hollywood itself, declaring that it would be difficult "to find better craftsmanship . . . at this time, in any art or country." He described as "brilliantly witty" Billy Wilder's tale of a histrionically demented has-been told from the point of view of a corpse, yet he felt compelled to offer a brief apology for the film's impurity of genre, the intervention of humor into what might have been a more somber project:

> It is true, I think, that they [Wilder and Charles Brackett, the producer and coscreenwriter] fail to make much of the powerful tragic possibilities which are inherent in their story; they don't even explore much of the deep anguish and pathos which are still more richly inherent, though they often reveal it, quickly and brilliantly. But this does not seem to me a shameful kind of failure, if indeed it is proper to call it a failure at all: they are simply not the men for such a job, nor

was this the kind of job they were trying to do. But they are beautifully equipped to do the cold, exact, adroit, sardonic job they have done.[1]

Variety, though, found the film to be more like a dirge: "There is scant relief from tragedy in any of the footage and the futile note is driven home when the dead writer continues his narration after his body has been hauled from the pool and tagged for the morgue."[2] Hollywood's legendary paper of record notwithstanding, Agee's reading is more accurate. In fact, if one follows the vectors of his reasoning, not to mention the logic of the film, *Sunset Boulevard* is one of the great comedies of its time.

Everyone from Carol Burnett to innumerable drag queens have replayed Gloria Swanson's unforgettable Norma Desmond as a comical figure. But by flailing their arms and emoting deadly pretense, Norma's campy mimics have merely overparodied mannerisms and attitudes that were already funny to begin with. In tone, in conceit, and especially in the treatment of its bizarre heroine and the town that made her what she is, *Sunset Boulevard* is downright hilarious. But to 1950 Hollywood, an industrial town in the process of breaking apart under the strain of massive economic upheavals, let alone accompanying political and emotional ones, a film in which a great star nearly rots to death before shooting a young talent in the back must have been quite unsettling. One can hardly blame *Variety* for lacking a sense of humor.

Sunset Boulevard is a ghastly sort of joke, the mocking kind that looks more like a sneer than a smile as it calls reason itself into question, but it's certainly no less comical for the depth of its attack. Consider what screenwriter Joe Gillis (William Holden) finds in the living hell of Norma Desmond's home: a great director finishing his career as a guilt-ridden servant, a swimming pool in which rats take the place of Valentino, and a vision of life wherein a monkey receives a proper and dignified burial in, of all things, a satiny white coffin upholstered in pink or "maybe red—bright flaming red. Let's make it gay!"

Gillis's unexpected encounter with the absurd expresses in character form what the audience meets in terms of genre disruption. As one critic described it, Wilder's fifties comedies "are visually just as gloomy as his dramas"—a logical artistic strategy, since for Wilder comedy may be set in disparate and often desperate circumstances: a faded star's mansion, a Nazi POW camp, a New York brownstone, or gangland Chicago at the site of the St. Valentine's Day Massacre.[3] With its voice-over narration, policemen, private detectives, and suspenseful score, the opening of *Sunset Boulevard* even appears to set the film in another genre, but comedy gradually takes over where crime fiction, film noir, or melodrama leaves off.

In a gesture of cosmic (in)opportunity that calls Hitchcock's wrong-man humor to mind, Gillis ends up in this creepy netherworld because his left front tire blows out in the middle of a high-speed chase, causing him to veer suddenly and fatefully into somebody's driveway in the magnificent 10000 block of Sunset Boulevard. Gillis speaks in the tough, terse language of film noir, and Franz Waxman's rhythmic score intensifies the suspense of the car chase, but the combination of tough talk and baroque romance is pointedly comical in its evocation of a Hollywood gone round the bend. In Wilder's blend of Dickens and noir, plausible realism and outlandish exaggeration, one can hear a governing snicker, what Milan Kundera calls "the Devil's laughter."[4] As Gillis describes it:

> I had landed myself in the driveway of a mansion that looked rundown and deserted. . . . It was a great big white elephant of a place, the kind crazy movie people built in the crazy twenties. A deserted house gets an unhappy look. This one had it in spades. It was like that old woman in *Great Expectations*—that Miss Havisham, with her rotting wedding dress and her torn veil, taking it out on the world because she'd been given the go-by.

Gillis thinks at this moment that he has failed to break into Hollywood. Just before spying "the credit boys" stopped opposite him at a light, he talks about heading back to Dayton, Ohio—specifically to face the derisive laughter of his coworkers at the local newspaper. But when his tire blows out, Gillis achieves what neither his glad-handing agent nor the bumbling, burping Paramount executive Sheldrake had been able to offer—namely, an entré to the *real* Hollywood, not just the one that produces movies and counts the receipts, but a nightmarishly gestalt version constituted by obsession, decay, money, insanity, myth, morbid romance, and, above all, the dry laughter of self-consciousness.

"You there. Why are you so late? Why have you kept me waiting so long?" The modern Miss Havisham responds from a second floor window, and while Gillis will eventually provide her with the long-lost suitor denied her fictional ancestor, for the time being she exists reductively as a pair of watching eyes shining through the dark with the look of one possessed, an appropriate metonymy for a washed-up movie goddess whose audience time and short memories have reduced to one. A gruff voice beckons Gillis to enter—it seems, strangely, that he is expected—and he does so despite his own weak protestations. Waxman's score, tense and percussive until this point, now takes on a musty lyricism as an unusual bald servant demands "Wipe your feet!" with Teutonic flair. The servant, Max (played by the fanatically flamboyant has-been Erich von Stroheim), directs Gillis up the stairs. As Gillis ascends and leaves the frame at the top of screen left, Max's head loomingly enters the frame from the right and, disembodied, solemnly intones, "If you need any help with the coffin, call me."

Wilder cuts to Gillis on the stairs: the remark has literally stopped him in his tracks. In a comic double take, a spontaneously ironic gesture that punctuates Max's line and emphasizes its grim humor, Gillis physically demonstrates the ironic perspective he has already revealed in language. The moment is short, taking no more than a few seconds, but Wilder uses it to interrupt Gillis's linear and (as it turns out) fatal progression toward Norma Desmond's heart-of-darkness boudoir with a comic theatrical convention: a character suddenly, through physical gesture, elevates himself from naive participant to ironic spectator.

Gillis's actions in this introductory sequence are also arresting in what they suggest about the hero's morbid state of mind. When Max orders him to go upstairs, he goes; when Norma escorts him in, he goes; when she demands that he leave, he doesn't go. Gillis evidently seems to find some gratification in this rotting world, something personally compelling, and thus he acquiesces willingly to his own apparent downfall.

Norma Desmond's gaudy, brocaded home—already called "crazy" by Gillis—is a monument to chaos, but it's the kind of chaos that has stultified into a way of life. Presided over by a madwoman and administered by a servile but nonetheless domineering male, the house presently serves as funeral chapel for a monkey. The chimp's identity, like that of the cadaver floating in the swimming pool, remains a mystery at this point in the film, but it is the second time that the spectator has been brought to the quintessence of Hollywood grandeur to discover a dead body. To Gillis, though, the arrival constitutes something of a triumph. Due only in part to a desperate flight from creditors and a flat tire, Gillis's arrival at the Desmond estate is also a culmination of his goal as former Dayton newspaper hack—in other words, to be a successful Hollywood hack. The fact that he enters the house as an undertaker and leaves it as a corpse only adds to the sense of his accomplishment. In any event, the cultural archaeologist finds yet another fifties chimp in this sequence—the cherished child-substitute of a childless woman. But because he is more ironic than his contemporaries, Wilder doesn't indulge his adopted culture's chimp mania. He kills the monkey off before the story begins, but he keeps the corpse around long enough to make a sardonic point.

Norma, whose entrance Wilder still delays for one more moment, speaks offscreen: "This way!" Gillis turns and sees a strange but vaguely familiar woman dressed in mourning black. Her eyes shielded by dark glasses, her hand clutching a precious cigarette holder, she beckons him even deeper into this seemingly endless house. "In here," she gestures with her hand and proceeds to deliver a line that (as a description of the whereabouts of the mystery corpse) can only be considered humorous: "I put him on a massage table in front of the fire. He always liked fires, and poking at them with a stick." A massage table, where all stars and starlets are rejuvenated. A fire, presumably to keep the stiff warm. Until the monkey's face is revealed under the coverlet, the audience is skewed first into wondering what kind of companion would enjoy poking at fires with a stick, and next what kind of person would relay this information in such a casual and accepting manner.

The answer to the first question comes when the blanket is drawn back to reveal the dead monkey, but the second one demands a more gradual revelation, and indeed the remainder of the film takes up the issue of what Hollywood stardom is all about. Throughout the film, Swanson employs a certain dramatic gesture: she tosses her hands open, flicking her wrist at the same time in an expression of possession and command, the kind fairy godmothers might use to grant a wish. As the film progresses, Norma grants Gillis his fondest wish by making him a well-paid scriptwriter with a mansion and his own live-in living legend, but in this scene the gesture implies that the morose and elaborate scenario being played out within the mansion's crumbling walls is almost entirely the product of Norma's imagination. Like Miss Havisham's, Norma's will is stronger than that of the world that confines her. This star's extraordinary determination, the product of a fiction-generating system that created stars and distributed their carefully structured images all around the world in order to reap a nice profit, can impose its hegemonic vision in however distorted a manner it chooses. And it is clearly a vision that rides on contradiction—between youth and age, sex and death, power and impotence, beauty and ugliness.

On the Road

One of the film's most delightful offscreen ironies is that Paramount Pictures sent Gloria Swanson on a promotional tour not only for the benefit of *Sunset Boulevard* but for the greater glory of the industry as a whole. By the late 1940s, Hollywood had come to understand that its public image had deteriorated along with its box-office receipts and that industry-wide measures had to be taken to stem the tide of public relations dissolution. In 1947 the first round of HUAC hearings into the putative communist infiltration of Hollywood had served to cast grave doubt on the industry's political morality, at least insofar as morality was judged by HUAC; this was a trend that obviously continued in full force through 1953 and beyond. But politics wasn't Hollywood's only image problem. In the spring of 1949, only a little more than a year before *Sunset Boulevard* was released, Ingrid Bergman's affair with Roberto Rossellini had provoked a general public scandal, and by the end of 1949 the woman who had most recently played St. Joan was revealed to be pregnant by her lover. Hollywood's reputation took a drastic beating along with Bergman's. As a specific consequence of the scandal, for example, a measure was introduced in the United States Senate designed, as *Variety* put it, "to license motion pictures and the actors appearing in them."[5] Sen. Edwin C. Johnson (D, Colo.) evidently believed that Bergman's "moral turpitude" was a threat to the nation's youth of the sort that could be prevented in the future by government regulation of actors. (Johnson called *Stromboli* "a stupid film about a pregnant woman and a volcano.") The measure never went anywhere, but its very existence, not to mention the whirlwind of moral indignation that produced it, provides good indication of the nation's cultural pulsebeat.

Secret communists and fellow travelers here, married Nordic movie stars impregnated by hairy Italian neorealists there, and the threat of television everywhere. The industry needed to strike back in self-defense. But in terms of orchestrating what would later be called a proactive response, Hollywood was less prepared than it might have been in earlier times. The film industry's well-chronicled economic woes in the period resulted among other things in a drastic reduction of public relations personnel. Between July 1947 and March 1950, Paramount Pictures cut its publicity staff from thirty-four to eighteen, Metro-Goldwyn-Mayer trimmed back from forty to twenty-five, and Warner Bros., which had previously led the pack in sheer numbers, sliced its force all the way down from forty-two to fifteen.[6] At the same time, in a damaging confluence of economic conditions, corporate strategy, current events, and changing public taste, gossip and scandal were taking over where organized studio publicity had perforce left off. In late 1949 this trend toward the unauthorized publicizing of private lives caused Ronald Reagan, then president of the Screen Actors Guild, to defensively blast the growing international corps of professional gossips for not "bring[ing] out the fact that this community consists in the main of hardworking, churchgoing family men and women who rarely if ever break into the headlines and who proportionately are engaged in more charitable activities than any other group in the nation."[7]

It was precisely during this time of promotional upheaval that Gloria Swanson, only too glad to be back in the public eye after a more or less unbroken sixteen-year absence, seized on the chance to shill for an industry that had once tossed her aside but that now needed her to inject some old-time glamour and star presence into Hollywood's national image. Swanson wasn't alone; so many actors were doing double duty as hucksters in 1950 that studios had to take special care that they didn't "step on each others' toes in a particular city."[8] But given the film she was ballyhooing, Swanson's case was unique. For her efforts, Paramount paid Swanson $1,000 per week as she gamely trooped around the nation on the dual mission of convincing the public that Hollywood was a healthy, thriving, trustworthy place and simultaneously promoting *Sunset Boulevard*, the nastiest, most derisive film about Hollywood ever to have been made at that point.

It is impossible to say whether or not Swanson convinced the public of Hollywood's positive value, but *Sunset Boulevard* and Paramount seem to have been helped quite a bit. Run at a cost of $75,000, Swanson's promo tour returned an estimated $250,000 of free advertising.[9] It must be noted, however, that although *Sunset Boulevard* was a "tremendous success" in cities, the film bombed in "the hinterlands." As *Variety* plainly noted (citing the opinions of Paramount executives) *Sunset Boulevard* was a "pic that must be keyed by publicity and exploitation and that it is impossible, no matter how big a job is done, to reach through the sticks."[10]

Contradiction and Confusion:
An Irrational Middle Ground

Swanson's successful venture into the realm of public relations demonstrates that even as Hollywood showed itself to be collapsing in the fall of 1950, the American film industry's cultural hegemony was still more or less intact and therefore continued to retain the power to bring together contradictory ideas and not only play them through but attempt to resolve them, however shakily, both on-screen and off. Embodying many of these oppositions, Swanson/Desmond serves by way of the magnitude of her image—she is, in a way, Hollywood itself, a connotation not lost on the executives who authorized the PR trip—as the living resolution to contradiction. A personality of such irrational, mythical proportion that she becomes herself a kind of ideology, Norma has scant use of reason: "I have decided to bury him in the garden. Are there any city laws against that? . . . I don't care anyway." Hers is a world of high surface drama masking or perhaps revealing more fully a substructure of insanity and despair. Admittedly, this may seem an unusual principle for comedy, let alone for a comedy's romantic leading lady. But *Sunset Boulevard* is a satire, not a romantic comedy, and its satirical thrust demands a sober foundation for the attack. In terms of the creation and transmission of culture, it would be difficult to find a more sobering and deserving foundation for satire than Hollywood and the art of cultural commerce.

As the magnet to which Gillis has necessarily gravitated as an aspiring screenwriter, Norma Desmond incarnates the farcical self-importance of Hollywood characterization much more thoroughly than either Sheldrake or Gillis's agent, who simply haven't lived there long enough to accrue Norma's desperate seniority. Her wealth is not limited to her finances, though the bountiful champagne and caviar she serves are certainly more than enough to convince Gillis that a prolonged stay might be worthwhile. More impressively, Norma's wealth is the wealth of Hollywood's past, the ornate narrative machinery that at this point in 1950 could be generated so convincingly that a dead man could speak and be heard and *believed*. Norma's famous declaration, "I'm still big! It's the pictures that got small," remains one of the most powerful statements about the legend of Hollywood and its prolonged decline, and Wilder intensifies the line's impact by granting Norma one of her all-important close-ups in which to deliver it. But Gillis then follows through on the subject of "pictures" with an observation of his own, a smirking comment that Wilder treats as a throwaway punchline: "Uh-huh. I knew there was something wrong with them."

To achieve his satiric comedy, Wilder plays with the real lives and screen mannerisms of Gloria Swanson and Erich von Stroheim, not to mention the less biographical, more popularized history of Hollywood mythmaking that nearly every American audience member could understand by the early 1950s. But he also festoons Swanson's character with a peculiar mixture of comic exaggeration and pathetic irony. In other words, he turns her into a clown. Norma's thickly applied makeup may on one level recall and play upon the conventions of silent cinema, but in the sheer excess of its application, in particular the dark and preternatural lips, Norma Desmond's greasepaint evokes Emmett Kelly at least as much as it does *Queen Kelly* (1929), which is only to say that by 1950 the conventional makeup of silent screen stars could be used to ridicule them. (In fact, *Sunset Boulevard* incorporates some footage from the earlier film. *Queen Kelly* had never been released commercially in the United States, but a print of the film surfaced at the Museum of Modern Art in New York around the time *Sunset Boulevard* was released. As *Variety* titled its reporting of the event, "1929 Swanson Fiasco Is Finally Reviewed as a Museum Piece.")[11]

Reading *Sunset Boulevard* not just as a satirical melodrama but as a generic comedy might fly in the face of its reputation, but the problem of classifying films within genres has yet to be resolved. For example, in an infamous (though to my mind ingenious) assessment of Howard Hawks's films, Robin Wood claims that *Scarface* (1932) belongs with Hawks's comedies. Richard Corliss describes *Sunset Boulevard* as "the definitive Hollywood horror movie," with Gloria Swanson playing Dracula to Gillis's Mina

Harker, a provocative gender reversal that Corliss does not pursue. Both Peter Wollen and Will Wright have attempted to classify narrative operations within individual films and genres by following the classifying model devised by Vladimir Propp for use in folktales, but the issue of classifying genres themselves has not been solved. Wollen himself once suggested that scripts be fed into computers in order to classify them, but this would only classify the scripts, not the films.[12]

Simply put, it's easy to call a given film a comedy when someone else—a scriptwriter, a studio's publicity department, another critic—says that's what it is. A less passive way of approaching comedy, especially in cases like *Sunset Boulevard*, is to see how a scenario that might well have been melodrama or even tragedy turns instead into an affirmative comic vision, one in which relentless incidental punchlines and absurd motifs (the dead monkey, the talking corpse, Max, the lips, and so on) act as ironic critical tools rather than merely as entertaining but dismissible sidelights. The joke of *Sunset Boulevard* is Hollywood itself, and while Wilder consistently subjects the real movie industry to the full force of his sarcasm, he also turns it into a maelstrom of irrationality, a comic universe unto itself. To Wilder, Hollywood is a series of bad jokes. Gillis tells Norma about his previous work: "The last one I wrote was about Okies in the dust bowl. You'd never know it, because when it reached the screen the whole thing played on a torpedo boat." As Gillis delivers the line, Norma is leading him into the living room where she will present her own ridiculous script. Being a product of the business Gillis sarcastically but truthfully describes, Norma does not see the humor in the situation and simply keeps walking, never even turning her head. Gillis evidently does not find his script's metamorphosis very funny either, though he inflects the line with unmistakable irony. But while contemporary Hollywood was not a laughing matter to either of the characters, Wilder obviously found it most amusing and presents it as much for its ironic commentary value as for expository reasons.

In Sheldrake's office, Gillis pitches his idea for a baseball script called "Bases Loaded." The idea meets with no enthusiasm at all until Sheldrake (Fred Clark), who has been belching and drinking bicarbonate and water throughout the scene and who is now on his way to the couch to lie down, says:

Sheldrake: Of course, we're, uh, we're always looking for a Betty Hutton. Do you see it as a Betty Hutton?
Gillis: Frankly no.
Sheldrake: Now wait a minute. If we made it a girls' softball team, added a couple of numbers, it could make a cute musical! (*He raises his left arm as if to indicate a marquee, and intones dramatically*) "It Happened in the Bullpen: The Story of a Woman."
Gillis: (*smiling painfully*): Are you trying to be funny? Because I'm all out of laughs.

The dialogue is mildly amusing, especially considering that Sheldrake has been introduced as "a smart producer." But what makes the scene genuinely comedic—and genuinely typical of the kind of humor *Sunset Boulevard* is built on—is its lack of a conclusion: Sheldrake does not make it clear whether or not "It Happened in the Bullpen" is a joke or a plausible scenario for next year's production schedule, and Gillis, just as he will be in the presence of Norma Desmond, is left completely in the dark about whether or not he's supposed to break up or break down. This is the Devil's laughter, as Milan Kundera describes it:

Things deprived suddenly of their putative meaning, the place assigned them in the ostensible order of things . . . make us laugh. Initially, therefore, laughter is the province of the Devil. It has a certain malice to it (things have turned out differently from the way they tried to seem), but a certain beneficent relief as well (things are looser than they seemed, we have greater latitude in living with them, their gravity does not oppress us).[13]

Impervious to the Outside World

Owing to the baroque overdetermination of a perverse film about a perverse culture as reflected perversely on screen, the comedy necessarily becomes intricate and self-enclosed. In their book-length study of Wilder, Neil Sinyard and Adrian Turner also note the film's self-referential involutions, and while it may not be necessary to say that Norma's swimming pool is specifically a symbol of her womb in order to make a point about the film's complexity, the two critics do offer an astute reading of the inscription "Mad About the Boy" on the silver cigarette case Norma bestows upon Gillis. As a reference to a popular song on the surface, the inscription also provides a dig against Gillis (the boy, compared to his older keeper), alludes to William Holden's first starring role (*Golden Boy*, 1939), and gives a premonition of Norma's madness.[14] But Sinyard and Turner, on the brink of the more overarching point, still fall short; it's not just that Wilder and Brackett constructed a highly detailed film, but that their film is so profoundly self-enclosed that, being *the* Hollywood tale par excellence, such self-enclosure makes the cinema as inevitable and inescapable as death itself. There is simply no way out of it—which is, of course, what the narrator discovers. What makes this vision comic, of course, is the treatment of this discovery. Rather than building a tale of performance, memory, and self-enclosure toward the orchestral tragedy of, say, *Lola Montès* (France–West Germany, 1955), Wilder finds humor in the paths his hero and heroine take to the morgue and the asylum, respectively. This may be the difference between a film *set* in a circus and a film *constituted* by circus, the former possibly being tragedy, the latter necessarily being comedy.

In his 1928 essay "Humor," Freud offers some speculative, nonclinical, but essential comments about the psychological function of humor. For Freud, there are no two ways about it: "Humor is not resigned; it is rebellious." Clearly, there can be few things more rebellious than a talking corpse, but in light of Gaylyn Studlar's theory of masochism and pleasure, Freud's view of humor takes on an even more provocative shading:

Obviously, what is fine about it is the triumph of narcissism, the ego's victorious assertion of its own invulnerability. It refuses to be hurt by the arrows of reality or to be compelled to suffer. *It insists that it is impervious to wounds dealt by the outside world, in fact, that these are merely occasions for affording it pleasure.* . . . It signifies the triumph not only of the ego, but also of the pleasure principle, which is strong enough to assert itself here in the face of the adverse real circumstances.[15]

For Studlar, Freud was wrong in seeing the masochist involved simply in a search for pain; in Studlar's view, the masochist always seeks pleasure. Thus, oddly enough, when Freud describes the humorist, he parallels Studlar and Theodor Reik describing the masochist: "There is no reversal of aim. Pleasure is arrived at 'by another road, by a detour,' since the masochist 'submits voluntarily to punishment, suffering, and humiliation, and thus has defiantly purchased the right to enjoy the gratification denied before.'"[16] In other words, what may seem to be misery is actually a celebration, as the blows struck by a heartless world are transformed into pleasure.

Inverting the basic terms of human existence, flipping them on their heads, is one of comedy's aims. And the deft substitution of pleasure for pain is one of the most gratifying consequences. In *The Seven Year Itch* (1955), for instance, when Tom Ewell's character entertains himself with a fantasy-parody of the erotic beach scene in *From Here to Eternity* (1953), ridiculous sex achieves even more of what the dramatic original offered—namely, a way of staving off impending doom. When *From Here to Eternity*'s characters (Burt Lancaster and Deborah Kerr) roll around in the surf, they find intense sexual pleasure by momentarily dismissing (and symbolically conquering) the threat of mass death which hangs over the film in the form of World War II. In the parody sequence in *The Seven Year Itch*, Wilder characteristically parallels wartime doom with the domestic 1950s when he has neurotic New Yorker Ewell nearly drown after making out in the waves with his wife's best friend, his way of staving off the boredom of his marriage. Although Wilder's sequence works as a triumphant melodramatic fantasy, enabling both the Ewell character and his surrogates in the audience to engage vicariously in an unlikely sexual scene, it is also comically painful, as Ewell's character, Richard Sherman, demonstrates with perfect clarity that he's no Burt Lancaster. This recognition could be harsh, but Wilder's humor turns it around. For Sherman, the world of pleasure is not accommodating on its own, especially if you're a short middle-aged man with an unexceptional face and a pear-shaped physique, the antithesis of muscular male pinup Lancaster. Instead, pleasure must be created out of the materials at hand—in this case, the pain of seeing yourself for what you are.

Turning pain into pleasure is one of the hallmarks of Jewish humor. Wilder's dark comedy, sometimes mistaken for garden-variety cynicism, is urbane and morbid and, like Freud's humor, bears more than a trace of the Viennese Jewish culture in which he was raised. Wilder supposedly met Freud in what is in retrospect a dry comedy routine, given the two personalities involved. As a young reporter, Wilder is said to have shown up at Dr. Freud's residence on the Bergasse and to have presented his card; Freud emerged, fresh from lunch, with a napkin tucked under his chin and sent the reporter summarily away.[17] But Freud and Wilder meet continually and more significantly in their shared sense of humor. In "Humor" Freud tells the joke of the prisoner being taken out to the gallows on Monday morning and remarking, "Well, this is a good beginning to the week."[18] Like Freud's prisoner, *Sunset Boulevard* revises the terms of reality to allow consciousness to remain superior when experience turns ever more sour. A subversive comedy, *Sunset Boulevard* is a rebellion of morbidity against a world only superficially alive.

Being unexpected, *Sunset Boulevard*'s humor is also constituted by a kind of suspension—a hesitation of laughter, an insecurity of meaning. This nervousness about how to take a joke affects the film's characters as well as its audiences. In their third scene together, when Gillis is seated in the dark, heavily decorated living room reading Norma's script, Gillis once again faces uncertainty about the proper way to read reality—Hollywood as theater of the absurd:

It sure was a cozy set up. That bundle of raw nerves, and Max, and a dead monkey upstairs, and the wind wheezing through that organ every once in a while. Later on, for comedy relief, the real guy showed up with the baby coffin.

Of course, the pet mortician's arrival provides little of what one would typically call relief, since Wilder shoots it, as he shoots other sequences inside the Desmond mansion, with an eye toward deadening the premises graphically. He cuts from a slightly high angle shot of Gillis, with Max visible on screen right (having just closed the curtains, as if either Gillis or the film itself needed to be closed in any more) to an extreme long shot of the front door with Max moving stiffly toward it. Wilder presents the door dead center on the screen, framing it with the drab and overblown symmetry of the foyer's architecture, and the sheer stillness of the shot—broken only by Max's movements—is scarcely what one might expect to be the right look for "comedy relief." When Max opens the door and the mortician enters bearing a tiny coffin, Wilder does not cut any closer, thereby leaving the character faceless and featureless, an object in a bizarre ritual the likes of which have eluded Gillis previously but which now have completely enveloped him. Still in extreme long shot, the mortician follows in Gillis's tracks and solemnly marches up the stairs. Rather than signaling any kind of tonal break, any traditional "relief," the sequence actually forces Gillis further into the morbid abyss of haute-Hollywood ritual by completing the character's transformation—begun with the double take on the stairs—from outside observer to ironic participant.

Gloria in Excelsis

If in practice Wilder defines the comedy of *Sunset Boulevard* as the radical ambiguity between what is funny and what isn't, a distinction similar to the blurry line between pleasure and pain, Norma Desmond is surely the film's reigning centerpiece. In a certain sense she operates as Wilder's deus ex machina, for one must accept the possibility of her existence before one can enter into her world. Only after accepting that such a grotesque character could easily emerge from the American film industry—not just that the system of production called Hollywood could produce a personality so fraught with garish despair, but that such a personality would be viewed with inherent and empathic understanding by an audience harboring similar aspirations toward fame and financial success—can one grant Norma Desmond the emotional weight she needs to seduce an out-of-work writer half her age. As grotesque as she is, Norma must remain desirable.

One key reason is her stardom. As a number of critics have noticed, Norma still *is* big, whereas heroes like Gillis are small. But the enormity of her gestures and the exaggeration of her speech convey more than just a set of silent-film conventions. From the insane coalescence of plausibility and nightmare comes the film's deepest comedy. Just as Gillis cannot pin down whether or not Sheldrake is making a joke about Betty Hutton and her girls' softball team, no one has yet determined the level of conscious intent with which Gloria Swanson portrayed her character. Swanson herself wrote that "the scene where Norma plays bridge with a few old friends came closest to giving us all the creeps, but it reminded us too, once again, of exactly who we were." Swanson was also concerned about the number of similar roles she was offered after *Sunset Boulevard*'s success: "I could obviously go on playing it in its many variations for decades to come, until at last I became some sort of creepy parody of myself, or rather, of Norma Desmond—a shadow of a shadow," though the original shadow, of course, was Swanson herself.[19] No matter how thoroughly one admires the effectiveness of the performance, a certain disbelief at the extent of Swanson's self-parody confuses any simple distinction between performer and character. Moreover, what Norma considers funny might be considered rather more painful to others less caught up in Hollywood madness. When she discovers that Gillis is a writer, she makes a little joke:

. . . writing words, words, more words. Well, you've made a rope of words, and you've strangled this business, ha ha! But there's a microphone there to catch the last gurgle! And Technicolor to photograph the red swollen tongue!

Were it not for the "ha ha" (which Swanson intensifies through an odd delivery that gives it a frightening spontaneity), one might interpret the line as being merely (if hideously) bitter. And it is bitter, there is no doubt. But the industry's grotesquerie amuses her, whereas her own does not. Perceiving this paradox, Gillis once again delivers the punchline, a throwaway remark that is nearly overshadowed by the force of Norma's dramatic delivery: putting his finger to his lips, he cautions, "Ssshhh—you'll wake the monkey."

Norma's insanity, readily accepted by audiences in 1950, is easy to diagnose. This character, described by James Agee as "half mad, suicidal, with the obsessed narcissistic arrogance of the once adored and long forgotten," has been churned up out of Hollywood history and gilded with the morbidity of Hollywood in decline.[20] Her passion for filmmaking is essentially necrophilic, and as a result she has spent years cranking out scene after scene for a Salome epic, a grandiose period piece with which she plans to continue her career. "Comeback?!" she snaps with a panicky air—"I hate that word!" Here again, Wilder disrupts the pathetic with the comedic by exaggerating Norma's emotions well beyond the point at which they can be taken at face value. When Norma describes the Salome story, she naturally gives it everything she's got—which in Norma's case includes (in medium close-up) pantomiming the act of grabbing John the Baptist's severed head from an equally invisible gilded tray and, as Norma puts it (slowly, and with relish), "kissing his cold, dead lips." That Gillis responds by saying "They'll love it in Peoria" only adds yet another overtly comic fillip to Norma's performance, which has culminated with a final exultant smile as she kisses the imaginary head. She immediately snaps out of character upon Gillis's smart-aleck comment and with the dismissive tone of someone with an inordinate amount of confidence adds, "They'll love it everywhere!" This joke, of course, is on Norma, though her eventual affair with Gillis—specifically a Salome-like murder of love—was in fact quite a popular story across America in 1950. They *did* love it in Peoria, if not its rural surroundings; *Sunset Boulevard* ranked twenty-ninth out of the 383 films released that year. This may not seem like much in the 1990s, when only a tiny handful of megabucks blockbusters are considered successful, but in the context of 1950, *Sunset Boulevard* was a hit.

Norma Desmond: Modernist Heroine

Female grotesquerie, one of the decade's most conspicuous cultural trends, did not originate with Norma Desmond, but she is surely one of the category's shining lights. Possessive to the point of murder, emotive to the point of inanity, Norma is hardly a feminist ideal. And yet her distorted character, dependent as it is upon a history of sexual idealization and constriction, is nonetheless a fairly noble modernist heroine. Norma dominates not only the lives of Max and, eventually, Gillis; she dominates the film itself and every frame in which she appears. In close-up, Norma's fortissimo emotions are amplified even beyond their already excessive limits. Even in high-angle full shot (as in the scene in which Gillis returns to her bedside following her suicide attempt), Norma's languorous and submissive attitude, intensified by the tools of the theatrical trade she has plied throughout her life, becomes the emotional focus of the shot despite the fact that Gillis takes the traditionally dominant position. In triumph and in despair, Norma Desmond reigns; elevated to the level of heroism, the sheer lunacy of her vision becomes a kind of artistic conquest.

Molly Haskell has written of Gloria Swanson/Norma Desmond:

Swanson's [love of a younger mate] is not only unreciprocated but ugly and embarrassing as well. As a gargoyle of vanity and manipulation, she crystallizes the most artificial aspects of her screen persona into an image that has become hers for posterity. Just as the Marion Davies of *The Patsy* and *Show People* was usurped by the caricature of her in *Citizen Kane*, Gloria Swanson, the comic sport of the early silents, has been supplanted by the campy vamp of *Sunset Boulevard*.[21]

One could argue that Swanson became much more of a comic sport than ever before, but Haskell's point about cross-generational love is well founded. In *Love in the Afternoon* (1957), as Haskell notes, Wilder pairs an aging Gary Cooper with a youthful, even pixie-ish Audrey Hepburn toward the wistful expression of an autumnal romance. In contrast, when the gargoylish Swanson/Desmond falls desperately in love with virile, muscular Holden/Gillis—whom Wilder specifically displays as sexually desirable in a swimsuit scene by the pool—the love of an aging woman for a younger man becomes expressly vampiric. For Wilder, Gary Cooper is an elegant figure of redemption and grace. Gloria Swanson, on the other hand, is a succubus.

In terms of sexual humiliation, however, both Gillis and Norma fare better than Max, who comes off as more of a harem eunuch than a butler. The fact that Max is a former husband relegated to the position of asexual servant somewhat tempers the degree of monstrosity Wilder heaps upon his heroine; she, at least, has retained a powerful sexual drive which she can satisfy by way of her money and status. Max, on the other hand, has no such drive and no such power. Ruined long before Gillis enters the scene, Max (the character James Agee strangely called "the one thoroughly sympathetic role") is in point of fact the only one who is ceaselessly pathetic: the Hollywood failure, the laughingstock Gillis feared he would become in Dayton.[22] That Max had once been a great film director is one of Wilder's more self-revealing jokes.

One of the few *light* comedy scenes in *Sunset Boulevard* occurs when Norma puts on a little show in a ghastly attempt to seize Gillis's interest for the evening. The scene opens with a shot of a twirling parasol—or what turns out to be a parasol, for what is visible on screen is a black spinning vortex circling the center of the image, the metaphorical morass from which Gillis can now no longer escape. The camera pulls back as Norma pulls the parasol away to use as a prop in the bathing beauty dance she performs for Gillis, who responds by musing morosely on the subject of the futility of Hollywood screenwriting. Norma throws herself on the couch next to him in a painful effort to cheer him up, then disappears only to return dressed as Charlie Chaplin, complete with black hat and walking stick with which at one point she raps herself across the face.

The Chaplin sequence is comical for several reasons, not the least of which is that Norma's whimsical impersonation of the Tramp reveals a genuine talent for comedy. More significantly, the sequence builds from the simple humor of imitation into a more operatic comedy of Hollywood manners. Max interrupts Norma's Chaplin routine to tell her important news: first, that Paramount is calling and, second, that the call did not come from Mr. DeMille himself:

> Norma: How do you like that? We've made twelve pictures together. His greatest successes! (*she slams the walking stick against the wall*)
> Gillis: Maybe he's busy. Maybe he's shooting.
> Norma: Ha ha! Oh, I know that trick. He's trying to belittle me! He's trying to get my price down! I've waited twenty years for this call. Now DeMille can wait 'til I'm good and ready! (*she throws her hat on the floor*)

Neither the dialogue as written nor the emphasis Swanson and Holden place on it are particularly amusing—especially not the "ha ha," which is a good deal more flatly bitter than in the earlier scene. The verbal elements here are more melodramatic than comical, but whatever pathos the sequence might evoke is radically tempered by the fact that Norma Desmond is at that moment wearing a ridiculous fake mustache. Expressed through (and despite) the tiny hairpiece, by this time associated as much with Hitler as with Chaplin, the histrionics in which Norma engages become farcical despite themselves.

A Classical Comedy?

Regardless of the degree to which comic elements modify the drama of *Sunset Boulevard*, the film's structure is classically comic in its own perverse way, for it affirms a better social order than the one it satirizes. In Northrop Frye's scheme of things, *Sunset Boulevard* replaces an inadequate world with a more gratifying one.[23] The original setup of the film, its "gimmick," as Gillis might call it, was actually *too* funny and had to be scrapped in favor of the final version. *Sunset Boulevard* originally began with a talking corpse on a morgue slab:

> I shot a whole prologue, a whole reel. . . . [It was] very well shot and quite effective. A corpse is brought into the morgue downtown—and I shot it there too—and it's the corpse of Holden. There are about six other corpses there under sheets. Through a trick we see through the sheets to the faces and they are telling each other the events leading to their deaths. Then Holden starts telling his story. We previewed the picture, with the original first reel. . . . The corpse is brought in on a slab, a name tape is put on the big toe of the corpse and once the tag went on the toe, the audience broke into the biggest laugh I ever heard in my life. I said, 'Oh my God!' and the picture just went straight down. It was a disaster. So that whole sequence went out, but we kept the notion of a man telling of the events which led to his demise.[24]

The revised strategy, in which Holden's identity as cadaver/narrator isn't revealed until the end, does not change Wilder's morbid premise, the original gimmick that cracked the audience up. The problem with their response was not their laughter but the point at which their laughter occurred, the way it colored the rest of the film. Had Wilder not wanted comedy at all, I think it's safe to say that he would most likely have eliminated the talking cadaver.

The morgue sequence, which Wilder described as one of "the two best scenes I ever shot," is shocking enough on the story level that one wonders how Wilder could be so flabbergasted by the preview audience's reaction. (Wilder's other favorite is the gas-chamber finale from his 1944 film noir classic *Double Indemnity*, also cut and replaced because of nervous audiences.) But when William Holden describes the dialogue Wilder gave the cadavers, the director's professed surprise makes even less sense:

> The corpse lying next to me asks me how I died and I say I drowned and he asks how can a young guy like you drown and I say, 'Well, first I was shot in the back,' and then he says, yeah, he was shot also. He was a Chicago gangster killed in Los Angeles. Then a little kid on a slab across from me says 'I drowned too, swimming with my friend off the Santa Monica pier. I bet him I could hold my breath two minutes.' Some dame is over by the kid and she says he shouldn't be unhappy as his parents will come and take him to a nice place. Then from way down there's this great big Negro corpse and he says, 'Hey, man, did you get the final score on the Dodger game before you got it?' And I say no, I died before the morning papers came out.[25]

By rearranging the revelation of Gillis's dual identity as participant and ironic commentator, Wilder turned a joke that descends into tragedy (the final shot of the first version was to have been "of a weeping Nancy Olson hovering over Holden's corpse like Robinson over MacMurray's" in *Double Indemnity*) into a humorous crime drama that ascends satirically into comedy.[26]

At the end of the film, the comedy becomes all the more vigorous because it is preceded by one of the most morose scenes in Wilder's career. Norma, who has ranted, cooed, shrieked, and simpered throughout the film, has placed a call to Betty Shaeffer (Nancy Olson), Gillis's cowriter and backdoor lover, but Gillis has taken the phone away from her. Desperate and defeated, she cries, "Don't just stand there hating me! Shout at me, strike me, but don't hate me! Say you don't hate me, Joe!" Not a bit of humor here, as Norma's despair is so great that she abandons all of her exaggerated gestures and simply breaks into tears.

But after Betty arrives, after Joe graphically demonstrates to her his present occupation as a live-in hustler, and after he begins to pack up and head back to the derisive laughter of Dayton, Ohio—from then on, *Sunset Boulevard* is almost nothing but comedy. Norma, in black, her eyes bugging out, gazes up at an invisible camera or screen (the distinction between the two is now completely blurred) and, in a whisper, intones: "No one ever leaves a star. That's what makes one a star." As Gillis walks in front of the house, in long shot, Norma appears at the door brandishing a gun. She shoots him in the back, just as nebbish hero Richard Sherman fantasizes that his wife will shoot him in *The Seven Year Itch*. As Gillis approaches the pool, she shoots him again, and again, and still in long shot he falls into the pool from which he originally began to speak—a shocking joke in itself. But Norma delivers the punchline: in medium shot, again gazing into the air with a satisfied expression, she whispers, "The stars are ageless, aren't they?"

Wilder then dissolves to a blurry image of patterns of light, then to the underwater shot of Gillis staring down from the surface, and once again the force of Hollywood narration is strong enough to wake the dead:

> Well, this is where you came in. Back at that pool again, the one I always wanted. It's dawn now, and they must have photographed me thousands of times. Then they got a couple of pruning hooks from the garden and fished me out, ever so gently. Funny how gentle people get with you once you're dead.

Gillis's direct address to the audience also suggests a certain commonality of status between spectator and corpse that the corpse, for one, treats as being perfectly ordinary, mundane, as natural as talk itself. Gillis's postmortem state of mind is identical to what we have seen of his live one, except that Wilder obviously felt that the dead version was better qualified to reach the mass American audience in 1950. Gillis therefore presents a most uplifting triumph over death— an even more immediate one than that afforded indirectly by procreation of the species, the implicit but absolute goal of romantic comedy as described by Northrop Frye and a host of other heterosexually valued critics.

Sunset Boulevard hardly needs literary antecedents to bolster its reputation, but the ending of one of Vladimir Nabokov's greatest comedies, *Laughter in the Dark*, is too appropriate to ignore. Like *Sunset Boulevard*, *Laughter* ends with a revelation of artifice accompanying the hero's death; "What a mess life has been," says Albinus immediately before dying, and Nabokov promptly supplies "stage directions" for the "last silent scene."[27] For Nabokov, the elevation of violent death into comedy peaks when the body of the hero becomes a prop for a theatrical production of his life; for Wilder, less of an aristocrat, the transformation is complete upon the entrance of a Paramount newsreel unit and Hollywood's ubiquitous Hedda Hopper. A policeman is trying to call the coroner:

Cop: Coroner's office. I want to speak to the coroner. (*irritated*) Who's on this phone?

Hedda: I am. Now get off! This is more important. This is Hedda Hopper speaking. I'm talking from the bedroom of Norma Desmond . . .

The conclusion of *Sunset Boulevard*, with Norma descending the stairs in her final performance, is Hollywood artifice at its most self-conscious. The last shot, the close-up for which Norma is all too ready, is in fact not a close-up but a shot of varying subject-camera distance in which a lunatic waving her arms in a variation of the fairy godmother gesture advances toward the camera staring the audience directly in the face. Her image, looming larger and larger in the frame, actually blurs before it reaches a close-up, but then a close-up's magnitude of expression would be excessively redundant even for this overdetermined tale. And even though the heroine is insane and the hero is on his way to the morgue, the lovers have nonetheless consummated their union—not in the pedestrian world of ruined glamour and failed careers, but in the much more vivid realm of the silver screen. Norma succeeds in orchestrating her greatest cinematic triumph, and Gillis succeeds in narrating the story and, just as winningly, conquering death. The society affirmed by this comedy's conclusion is constituted entirely by artifice in the form of the perennially dying but never dead movie screen, where resurrection takes the form of voice-over narration and a starring role in a newsreel. Gillis's desire—to prostitute himself and write for Hollywood—is thoroughly satisfied by the end of the film, and consequently even Northrop Frye would be forced to conclude that *Sunset Boulevard* is a classical generic comedy: "The obstacles to the hero's desire, then, form the action of the comedy, and the overcoming of them the comic resolution."[28] Given the film's dismal depiction of American life and values, Gillis's successful Hollywood death provides the happiest of happy endings.

Prisoners: *Stalag 17* and *The Seven Year Itch*

Getting Darker

The oddball position of *Sunset Boulevard*, its elusive role in Wilder's comic vision as well as its role in fifties comedy in general, becomes clearer when it is compared to Wilder's next hit, *Stalag 17* (1953). Wilder had followed *Sunset Boulevard* with the critically and commercially disastrous drama *Ace in the Hole* (aka *The Big Carnival*) in 1951. (The film has since found an appreciative audience; its cynicism about media circuses now seems quite prescient.) But if the development of Wilder's career as a *comedian* is any indication, screen comedy was being transformed into—and accepted as—a considerably darker genre. *Stalag 17* is no lighter in spirit than *Sunset Boulevard*, but by a peculiar blend of contemporary tastes, critical preconception, and modern academic routine, *Stalag 17* is flatly "a comedy." So said the ads, and so say the critics. Neil Sinyard and Adrian Turner provide a symptomatic case in point, especially because they refer to two other critics to make their case: "Joseph McBride and Michael

Wilmington have suggested that *Ace in the Hole* is more of a concentration camp film than this one; and indeed, *Stalag 17* is hardly a war film at all, being unmistakably Wilder's most successful comedy up to that date."[29]

How peculiar. *Ace in the Hole*, in which a lone man lies trapped in a cave while hundreds of campers arrive in station wagons and mobile homes as freely as they might go to a zoo, becomes "more of a concentration camp film" than a film that takes place entirely within the confines of a "concentration camp," which is in point of fact not a concentration camp but rather a camp for prisoners of war. "Hardly a war film at all"? I think it's a safe guess to say that in 1953, less than a decade after the Allied victory, when audiences saw Nazis gunning down two American POWs, displaying their dead bodies to the other prisoners in a public show of force, and parading the corpses' hearse (a dingy wagon) past the prisoners while the exhausted and demoralized men are forced to destroy their own escape tunnel, most of them thought they were seeing a film about the war. There is no critical debate about it, though: *Stalag 17* is a comedy.

The Seven Year Itch and *Stalag 17* were originally Broadway plays with critical reputations already in tow even before filming began, and with other moderately well-known authors' names attached to the projects, both films have tended not to attract the attentions of Wilder's admirers as much as projects which he originated himself. But there is something to be said for seeing these two films as products of their age rather than simply as products of Billy Wilder, who didn't have to dig deep in these two popular stage comedies to find the morbidity and despair often credited to him alone. In any case, since Wilder's fifties comedies offer some of the decade's harshest and most overt attacks on American social and sexual conventions of the period, the nature of the attacks as well as the nature of Wilder's humor are particularly illuminated when comparing what is and isn't Wilder's in these two adaptations.*

---

* Rather than detailing each of the revisions Wilder made—and in both *Stalag 17* and *The Seven Year Itch* the changes are substantial—I will concentrate on some added scenes, lines, and structural devices that bear retrospectively on *Sunset Boulevard* and look ahead to *Some Like It Hot*.

Violence toward oneself or toward others underlies both of these transitional comedies, and Wilder intensifies this pervasive sense of pain and potential death whenever possible. The playwrights, Donald Bevan and Edmund Trzcinski, begin *Stalag 17* with the two escaped prisoners already dead. Wilder instead turns the event into an action sequence that ends in disaster, choosing to begin his comedy with a harshly lit low-angle shot of the camp in which two barbed wire fences spread out from the center of the frame, seemingly enclosing the audience, and in which an armed guard with a fierce dog advances menacingly toward the camera. This shift in plot structure and mise-en-scène is hardly explained solely by the change in media, for Wilder might just as easily have begun with exterior shots only to enter the barracks to discover the prisoners discussing their dead friends. Rather, Wilder's version suggests the possibility of escape only to dash the hope violently in a burst of gunfire, thereby providing a concrete and visible reason for the hopeless morbidity on which the film's humor stands.

Unlike the Broadway versions, Wilder's *Stalag 17* and *The Seven Year Itch* begin with voice-over narrations. As with *Sunset Boulevard* and *The Apartment* (1960), these direct addresses from screen to audience serve an expository function by setting up the time and place of the narratives, but they also provide a subtle shading of artifice to the representations. Wilder never employed anything as outrageously artificial as the talking Oscar statuette who befriends the audience in the opening moments of Frank Tashlin's *Susan Slept Here* (1954)—at least Joe Gillis's corpse had been animate at one time or another. But in each of these films in which narrators mediate by direct address, the audience's perception depends upon the existence of a third party, a character (or, in the case of *The Seven Year Itch*, simply a voice) who is able to participate in the fictional world but also stand apart from it, albeit fictitiously. This middle ground between unabashed comic fiction and the hazy reality of a dark movie theater is in all cases the province of ingratiating storytellers who draw the audience in by telling simple facts: this is Sunset Boulevard, this is a POW camp, this is Manhattan, and so on. Oddly, however, each of the voices in Wilder's comedies has a Cassandra-like tendency to foretell calamity, and the friendship they offer to the lonely spectator looking for a few words of wisdom from the screen turns out instead to be an introduction to doom-filled worlds of stress and violence, frustration and death.

Gays in the Military

"Sprechen Sie Deutsch? Then Droppen Sie Dead!" the prisoner Shapiro (Harvey Lembeck) tells the Nazi Schultz. "Raus! Raus!" Schultz orders, and prisoner "Animal" Krusawa (Robert Strauss) replies with a canine "Rowf! Rowf!" These lines, added by Wilder and cowriter Edwin Blum, help underscore the fact that the two most verbally impudent prisoners are a Jew and a Polak. "Animal," who owes his nickname to an especially rampant libido, is indeed no better off than a dog in this POW camp, but rather than simply acquiescing to his confinement he responds like Freud's prisoner by ridiculing his situation, thereby turning an intolerable reality into a source of pleasure. Shapiro, more cerebral than his friend, also makes a linguistic joke, but his combines both semantic and syntactic alterations to form a direct assault on his captors. It is worth noting that, in the play, "Animal" is the nickname of the Jewish character, Harry Shapiro, and the Krusawa character's name is Stanley "Stosh" Urbanek. For Wilder and Blum, apparently, a Jew is both too intellectual and too sexually repressed to be an animal, whereas the Pole, following stereotypical form, isn't terribly brainy and is consequently not libidinally challenged.

The union of Shapiro and Animal, based in part upon their ethnic identities—they're members of the two groups most decimated by Nazi genocide—reaches its most potent expression when Shapiro puts on a straw wig and transforms himself into a makeshift Betty Grable for Animal's pleasure. But Animal's libido rages so uncontrollably that it is able, like Lorelei Lee's lust for diamonds, to effect a radical change on the screen: his sexual desire is strong enough to superimpose the actual image of Betty Grable on top of that of his friend. This is an unusually complex instance of cross-dressing, with formal and psychological vectors extending in several directions at once: the mixed-gender audience is invited to look at the male Animal who looks at the male/female Shapiro, thereby causing the mixed audience to look at the male/female Shapiro/Grable as a funny transgender object of desire. If cross-dressing is, as Marjorie Garber suggests, a "category crisis . . . a failure of definitional distinction, a borderline that becomes permeable, that permits of border crossings from one (apparently distinct) category to another," the formal figure of the superimposition both underscores and complicates the cross-dress code's essentially formal figuration.[30] Like the Piggie/diamond in *Gentlemen Prefer Blondes* (released the same year, 1953), Shapiro becomes a visual joke, the pleasurable condensation not only of male and female but also of reality and representation, brute fact and unharnessed desire.

Yet this formal figure only reiterates what Wilder has already made clear: Shapiro and Animal are a couple. Wilder repeatedly sets these characters apart from the rest of the barracks as a team, and as a result the dance they perform together is therefore not without its own sexual foundation. Given the setting of *Stalag 17*, this is a neat way of working in a third group oppressed by Nazi terror—a small but distinct minority in terms of Nazi genocide, but one that was causing drastically increased concern—no, it was outright hysteria—in 1950s America. Of Germany's gay male population, estimated at 1.2 million before the war, between 50,000 and 63,000 were convicted of violating Nazi laws against homosexual conduct; of these, between 5,000 and 15,000 died of starvation and disease in concentration camps. As characters, Animal and Shapiro aren't "gay"; like most representations of homosexual desire on-screen, these characters' presumably heterosexual orientation is undercut, not overturned. For Animal, in fact, the sequence ends in disappointment and tears. Nevertheless, two points intervene. First, had these fictional characters been real human beings in Germany between the mid-1930s and the end of the war, what we see of their relationship could well have rendered them guilty of homosexual conduct and therefore subject to deportation to concentration camps. In Nazi Germany, not only was "plain touching" between two men an offense, but "a lewd glance from one man to another was sufficient grounds for prosecution."[31] The way Animal looks at Shapiro isn't just a lewd glance. It is a wolfish stare, and it leaves no doubt whatsoever about his sexual interest. Men in Nazi Germany died for less.

More important perhaps is the fact that these characters are simply that—characters. Can fictional creations really be said to be sexually *oriented* in an ultimate sense? Or instead, do they represent in a profoundly open-ended way the polymorphous sexuality at the foundation of the human psyche? Characters of course have no psyches; audiences do. Defined by the culture from which they arise, film characters of both genders appeal to their audience's infantile bisexual core in partial defiance of the particular repressions and expressions of their age. As a consequence, what must be examined in this case are not just the sexual pressures of a Nazi POW camp as expressed by the all-male dance, a frequent combat film convention, but rather the peculiar sexual interdictions of American culture in 1952–53.

Turning from fascism to democracy, we find historian Stephen J. Whitfield describing America's antigay preoccupation in the early 1950s as central to the period's ideology: "In an era that fixed so rigidly the distinction between Communist tyranny and the Free World, and which prescribed that men were men and women were housewives, perhaps only one peril seemed, if anything, worse than Communism."[32] Historian Jonathan Katz bluntly calls the 1950s a period of "full-scale, national anti-homosexual witch hunts." Historian John D'Emilio concurs: "The 1950s were a grim period for gay men and lesbians. Neither before nor since has oppression against us been so intensely concentrated."[33] Katz cites a *Newsweek* book review from 1949 as documentary evidence of rapidly escalating sexual oppression:

> The sex pervert, whether a homosexual, an exhibitionist, or even a dangerous sadist, is too often regarded merely as a "queer" person who never hurts anyone but himself. . . . The semihysterical, foolishly sympathetic, and wholly unscientific attitude of any individual

engaged in social work and criminology to regard sex perverts as poor unfortunates who are suffering from disease and cannot help themselves, has a tendency to feed their ego. [An "expert"] suggests that the sex pervert be treated, not as a coddled patient, but as a particularly virulent type of criminal.[34]

Witness also *Time*, 1956:

The full-grown homosexual wallows in self-pity and continually provokes hostility to insure himself more opportunities for self-pity; he is full of defensive malice and flippancy, covering his guilt and depression with extreme narcissism and superciliousness. He is generally unreliable in an essentially psychopathic way and (unconsciously) always hates his family. There are no happy homosexuals.[35]

And *Commenweal*, 1954: "The homosexual is a freak of nature as is the albino or the midget."[36]

D'Emilio chronicles the fact that in the first few years of the 1950s gay men and lesbians in the military were purged with even greater force than they had been previously, a trend that continued through the next decade and, obviously, beyond. In 1952, the year before *Stalag 17*'s release, approximately 2,000 men and women were dismissed from the military on grounds of homosexuality. This is *twice* the number of dismissals from even a few years before. By the 1960s the figure had risen to 3,000 per year.[37]

In its double historical context of Nazi physical violence and American emotional violence against gay people, Wilder's work is genuinely radical. The dancing scene, built by Wilder and Blum into a far more significant event than the stage play's parallel moment, provides an especially nuanced instance of how a kind of gay desire found expression on-screen in a period of extraordinary antigay oppression. The stage play itself is simply further evidence of the period's endemic fear and loathing; at one point, Sefton (the William Holden role) calls Dunbar (played by Don Taylor in the film) a "friggin' pansy," a gratuitous if conventional line, and later Herb, the youngest soldier in the barracks, responds to being kidded by Shapiro and Stosh about the size of his penis by lashing out at them: "What's the matter with you guys, are you queer or something?" Bevan and Trzcinski originally brought Stosh and Shapiro together as a couple, but they were disconcerted by the sexual tension they created; Wilder and Blum push this tension much further by treating it comically— not to put it down, but to make it pleasurable.

It bears repeating that, like the strange, out-of-the-blue moment in *Gentlemen Prefer Blondes* when Mr. Esmond and the taxi driver Pierre blow kisses to each other—gestures which on one level are grounded by character motivation but which at the same time seem to fly out of nowhere—neither character here is "gay," though the momentary pleasure in which Shapiro and Animal so obviously revel is pretty much exactly that. In terms of seeing specifically denoted gay characters on movie screens (an important self-affirmation by representation, a pleasure the heterosexual world takes quite for granted), American gay and bisexual men would have to wait for another Wilder comedy a few years later to see themselves (however fleetingly) openly self-identified on-screen. What contemporary audiences saw here instead was a momentary rupture in the American heterosexual male's painstakingly codified behavior toward his peers. This rupture toys with the straight male's fear of homosexual desire, a fear that early fifties culture did its best to exacerbate, and yet it is played for nervous laughter, not terror. To borrow Garber's phrase, it is a pleasurable crossing of boundaries, a melting of categories so powerful that it affects not only the content of the image but also its form, as fantasy literally imposes itself on physical fact to create an ideal image of desire: an androgynous polymorph incarnate, one that is based, better still, on a movie star. No wonder Animal greets it with a wolfish stare.

One may question why I invest so much expository time on a single moment. I hope that I can make two things clear: first, for gay men and lesbians these minor disruptions of what is largely a biased if not overtly hostile cinema constitute a rare triumph, and second, because they are so rare they are all the more powerful as defining moments in a director's vision. Sexual repression in the 1950s was scarcely limited to homosexuality. Throughout the film, Wilder plays off the more generalized, even amorphous kind of American repression that limits the expression of *any* kind of sexual desire only to ritual: the telescopic peep show that Sefton operates, the elaborate ruse used by Shapiro and Animal to work their way into the Soviet women's camp, and finally the comic dance sequence all provide some form of sexual release, but they are highly structured, painfully focused moments that remain divorced from the rest of the men's experience. Still, the simultaneous repression and expression of homosexuality remains in the forefront because it flies directly in the political face of the era—and well beyond. Critic Robert Mundy, for instance, writing at the height of the sexual revolution in the late 1960s, takes the position that because the two dancers are men, "the sexual function [of dance] is undermined." Mundy's assumption of heterosexual *rightness* is so thorough that he doesn't even bother to explain himself.[38]

In terms of the increasingly imminent appearance of gay sexuality on screen in the 1950s, a subtle but potent revision from Broadway to Hollywood is the difference between the barracks' response to the camp crier's line, "Next—all men from Texas will meet behind the north latrine." In the play, stage directions call for the men to boo because they hate the Texans for being con-men, punningly calling them "crap artists." In Wilder's version, however, the prisoners respond with insinuating amusement; the men from Texas seem to have a reputation for meeting behind the north latrine. Keep in mind that although these rapacious Texans remain safely offscreen, they aren't being characterized in the same way as, say, the "10,000 faggots" described in 1952 by New York newspaper columnist Lee Mortimer as having poisoned the government by their very presence.[39] In *Stalag 17*, the equally offscreen "faggots" are war heroes.

In *The Seven Year Itch*, too, gay men (or, more accurately, protogay men) make a brief, safe, but nonetheless refreshing offscreen appearance in the form of a passing reference to "those two guys on the top floor—interior decorators or something." And of course the crowning moment in Wilder's persistent interest in homosexuality as a threat to the mundane occurs not in the post-Stonewall *The Private*

Life of Sherlock Holmes (1970), in which Holmes humorously refers to an ongoing affair with Watson (Watson is horrified, but Holmes is very much at ease with the idea), but eleven years earlier in *Some Like It Hot* (1959), when Joe. E. Brown delivers his immortal acceptance of his lover's masculinity with the line "Nobody's perfect." In each case, gay desire finds its way onto the screen through comedy, which in Wilder's case was disruptive enough to allow the positive expression of precisely the kind of sexuality that Nazism tried to obliterate through physical force and that American law and culture attempted to suppress more insidiously through brutal psychotherapies, FBI harassment, job discrimination, and as Vincente Minnelli depicts with chilling accuracy in *Tea and Sympathy* (1956, from the timely 1953–54 Broadway hit by Robert Anderson), institutionally mandated intimidation.

An Army of Clowns

Wilder's disruption of social standards extends beyond nervous American sexual taboos. For Wilder, it's life itself that is under attack. The comedy of *Stalag 17* finds one of its most succinct expressions in the following bit of dialogue and the ensuing story revelation:

Schultz: Look at them, lieutenant. Everybody is a clown. How do you expect to win the war with an army of clowns?

Shapiro: We sorta hope you laugh yourselves to death.

Schultz: Yeah. (*He laughs hysterically in close-up*) He he he he he he he he! (*Schultz stops laughing when he notices that the lightbulb cord has been fashioned into a noose*)

The noose is the spy's signal, and this is the first time the audience discovers the means by which the German spy transmits information to his superiors—the device, in other words, that has spelled violent death for Johnson and Manfredi, the dead escapees, and which now threatens a similar fate for the heroic Lieutenant Dunbar. Death is everywhere, but Wilder sets up the revelation with an exaggerated reference to the salvation of humor: just like Norma Desmond, the men have all donned little black mustaches and are in the midst of performing a comedy routine. Here, of course, they are specifically ridiculing Hitler. They turn in unison, give a Nazi salute, and raucously babble in pig-German—"Gezuntheit! Gezuntheit! Everything is gezuntheit!" says one particularly loud voice. (In the play, only Harry and Stosh do Hitler imitations; Schultz's speech about the "army of clowns" is Wilder's addition.)

Modern despair could hardly find a better locus than a Nazi POW camp, with the obvious exception of a Nazi concentration camp. By recalling Ernst Lubitsch's Nazi comedy, *To Be or Not to Be* (1942), *Stalag 17* echoes Lubitsch's own comments vis-à-vis the appropriateness of blending comedy with the most unfunny of situations:

> I was tired of the two established, recognized recipes, drama with comedy relief and comedy with dramatic relief. I made up my mind to make a picture with no attempt to relieve anybody from anything at any time. . . . One might call it a tragical farce or a farcical tragedy— I do not care and neither do the audiences.[40]

The fact that audiences cared much less about the destruction of "recognized recipes" in *Stalag 17*, which was an enormous success, than they had with *To Be or Not to Be*, which failed critically as well as commercially, may have more to do with changing attitudes toward the war than with differing responses to the two directors' styles. But it also indicates that comedy itself had undergone a substantial transformation in the public eye. If genre expectations are like recipes, the cultural cookbook was now in a newly revised edition updated for the modern postwar kitchen. Darker in tone and more explicitly unnerving in its implications, commercially successful film comedy no longer had to be frothy to be funny. Not only that, it didn't even have to be funny to be comedy.

In this light, consider *Stalag 17*'s direct descendent, the television combat sitcom, *Hogan's Heroes*. Premiering in 1965, *Hogan's Heroes'* comedy had the benefit of time; the war was much more distant in memory, though brewing Vietnam anxieties probably played into its appearance in the mid-sixties. In any case, *Stalag 17's* commercial success eleven years earlier had proven that audiences would accept a POW camp as a setting for comedy. Missing from the television series, however, is much sense of darkness or threat. The TV Nazis are broad, incompetent comic buffoons. Jovial Sergeant Schultz and bungling Commandant Klink are not like their big-screen counterparts; they're the sieg-heiling parody Nazis found in Wilder's mustache scene elevated to the level of main characters. As is often the case, television's presence in the home seems to demand a curtailing of any malignancy of content.

Wherever it's expressed, comedy provides in art what is denied in life—namely, a way out, a challenge not only to artistic standards but to cultural constrictions and social terrors. In *Stalag 17* the social locus of comedy is an indisputably terrifying history of worldwide carnage and misery; in *Sunset Boulevard* it's Hollywood; in *The Seven Year Itch* it's marriage. One does not have to conflate the three arenas to see that they are not simply the products of the vague cosmology known as "the modern condition" but rather of specific power relationships that thrive on oppression. Prisoners of the Nazis, prisoners of highly constrained commercial entertainment, prisoners of a system of sexual regulation: in this way, black comedy links marriage to World War II. Little wonder that contemporary critics tended to find Wilder's most emblematic trait to be his bad taste.

Shot in the Back—Again

In a way, only the particular threat of death at the hands of the Nazis separates the dark humor of *Stalag 17* from *The Seven Year Itch*, but if one substitutes "a wife" for "the Nazis," as Wilder more or less did in the latter film, the distinction between the two begins to collapse in a most uncomfortable manner. The severe decline of playwright and coscreenwriter George Axelrod's critical reputation, together

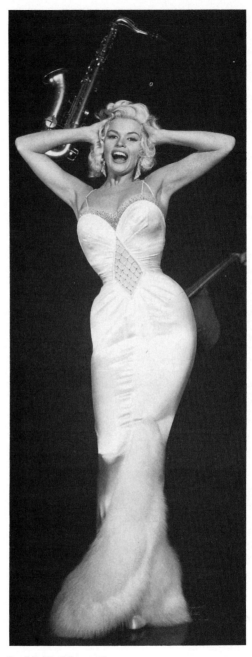

Rock 'n' Roll Dream Screen

Jayne Mansfield, the reigning queen of
hysterical laughter in the 1950s, basks in publicity
for *The Girl Can't Help It.*

(Courtesy of the Academy of Motion Picture Arts
and Sciences)

Bigger Than Life

Workmen prepare to put Marilyn in her place—on a billboard advertising *The Seven Year Itch* (1955).

(Courtesy of the Academy of Motion Picture Arts and Sciences)

How Drunk Is That Doggie in the Window?

Mr. Bascom (played by Baron) laps it up in this bit of publicity for *Hollywood or Bust* (1956).

(Courtesy of the Academy of Motion Picture Arts and Sciences)

The Body as Parody

Jayne Mansfield's costume in Raoul Walsh's comedy *The Sheriff of Fractured Jaw* (Great Britain, 1959), is especially vulgar, even for Jayne Mansfield; not only do lace breastplates define her upper torso, but her pubic hair finds a fashion tease in the form of black netting.

(Courtesy Photofest)

Front and Center

Breasts, both real and fake, played a prominent role in the marketing of *Some Like It Hot* (1959).

(Courtesy Photofest)

Designing Women

Ribbons, satin, jewels, and a pair of massive breasts make Bob Hope a stylish fashion icon in Paramount's comedy *Casanova's Big Night* (1954). Note that each breast is almost as large as Hope's head.

(Courtesy Photofest)

Double Drag

Milton ("Mr. Television") Berle can't resist flirting with a startled Desi Arnaz, while a miffed Lucille Ball chomps a cigar in disgust in a segment of Desilu Playhouse from the late 1950s.

(Courtesy Photofest)

Hey Big Spender

One aspect of fifties culture is dramatized with appalling precision in this image of television star and cultural phenomenon J. Fred Muggs donating what appears to be a nickel to the March of Dimes's campaign to cure polio as June Lockheart, permanent panelist on television's *Who Said That?*, looks on in strained enthusiasm.

(Courtesy Photofest)

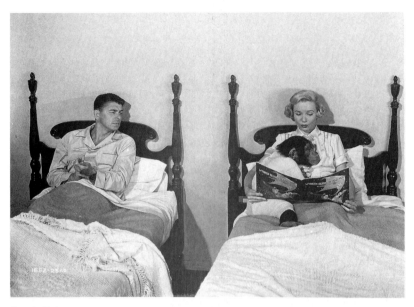

Family Values

Ronald Reagan, already exiled to a classic fifties twin bed, seems especially perturbed by Diana Lynn's loving attention to Bonzo's developmental needs in the immortal *Bedtime for Bonzo* (1951).

(Courtesy Photofest)

A Monkey's Uncle

Chimp star Pierre, in a timely Gorgeous George wig, makes Jerry Lewis cry uncle in *My Friend Irma Goes West* (1950).

(Courtesy of the Academy of Motion Picture Arts and Sciences)

Second Childhood
Portly Charles Coburn shows Baby Boopkins how to get the job done in *Yes, Sir, That's My Baby* (1949).

(Courtesy Photofest)

Bedtime Story
Lucy and Desi may have had to sleep in twin beds during the 1950s, but Bob Hope and Trigger had enough room to cuddle in *Son of Paleface* (1952). The horse appears to resent Hope's having hogged the blankets.

(Courtesy of the Academy of Motion Picture Arts and Sciences)

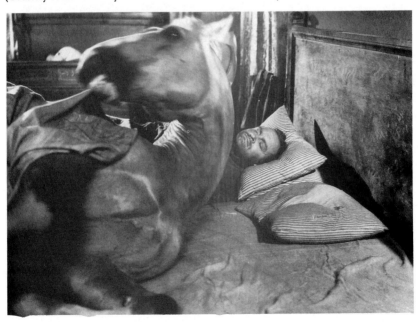

Great Gams:

Miss Laurel (Marilyn Monroe) shows off her acetates to Barnaby Fulton (Cary Grant) in *Monkey Business* (1952).

(Courtesy Photofest)

Fur is Murder:

Persian lamb was a becoming addition to anyone's wardrobe in the early 1950s; here, a reporter and photographer track down Barnaby and Edwina Fulton (Cary Grant and Ginger Rogers) after Barnaby's night in hell in *Monkey Business* (1952).   (Courtesy Photofest)

Gaze Meets Gaze

To sell *Gentelmen Perfer Blondes* (1953), Jane Russell and an unidentified muscle-boy demonstrate the multidirectional nature of visual pleasure in Twentieth Century-Fox's publicity appeal to both genders and all sexual orientations.

(Courtesy of the Academy of Motion Picture Arts and Sciences)

New Order in the Court

In *Gentlemen Prefer Blondes* (1953), the lurid realm of showgirl theater reaches its zenith as Jane Russell, Playing Dorothy, plays Marilyn Monroe playing Lorelei, thereby stupefying yet another mealy male (Marcel Dalio).

(Courtesy Photofest)

Cutting Room Floor:

William Travilla's kinkiest costume for Marilyn Monroe in *Gentlemen Prefer Blondes* (1953) was designed for an elaborate musical number that ended up being cut from the film.

(Courtesy Photofest)

Material Girl:

Lorelei Lee (Marilyn Monroe) ponders the position of women amidst a graphic display of patriarchal romance, including some kinky light fixtures.

(Courtesy the Academy of Motion Picture Arts and Sciences)

The Director's Task:

As Paramount's original caption puts it, "Billy Wilder embraces Gloria Swanson in an almost stranglehold on the set of *Sunset Boulevard* [1950]."

(Courtesy of the Academy of Motion Picture Arts and Sciences)

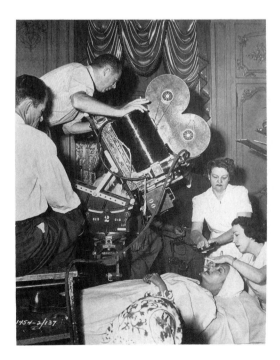

Total Makeover:

Billy Wilder bears down on Gloria Swanson during the filming of Norma Desmond's cosmetic comeback in *Sunset Boulevard* (1950). The cosmetologist holding the magnifying glass doesn't seem to like what she sees.

(Courtesy of the Academy of Motion Picture Arts and Sciences)

Young Beefcake, Old Cheesecake:

Gloria Swanson, looking quite fit in a spectacular Edith Head creation, is still treated as a depressing succubus feeding off virile William Holden, displayed to his best sexual advantage in *Sunset Boulevard* (1950).
(Courtesy Photofest)

The Devil's Laughter:

Norma Desmond (Gloria Swanson) may descend into madness near the end of *Sunset Boulevard* (1950), but is it possible to watch her go crazy without smiling? (Courtesy Photofest)

Wish Fulfillment:
Shapiro (Harvey Lembeck, *left*) may be apprehensive, but "Animal" Krusawa (Robert Strauss, *right*)is ecstatic in this promotional photo from *Stalag 17* (1953).

(Courtesy of the Academy of Motion Picture Arts and Sciences)

Domestic Comedy:
Richard Sherman (Tom Ewell) faces his own mortality, in the hands of his wife (Evelyn Keyes), in *The Seven Year Itch* (1955). She's about to shoot him in the back.
(Courtesy Photofest)

The Freudian Fifties:

Sometimes a cigar is only a cigar, said Freud, and sometimes a kayak paddle is only a kayak paddle; whatever it is, Tom Ewell appears to be enjoying himself in this production still from *The Seven Year Itch* (1955).

(Courtesy of the Academy of Motion Picture Arts and Sciences)

A Perfect Fantasy:

Doris Day, looking smart in a Jean Louis suit, seems to be finding that self-love is the greatest love of all, but in fact she's imagining a future with Rock Hudson in *Pillow Talk* (1959).

(Courtesy Photofest)

On Display:
Rock Hudson gives his fans some beefcake in *Pillow Talk*, the 1959 sex comedy hit.   (Courtesy of the Academy of Motion Picture Arts and Sciences)

Star Treatment:
Some Like It Hot's two male stars can't relax on the set without an eager studio photographer creeping up behind them, though one has to admit it couldn't have been a better setup.

(Courtesy Photofest)

Dolled Up:
Jerry/Daphne (Jack Lemmon) and Osgood (Joe E. Brown) are well equipped for a night of passion in *Some Like It Hot* (1959).

(Courtesy of the Academy of Motion Picture Arts and Sciences)

Killer Kid:
Jerry Mathers, television's beloved "Beaver," shoots to kill in this provocative publicity still for *The Trouble with Harry* (1955).

(Courtesy of the Academy of Motion Picture Arts and Sciences)

Dreamwork as Work:
Miss Gravely (Mildred Natwick) attempts to come to terms with Harry's apparent murder in *The Trouble with Harry* (1955).

(Courtesy of the Academy of Motion Picture Arts and Sciences)

Close Inspection:
Sam (John Forsythe, *left*) and the Captain (Edmund Gwenn, *right*) give Harry's naked corpse a final once-over in *The Trouble with Harry* (1955).

(Courtesy of the Academy of Motion Picture Arts and Sciences)

Model Wife:

Barbara Bel Geddes prepares the perfect meal and serves up the perfect murder in the "Lamb to the Slaughter" episode of *Alfred Hitchcock Presents*.

(Courtesy Photofest)

Gorgeous Jerry

Jerry Lewis promotes *My Friend Irma Goes West* (1950); Paramount's original caption reads, "Go away, big boy, you bother me."

(Courtesy of the Academy of Motion Picture Arts and Sciences)

Cleaning Up Their Act:

"Things like this make sense in a Martin and Lewis movie," explains Paramount's original caption for this still from *Artists and Models* (1955).

(Courtesy of the Academy of Motion Picture Arts and Sciences)

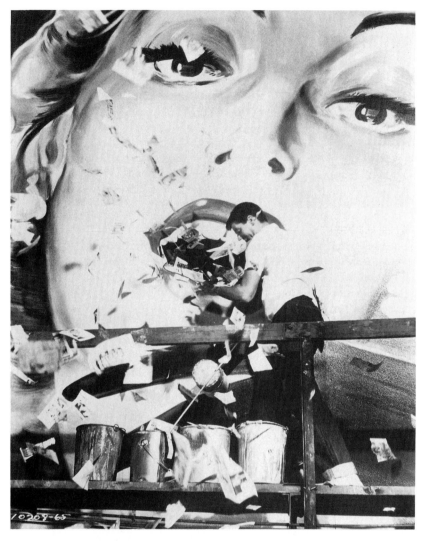

Out of the Mouths of Babes

An ideal fifties titan-woman spits out Eugene Fullstack's (Jerry Lewis) comic book collection in the beginning of *Artists and Models* (1955).

(Courtesy of the Academy of Motion Picture Arts and Sciences)

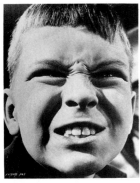

Baby Boom:

George "Foghorn" Winslow in a promotional photo for *Artists and Models* (1955), in which he plays a typically violence-prone child of the 1950s; Winslow also appears in *Monkey Business* (1952) and *Gentlemen Prefer Blondes* (1953), in each case as a stolid parody of adulthood.

(Courtesy of the Academy of Motion Picture Arts and Sciences)

By the Numbers:

Longtime Hollywood columnist Sidney Skolsky enthusiastically notes the measurements adorning Jayne Mansfield's slantboard on the set of *The Girl Can't Help It* (1956); note the other custom decoration at the top of the board.

(Courtesy of the Academy of Motion Picture Arts and Sciences)

Temperature's Risin'

The mere sight of Jerri Jordan (Jayne Mansfield) causes an iceman and his ice to lose their cool in *The Girl Can't Help It* (1956).

(Courtesy Photofest)

Home Delivery

Jerri (Jayne Mansfield) brings some vitality into the life of Tom Miller (Tom Ewell) in *The Girl Can't Help It* (1956).

(Courtesy Photofest)

Star Quality:

Rita Marlowe (Jayne Mansfield) and Shamroy in *Will Success Spoil Rock Hunter?* (1957). (Courtesy Photofest)

Corporate Rock:

Gangster/recording executive "Fats" Murdock (Edmond O'Brien) struts his stuff to the accompaniment of a jailbird back-up band in *The Girl Can't Help It* (1956).

(Courtesy of the Academy of Motion Picture Arts and Sciences)

Recovery

Suffering a typical fifties hangover, Tony Randall tries to put a bad night behind him in *Will Success Spoil Rock Hunter?* (1957).

(Courtesy of the Academy of Motion Picture Arts and Sciences)

Bananas:

Jayne Mansfield's real-life husband, former Mr. Universe Mickey Hargitay, makes a spectacle of himself as Bobo Branigansky, jungleman boyfriend of Jayne's Rita Marlowe in *Will Success Spoil Rock Hunter?*(1957).

(Courtesy of the Academy of Motion Picture Arts and Sciences)

with fairly rigid notions on the part of most commentators about what is and is not "cinematic," have contributed greatly to the dismissal of *The Seven Year Itch*. Still, Wilder's adaptation of an extant property once again shows that his comic vision didn't offer a raw departure from other popular art so much as it provided a more articulate critique.

Although Axelrod is credited as cowriter on the film, Wilder's influence is quite evident when comparing the film's script with that of the play. Indeed, Axelrod appears not to have been thrilled with Wilder's revisions. In his play *Will Success Spoil Rock Hunter?*, which Frank Tashlin all but discarded when filming it, Axelrod makes several snide if oblique references to Hollywood's directing and screenwriting habits. But whatever he did to Axelrod's play, Wilder never did work out the playwright's ga-ga guyism. In both play and film, the degree of overdeveloped innocence The Girl projects marks her as an imaginary creature. She's an infantilized hypersexual woman cast in the mold of heterosexual male desire—*not* the desire of real straight men, but a kind of *über*heterosexual imperative that forces such men into impossible constrictions. To my mind, neither the play nor the film comes to terms with this woman in the slightest. Here and elsewhere, men (writers, directors, fictional characters, audiences) remain mystified by the objects of their hysterical attentions.

But because it is darker in tone than Axelrod's play, Wilder's film presents a deeper justification for Richard Sherman's panic than the relatively one-dimensional fear of adultery on which Axelrod dwells. For example, one of Axelrod's recurrent jokes concerns *The Scarlet Letter*. Mentioned as one of the books Sherman's boss wants to reissue, Hawthorne's tale of public shame and personal suffering becomes one of the play's most persistent leitmotifs. At one point, stage directions even call for a bright red A to be projected onto Sherman's clothing. In the film, however, Wilder abandons Puritanism for romantic degeneration in the form of Oscar Wilde's *The Picture of Dorian Gray*. In a scene as noteworthy for its performances as for its dialogue, Sherman's boss (who does not appear in the play) shouts himself hoarse describing the peculiar relevance of *Dorian Gray* to America in the 1950s:

It's a natural, Sherman! Look at what we'd be giving them for a quarter—violence, lust, and corruption! The story of a young man. On the surface, clear-eyed and healthy. Just like you, Sherman! But underneath—ah, dry rot! And the termites of sin (*wheeze*) and depravity (*wheeze*) gnawing at his soul!

The fifties' enthusiasm for merchandising, a topic to be taken up more fantastically by Frank Tashlin, here becomes so powerful that a corporation man cannot convey it without shouting. And what he is yelling about is the idea that readers of two-bit paperbacks all across the country would find something personally timely about a book that describes its beautiful but artfully concealed protagonist as "gazing at the picture [of himself] in sickened horror," seeing in it "the visible emblem of conscience," and finally becoming precisely what the portrait had accurately depicted him as being—"withered, wrinkled, and loathesome of visage."[41]

Freud may have constructed the most widely compelling modern tableau in which an apparently calm and ordinary-looking individual stands horrified before the monstrous, dreamed-up manifestations of his or her repressed desires, but his was by no means the original. What Sherman fears throughout the film—and what, by extension, all of America is assumed to fear and, more important, to want to *buy*—is not the public scrutiny of Hawthorne's Puritan New England as much as it is a baroquely fashioned and romantic vision of internal degeneration and self-loathing. As Wilder pointed out to his contemporary public's amusement, lurking beneath the placid, easygoing, and utterly artificial surface of well-decorated fifties homes and workaday corporate routines was "dry rot," decay, and torment. The film's unsatisfactory ending—Sherman taking the truly American way out by running away from his traumas and temptations, refusing to resolve or even indulge them fully, and rushing off to join his wife—isn't nearly convincing enough to dispel the lurid fantasies and anxieties that permeate this story of middle-aged frustration.

A few of Wilder's seemingly minor additions to the script crystallize the extent of Sherman's problem. *Before* he meets The Girl, before the great void in his life finds a fantastic physical expression, Sherman talks compulsively to himself in a neurotic effort to replace his vacationing wife. The charade peaks when he plays both parts in the conversation:

> What happened at the office today, dear? What happened at the office? Well, I shot Mr. Brady in the head, made violent love to Miss Morris, and set fire to 300,000 copies of *Little Women*. That's what happened at the office.

Proletarian revolution, free lust, and the incineration of Louisa May Alcott's vision of family life: a nice fifties dream. Soon afterwards, he crashes painfully to the floor, having slid on his little boy's discarded roller skate. His reaction is especially strong: "RRRRRRicky!" he growls murderously, as if his anger and frustration toward his son has been building for some time. Throughout the film, Sherman's reactions toward his wife and child are much more extreme than their behavior toward him. In humiliating contrast, they treat him not as the family's patriarch but as an inconsequential necessity, a bill-paying drone whose existence merely enables *them* to achieve full flower as American consumers.

In terms of comedy, the most potent revision occurs in Sherman's murder fantasy when his raging guilt causes the specter of his wife to appear armed with a gun. In the play, Axelrod describes the sequence as follows:

> **Helen:** You should have thought of that before. . . . Goodbye, Richard. . . . (*She fires . . . five times. . . . He sinks slowly in motion picture fashion, clutching his middle*)
>
> **Richard:** (*in agony*): Helen . . . I'm going . . . fast . . . give me a cigarette . . .

Wilder makes the shooting a great deal more violent, with Helen blasting Richard repeatedly *in the back* as he climbs the stairway. And rather than sinking "slowly in motion picture fashion," Wilder has the motion picture Sherman collapse and tumble down an entire flight of stairs, at which point Helen shoots him one more time for good measure. Only then, after an act that must be considered exceptionally brutal for a romantic comedy, does he deliver his line. It certainly would have been possible to film the sequence precisely as the parody shoot-out Axelrod's original material demanded, but Wilder chose instead to shoot this murder every bit as harshly as he did the double murder sequence in *Double Indemnity*, the only difference being that in the comedy killing, the woman reigns supreme.

As with the rest of Wilder's black fifties comedies, only because an event or a way of life is nightmarish does comedy intervene and, ultimately, take over. At a time in which Nazism and domestic breakdown could be topics for Broadway comedy, Wilder had little trouble finding source material. But in his original scripts, comedy and nightmare tend to unite even more raunchily to create a world of dark carnival where the basic terms of civilization are inverted. And there are few better illustrations of dark, inverted comedy in the history of film than *Some Like It Hot*.

Clothes Make the Man: *Some Like It Hot*

An Escapist Comedy

In 1959 *Some Like It Hot* ranked third in *Variety*'s list of box-office successes. The number one film, *Auntie Mame* (which came out at the end of 1958), tells the story of a woman so bored by traditions and proprieties that she spares no expense to escape from them. Disney's *The Shaggy Dog*, the tale of a boy who turns into a sheepdog, ranked second, and the Doris Day–Rock Hudson sex comedy, *Pillow Talk*, in which (among other things) an obstetrician believes in the possibility of Hudson's pregnancy, ranked fourth. For the first and only time in the decade, the four most commercially successful films of the year were comedies.

In varying degrees, each of these films deals with a radical escape from ordinary life. In the case of *Pillow Talk*, this takes the form of Doris Day's renunciation of celibacy. Typically for its era, a healthy amount of dialogue in that film is devoted to psychotherapy, but one does not have to be an analyst to get the phallic joke of the end credits sequence, where the words "The End" appear, only to be followed by the camera tilting up to reveal an ever-growing tower of pillows with the words "not quite" written on them. And as far as *Auntie Mame* is concerned, a surprising but telling contrast of cultural values can be seen in George S. Kaufman and Moss Hart's 1930s comedy hit, *You Can't Take It with You*. Filmed by Frank Capra in 1938, this stageplay-film adaptation also uses family eccentricity to express the urge to escape the tedium of American social expectations. In both films, the impending marriage of a member of the family's second generation to someone who represents "normal life" figures prominently. In the Roosevelt-era film, the marriage occurs, and the young couple's enduring love teaches both the eccentrics and the bride's stuffed-shirt parents a lesson of tolerance. But in the Eisenhower-era film, the prospective bride is every bit as much of a lockjawed twit as her pompous suburban parents, and the marriage is mercifully prevented. As its box-office receipts suggest, *Auntie Mame*'s comic escape from propriety is the late 1950s at its most conventional.

The enduring critical and commercial popularity of *Some Like It Hot* might lead one to believe that the film has been overanalyzed. Writers have in fact tended to knock themselves out trying to find ever more jazzy superlatives for the film, but something about it still makes many of them awfully nervous. In point of fact, this 1959 classic is still more daring than its criticism, mostly written during the sixties and seventies:

A different sort of tragic ending occurs in *Some Like It Hot*. While Joe and Sugar are romantically paired off, Jerry is unable to reassert his real personality. His troubling confession—"I'm a guy, I wish I were dead"—does not faze Fielding. When Fielding tells Jerry that "nobody's perfect," Jerry appears to be unable to escape his role as "Daphne."[42]

To avoid the pitfalls of female impersonation, Wilder holds a tight rein on Lemmon and Curtis. To the audience, they are indisputably males, and the screenplay has them complain bitterly about having to wear feminine garb; and this constant carping is one of the things that keeps the masquerade from growing obnoxious.[43]

Some of the best writers on cinema . . . have dwelled on the film at some length and supplied stimulating ideas. . . . None of them, however, has really accounted for what is surely the film's most remarkable achievement: its success in sustaining and developing its central conceit of transvestism which could have gone stale and tasteless in other hands.[44]

And, like the monkey mortician bearing his tiny coffin, here's Judith Crist for comedy relief:

For every raucous and or ribald masquerade joke there is another that involves a transvestite leer, a homosexual "in" joke or a perverse gag. Here is the prurience, the perversion, the sexual sickness that is obsessing the characters and plots of our films.[45]

Perhaps the hands and mind of a "transvestite" director might someday fashion a fresh and tasteful approach to the "conceit of transvestism" in a Hollywood feature film. An attempt was made in 1953, six years before *Some Like It Hot*, when schlock director Edward D. Wood Jr., himself a cross-dresser, made and starred in the notorious *Glen or Glenda?*, but then nobody has ever accused that film of being in good taste.

In any event, the authors of the third passage quoted above, Neil Sinyard and Adrian Turner, are so unnerved by "transvestism" that in an effort to dispel the evil it represents to them, they insist that it har–

bors an innate offensiveness that only genius can circumvent. This isn't surprising, for these critics' theories about sexual resolutions find an even more appalling formulation when they declare with a sour strictness worthy of Jonathan Edwards that "in *The Apartment* the reconciliation between Baxter and Miss Kubelik has been contaminated by contact with the older Sheldrake"—love as venereal disease. As far as *Some Like It Hot* is concerned, these critics are the unfortunate rule, not the exception. The film's commentators are often little more than walking, talking symptoms of the same cultural hysteria that produced and sustained the antigay assaults of the 1950s. As a result, their criticism is as worthy of psychoanalysis as any film.

As uncomfortable as it may be to admit, Judith Crist is the one who gets it right. As Rebecca Louise Bell-Metereau points out in her book *Hollywood Androgyny*, Crist hates what she sees, but at least she sees it.[46] *Some Like It Hot* did in fact open new sexual ground in American film. Crist's own take on the issue—Wilder acting as a sort of predatory queer converting an impressionable cinema into a sex-obsessed pervert—is obviously hogwash, but her response still merits points for its front-and-center honesty.

Pretty Boys

The tendency of many critics to perceive no possible role for "transvestism" other than as a dangerous but disarmed "metaphor" for heterosexual tensions is hardly surprising, though the film does go out of its way to block this conclusion. The comedic possibilities opened up by the nerve-wracking topic of "transvestism" are boundless, but when presented with the film's raging ambiguities and sexual contradictions, most of *Some Like It Hot*'s commentators haven't considered very many possibilities at all and instead find it imperative to apologize, rationalize, and squirm whenever they deal with the ways in which a big-budget Hollywood production of 1959 dealt with how men learn to destroy a constricting moral code—one that has brought them nothing but loneliness and frustration—by dressing in women's clothes. In his book on films of the 1950s, Peter Biskind suggests that the "transvestism" of *Some Like It Hot* became "harmless" the minute it became "humorous," but comedy must somehow be able to dispense with centuries if not millennia of satirical and socially disruptive content in order for this to be true. As usual, most critics use the term *transvestism* to mean a man in a dress—any man in any dress for any reason—but then labeling provides a ready way of containing the more anarchic and threatening ideas that manage to bubble up from underneath the labels anyway.

It is precisely the inability of human beings to constrict themselves to the limit demanded by American social regulations that *Some Like It Hot* takes as its timely central subject. And strange as it may seem, Hollywood finds itself way ahead of the historians and critics in terms of tapping into social progress. What Roland Barthes wrote almost twenty years later in his preface to Renaud Camus' novel, *Tricks*, is little more than an elegantly worded restatement of the "I'm a boy, I wish I were dead" scene from *Some Like It Hot*:

> to proclaim yourself something is always to speak at the behest of a vengeful Other, to enter into his discourse, to argue with him, to seek from him a scrap of identity: "You are . . ." "Yes, I am . . ." Ultimately, the attribute is of no importance; what society will not tolerate is that I should be . . . *nothing*, or to be more exact, that the *something* that I am should be openly expressed as provisional, revocable, insignificant, inessential, in a word: irrelevant.[47]

When Jerry (Jack Lemmon) initially makes his transformation into Daphne, the abruptness with which he moves from one seemingly unalterable gender to another makes him think about death. When Joe (Tony Curtis) tears him forcibly away from his newfound femininity, he thinks about death. Intolerable in both of these moments is the absence of categories, and the only option available to him is dying. Though he takes longer to get into the female role than his ladies' man buddy, Jerry ends up fighting very hard to keep it. And if "security" takes the form of explanatory labels (you are . . . , I am . . .), what else can one make of desperate Jerry's mirror-image laments? "I'm a girl, I wish I were dead," followed by "I'm a boy, I wish I were dead" does seem to imply that the middle ground is the safest, not to mention the liveliest.

To be fair, not all critics are so shortsighted. Brandon French gets the message: "What *Some Like It Hot* affirms is neither heterosexual nor homosexual nor even female, but rather the abolition of those absolute poles in favor of an androgynous continuum."[48] At stake in *Some Like It Hot* is the security afforded by rigid codes of conduct. And this security, like any product of repression, comes at a price: Joe's coy but bullying treatment of women, Jerry's hypochondria and weak will, the drab meanness of both of their lives. This repressive economy must necessarily collapse, and when it does—Joe finally understands that if he and Jerry do not put on dresses and transform themselves into what the world sees as women they will be slaughtered—the characters' interiority detonates their simple all-male facades. Rebecca Louise Bell-Metereau writes: "What is exceptional about the film is the thoroughness of the transformation from male to female. Wilder is willing to explore the reversal not only in its superficial aspects but also at the level of its transvestite and homosexual implications."[49]

Joe takes to his costume immediately, which is not surprising since the pouty pursed lips and upper-crust voice appear the second he picks up the phone, and thus these characteristics predate the dress and wig. In his big moment of reckoning, he takes the receiver, purses his lips, and in a smooth and confident falsetto voice says, "Hello, Mr. Polackoff? I understand you're looking for a couple of *girl* musicians." Because Joe's female identity preexists his cross-dressing, *Some Like It Hot* does not take the figurative space of cross-dressing as an end in itself, Marjorie Garber's brilliant observations to the contrary. For one thing, Tony Curtis, who had a reputation for being not only handsome but beautiful, simply builds in both appearance and performance on a foundation audiences had already perceived in the star's persona. Two years earlier, in Alexander Mackendrick's *Sweet Smell of Success* (1957), a woman thinks Curtis's character, a press agent, is really an actor because "He's so pretty, that's how." In Blake Edwards' *Operation Petticoat* (1959), too, Cary Grant as the seasoned submarine commander tells the newly arrived and pristinely (and fully masculinely) attired Curtis that he cannot become the supply officer because "it would ruin your manicure." In an era of male beauty on screen—from Dean, Brando, and Clift on the star level through Robert Wagner, Jeffrey Hunter, Robert Francis, and Tab Hunter as young hunk leads to Russ Tamblyn and Ricky Nelson in supporting roles—Curtis could move from male to female to male without any violence being done either to his own image or to the general image of masculinity he represented.

It is scarcely coincidental that all this attention to male physical beauty was occurring at precisely the time when gay men, the nightmare reality lurking behind these male actors' dreamy images, were being hounded out of their jobs and into psychiatric "treatments" designed to blast into oblivion whatever "femininity" their psyches managed to maintain. From Tony Curtis in drag to Tab Hunter in a swimsuit to stripped-down Gorgeous George and his marcel, beautiful male pinup types were attracting the gaze not only of women but of other men throughout the 1950s, and the nation responded by applauding, panting, and giggling—and by condemning gay men.

Hot, Cold, and Overboard

For all the discomfort *Some Like It Hot* has engendered among its enthusiastic but prudish defenders, its specific representations of sexuality has provoked the most glaring disagreement. On the hot side is Bernard F. Dick discussing the double seduction sequence with Joe and Sugar on shipboard and Jerry/Daphne and Osgood tangoing 'til dawn:

> Joe is romancing Sugar on board a yacht while Osgood is wooing Jerry/Daphne in a roadhouse. Wilder could have crosscut the scenes, but the effect of a double seduction occurring simultaneously—one succeeding, the other too ludicrous even to fail—would have been lost. Instead, Wilder used a swish pan, where the camera would swing from one place to the other—from the yacht to the roadhouse—cre-

ating a momentary blur. Since Joe is feigning impotence to win Sugar, a swish pan would literally throw the viewer off the yacht when the situation grew too intimate.[50]

For a seduction "too ludicrous even to fail," the union of Jerry and Osgood certainly has its staying power. Jerry longs for death after Joe forces to him to ditch Osgood, and Osgood looks far from jilted in the final shot. But for this critic, the heterosexual couple is not only *the* real and successful one but is also so searingly sexual that Wilder had to cast his audience into the drink to keep them from being burned.

On the cooler side is Molly Haskell, who describes Sugar/Marilyn's attraction to Joe/Josephine/Curtis:

> In Curtis she finds the sexual casualty (the would-be leading man to match her would-be leading lady) whose strengths match her weaknesses and weaknesses her strengths. They become "lovers" after their own fashion, while, in a parody of Marilyn's usual film fate, Lemmon plays sugar daughter to Joe E. Brown's sugar daddy, and one relationship is no more "heterosexual" or even sexual than the other.[51]

One notes in this passage a curious absence. The relationships described might be either "heterosexual," which Haskell reassuringly insists they aren't, or "even sexual," which they aren't as well. While it would be just as patent a distortion to describe either set of fictional couples as "homosexual," at least at this point in the film, what is lacking in both these conflicting hot and cold readings is an idea that is apparently unthinkable—namely, that the sexuality represented by all these fictive characters is so rampant that it cannot be contained by the gender imperatives of American society.

What is the cultural point of these mirror-image denials? To me, the point is painfully simple: the critic must not appear to be engaged in any way by the open sexuality of this comedy. From sophisticated discussions such as Haskell's to crude ones such as Crist's, the film's sexual dynamics must be explained away, denied, rendered "other," and dismissed. For male critics, often, this comes across as a particularly vulgar personal response to the homosexual panic the film obviously plays with. For almost every critic it is a political strategy designed to keep the social threat implied in and by nearly every frame of this film—namely, a categorical breakdown in gender definitions—from living on in the form of criticism.

In an interview, Wilder himself drew back from what he had wrought. His cowriter, I.A.L. Diamond, thoroughly denies the existence of what the interviewer quaintly calls "homosexual motifs," but Wilder is a bit cagier in his reply, at first denying and then revising the denial:

> *Diamond:* The whole trick in the picture is that while the two were dressed in women's clothes, their thinking processes were at all times a hundred percent male. When there was a slight aberration, like Lemmon getting engaged, it became twice as funny. But they were not camping it up. They never thought of themselves as women. Just for one moment Lemmon forgot himself—that was all. The rest of the time, Curtis was out to seduce Monroe no matter what clothes he was wearing.

> *Wilder:* But when he forgot himself it was not a homosexual relationship. It was just the idea of being engaged to a millionaire. It's very appealing. You don't have to be a homosexual. It's security.[52]

Diamond acknowledges the fact that the "slight aberration" struck the most pleasurable note, all the while defensively insisting that Josephine and Daphne were "a hundred percent male." Wilder, more ironically, attempts to deny the homosexuality by making Daphne's reaction seem utterly normal. In practice, however, Wilder treats cross-dressing as the material expression of cross-thinking and cross-feeling, and rather than denigrating one relationship by swish-panning away from the other as Dick claims, or removing both relationships from the realm of sexuality altogether as Haskell claims, he repeatedly *unites* the two men's experiences as they move toward a romantic resolution. The swish-pans do provide the most efficient unifying device. Simpler cutting back and forth between parallel scenes occurs relatively often, but as a formal figure Wilder's swish-pans have a double virtue: not only do they graphically *create* a spatial and emotional unity between two different spaces and sets of characters, but they also have a hilarious linguistic connotation, especially given the homosexual panic that underlies this film's comedy and most of its criticism. How better to express the blurry lack of sexual categories embodied by a couple of swishes?

Security

When these four characters all end up in a speedboat together at the end, only one physiological fact separates the couple in the back of the boat from the couple in front, and judging by the expression on his face, it's a fact that Osgood for one couldn't care less about. Jerry, on the other hand, undergoes something of a regression in that final shot; the trauma inflicted by Osgood's absolute self-assurance seems to throw him back to the period of his dark confusion—before he danced and sang and happily announced that the reason a guy would want to marry a guy was "security." The "security" joke comes in the middle of an extended comic sequence, and its force stems at least in part from the self-evident fact that there would be little "security" in this marriage, at least insofar as half the couple is implicitly lying to the other half about the nature of his genitalia. One corollary of the joke, however, is that even under the circumstances Jerry falls back on security as the rationale for this most precipitous of decisions. Unable to bear the categorical absence of a middle ground, he lunges toward marriage with Osgood. The sequence is worth quoting at length; it plays as follows:

Jerry: I'm engaged!
Joe: Congratulations! Who's the lucky girl?
Jerry: I am. (*he sings and shakes maracas*)

Joe:	What?!
Jerry:	Osgood proposed to me. We're planning a June wedding. (*sings, dances, shakes*)
Joe:	What are you talking about? You can't marry Osgood!
Jerry:	(*getting up from bed and entering two shot*): You mean he's too old for me?
Joe:	Jerry, you can't be serious.
Jerry:	Why not? He keeps marrying girls all the time.
Joe:	But, but, you're not a girl. You're a guy. And why would a guy want to marry a guy?
Jerry:	Security! (*sings, dances, shakes*)
Joe:	Jerry, you better lie down. You're not well.
Jerry:	Will you stop treating me like a child? I'm not stupid. I know there's a problem.
Joe:	I'll say there is.
Jerry:	His mother. We need her approval. But I'm not worried, because I don't smoke. Ha ha ha ha! (*sings, dances, shakes*)
Joe:	Jerry, there's another problem. Like *what are you going to do on your honeymoon?*
Jerry:	We've been discussing that. He wants to go to the Riviera, but I kinda lean toward Niagara Falls.

Joe presses further in what increasingly becomes a desperate quest to end Jerry's joy, and Jerry finally admits that his goal is a quick annulment and a handsome settlement. But even this ultimate recouping of the character's heterosexuality is not quite so ultimate, for it is here that Jerry mourns: "I'm a boy, I'm a boy, I wish I were dead. I'm a boy. Oh boy am I a boy." But Daphne doesn't depart without a struggle; she reappears in spirit if not in form very soon afterward when Jerry feels hurt and insulted that Joe could note with surprise, "These are real diamonds!" "Of course they're real," Jerry snaps. "What do you think—my fiancé is a bum?"

In the dialogue as written, Jerry's refusal to deny the possibility of a marriage with Osgood forms the most overt source of comic pleasure, and the relentless repetition of this denial is nothing if not a joyful expression of what would certainly have been considered a repellent affront to national morality (not to mention a violation of the law) outside the realm of fiction in 1959, let alone in 1929 when the film takes place. Every one of Jerry's lines reroutes the conversation away from the sexual interdictions of American society *explicitly* toward a homosexual union. Wilder then follows through by having Joe phrase his distress, his fear of what Jerry so excitedly seems to want, by declaring that Jerry must be sick; Jerry, who appears to be familiar on however unconscious a level with the strangely resilient idea that homosexual desire in the adult has something to do with arrested development (an idea that had more currency in 1959 than it does now that it's discredited), quickly replies that he is not to be treated like a child. He knows instead that the "problem" is Osgood's mother, ostensibly her hatred of smoking daughters-in-law, but on a deeper level her domineering and belittling treatment of Osgood (information supplied by Osgood, who also might have represented a fifties Freudian "invert") and its effect on their future together. Thus Osgood's biography virtually seals Jerry's gay fate, for it brings to the surface exactly what Wilder has been implying so far—that Osgood's persistence with Jerry/Daphne, treated as a kind of comic heroism, the triumph of lust over age, might be possible because Osgood has found in Jerry/Daphne exactly what he has been looking for all his life.

In what they suggest about Jerry's fears and desires as well as those of Joe and Osgood, Jerry's laughing, singing, joking, dancing, and rhythmically recalling the endless tangos and steamy subtropical frissons of the night before provide the tightest single comedy routine in the film. It would be difficult to find another expression of gay desire in film history that could be both so foresightedly euphoric and, at the same time, so specific in its articulation of popular anxieties.

As Bell-Metereau points out, Daphne tends to be rather more aggressive than Jerry:

When Jerry/Daphne dances with Osgood, it is clear that he relishes this chance to lead; he also appreciates the worshipful admiration he receives as Osgood's loved one. It is ironic that as a woman Jerry can play the man, whereas in his supposedly normal man to man relationship with Joe he is the cajoling, submissive female.[53]

But Wilder adds another level of meaning with his camera. Jerry begins the "security" sequence in bed, shaking and singing, seen in a high-angle shot that suggests a certain irony on the part of the director but more vividly implies that Jerry, now immersed in his femininity, has found a role that allows him to be as passive as he wants—a passivity that paradoxically gives him power. Joe, now dressed in his yachting outfit (which is every bit as ludicrous as the Josephine getup: a phony male compared to a phony female), completes the opposition in the early part of the sequence by being filmed in low angle as he paces behind Jerry's bed. However, the instant Joe demandingly asserts "You can't marry Osgood," Jerry jumps off the bed and Wilder films the rest of the scene in a two shot: on an equal level with Joe, Daphne proves to be quite assertive when challenged. Only when the equally falsely costumed Joe succeeds in destroying his dreams does Jerry reemerge with another death wish.

The Death Instinct

As is often the case with Wilder, death pervades this comedy, from its opening sequence in which the occupants of a hearse open fire on a police car to its open-ended ending, where the heroes are *still* escaping underworld execution. The notion of closure is subtly challenged by the final shot: to where are these characters racing? It's movement itself, expressed by a moving camera accompanying four moving characters, which "ends" the film, yet the movement is qualified by the fact that they all remain more or less in the same compositional spot on the screen. In Wilder's world, the line between movement/life and stasis/death is thin.

Throughout the film, Wilder links life and death, which is to say sex and death, with a peculiar relish that allows for jokes both obscure and thinly veiled. In a bit of comedy that may or may not strike anyone as particularly prurient when it occurs, a casket riddled with bullets gushes fluid all over a hearse, but the punchline doesn't come until the detective, investigating Mozzarella's Funeral Parlor and discovering a speakeasy with a wild floor show behind the solemn front room, declares, "If ya gotta go, that's the way to do it." In an especially elaborate joke, Wilder later inflects this sexual morbidity or morbid sexuality with a food fetish when Jerry, overwhelmed with the abundance of females in the band, enthusiastically describes a recurrent dream:

| Jerry: | I used to have a dream. I was locked up in a pastry shop and there was goodies all around. There was jellyrolls and mocha eclairs, and sponge cake, and Boston creme pie, and cherry tarts . . . |
| Joe: | Listen to me. No butter, no pastry. We're on a diet. |

By 1959 it would seem that the "simplified Freudianisms" of the past decade had reached the point at which general audiences could be assumed to understand this dream joke without further explanation. All the products in Jerry's bakery are obviously and overtly sexual, as the hungry yet satisfied smile on Jerry's face suggests. But while sex jokes were hardly new to the cinema, Wilder treats Jerry's dream work as being comical *as dream work*. Moreover, Joe knows exactly what Jerry means; he insists that nothing can be eaten, that abstinence is their only salvation, and thus he dispenses with psychological jargon in favor of a mutually understood metaphor that would not exist without the reductive appeal of popular psychology.

The joke does not play itself out until near the end of the film, when an enormous confection—a giant cake—is delivered to the head gangster, Little Bonaparte. Instead of the traditional nubile woman who serves as the lewd creme filling, out pops a thug who blows the birthday boy away with a machine gun. Joe (in "reality") and Jerry (in dream) treat women as little more than "goodies" available for purchase, and the grotesque mass murder perpetrated by the relentlessly and satirically masculine gangsters forces them to reexamine themselves and their view of women. Little Bonaparte, as the gang leader, is thus destroyed by the same metaphor expanded to outrageous proportions. As Brandon French puts it, *Some Like It Hot* depicts "a male world so predatory that the resumption of androgyny becomes a matter of life and death."[54]

Sugar Kane, whom Haskell rightly describes as being "as much 'in drag' as" Joe and Jerry, is the only human confection to remain intact by the film's end.[55] As Wilder noted years after completing *Some Like It Hot*, the profusion of writing about Monroe is staggering: "I think there have been more books on Marilyn Monroe than on World War II, and there is a great similarity." Also worth repeating in the World War II vein is Tony Curtis's famous description of what it was like to kiss the reigning sex goddess: "It was just like kissing Hitler." There is little need in this particular study to elaborate upon or challenge the Monroe industry's evaluation of her performance here. It bears mentioning, however, that Sugar's own description of her past furthers the same confection metaphor, only this time it's told from the woman's point of view. "I always get the fuzzy end of the lollipop," she declares, and if one is prone to making sexual associations to metaphors, the oral interest Sugar describes seems particularly graphic—and none too pleasurable from her point of view.

Drinking heavily throughout the film and thus acting in a timely fifties haze, Sugar forms a kind of tragic counterpoint to the giddiness of Daphne and Josephine. Just as their costumes and mannerisms are constructed from a painful history of female subjugation built on idealized images and sexual constraints ("I don't know how they walk in these things" says a hurting, frustrated Jerry about Daphne's new high heels), Sugar's life, like Monroe's career, is a costume. But it's one that couldn't be removed without extraordinary violence against herself; she *is* her drag. Once again cast as a "showgirl," Monroe plays her character as self-display in the role of self-display, and this career in the service of male pleasure has brought her character little more than a depressed self-contempt, the source of which is patently obvious to Sugar. And Wilder *still* never comes to terms with her. If the film has a central deficiency, it is Wilder's inability to move Monroe's character beyond a sort of paralyzed observation of her own image. Because they are male, Joe and Jerry are granted far more latitude.

Audacity and Redemption

In an "audacious" scene that has caught the eye of a number of critics, Joe, dressed as Josephine, tops off Sugar's tearful on-stage rendition of "I'm Through with Love" by walking onto the stage, kissing her, and telling her in all sincerity, "None of that, Sugar. No guy is worth it." Lesbian panic, on which some of the women's scenes' most anxious comedy hinges, simultaneously peaks and disintegrates in an instant, since from the heroine's perspective the line and kiss are delivered by a trusted and loving woman. Sugar initially reacts with a purposefully ambiguous look of shock: is she surprised that Josephine is Joe, or that Josephine kissed her, or (as is most satisfying) both? Whatever one's reading, Sugar can scarcely be blamed for being shocked. She has just discovered not only that her friend Josephine cares more for her than any of the men who have forced her to suck the fuzzy end of the lollipop but also that the categories of sexual definition that have enslaved her are in point of fact much more malleable. It is this transgender aspect of the scene, the first of the film's two sexually open-ended climaxes, that is truly "audacious," not simply the fact that "a woman" is kissing another woman.[56]

Critical discourse is most enervating when it comes to the film's ending. "Nobody's perfect" might well be the most succinct single expression of Wilder's vision of an ideal America in the fifties. As late-seventies film theory might phrase it, it is understood that the Wilder-text (if such an entirety can be deduced without reference to the author-ideal) is predicated upon and even generated precisely by the moral code this utterance represents; as conclusive aphorism, it bears not only textual but intertextual connotations, here expressed as equivocal desire in the form of an object-choice that refuses to name itself. Call it what you will, the remark has provoked odd responses:

Jerry, with elaborate flamboyance, tears off his wig to disclose his true gender—and nothing happens. Small wonder that Osgood is not only unperturbed but *unconvinced*. (Neil Sinyard and Adrian Turner)[57]

Finally, he [Jerry] yanks off his wig and says, "Damn it, I'm a man." "Well, nobody's perfect," Osgood replies in a line that is certainly the kiss off to sexual stereotypy. (Bernard Dick)[58]

In a way, *Some Like It Hot* tells . . . how Joe. E. Brown trapped Lemmon into the awful transsexual consequences of an effeminate movie presence. (Richard Corliss)[59]

Since Osgood explicitly tells Jerry that Jerry's identity as a man does not in any way dampen Osgood's tremendous sexual drive, it is truly queer that none of these writers can bring themselves to mention the unmentionable. Osgood (1) remains unconvinced, (2) kisses off stereotypes, and (3) represents the "awful" and "transsexual" outcome of effeminacy. Sinyard and Turner must be willing to dispense with what is certainly one of the widest grins ever seen on film in order to propose Osgood's lack of faith, and Dick scholastically finds the triumph of Osgood's reaction to be merely a witty comment on "stereotypy." But neither of these responses, as incomplete as they are, reach Richard Corliss's level of evasion. First of all, "transsexual" is the wrong word. Nobody has (or has had) a sex change operation, nor does anyone appear to want one—especially in the fictive world of 1929, over twenty years before Christine Jorgensen brought the issue into popular consciousness. Second, Osgood's face is not especially "effeminate" by most standards of what constitutes femininity in the West. But then Corliss has already claimed that both Curtis and Lemmon are themselves "effeminate." And given the fact that Sweet Sue's manager, Beinstock (called "Beanstalk" by Sinyard and Turner) has a similar lack of ruggedness, one assumes that every non-Mafioso in the film is "effeminate" too. Which of these characters present "awful" consequences, however? None does—except, according to Corliss, poor Osgood, the one who doesn't care if his lover is a guy.

"Curtis," Corliss goes on to declare, "is far more comfortable as [Cary] Grant than as a girl." Given the speed and grace with which Joe becomes Josephine, Corliss's impression is bluntly wrong, more a measure of the critic's panic than Curtis's sense of humor. And Corliss is still not finished: "Curtis' masculinity is asserted for good when, again dressed as a girl and in the middle of the final chase sequence, he stops to hear Monroe singing 'I'm Thru with Love.'" The end result becomes an assertion of masculinity for Corliss because the moment marks a heroically heterosexual "redemption." This is a particularly striking example of how critical discourse can be put to the service of sexual and social prejudice, which here takes on the language of religion.

If one must argue the merits of the film as a heterosexual gospel, Joe is "redeemed" when he sees the extent to which his romance with Sugar has been on his own (masculine) terms, the pain he has inflicted on her, and his own culpability. Since he is dressed as a woman at that moment, this most crucial step in his development may have something to do with overcoming the brittle, empty masculinity of his past as Joe and of his yachting persona as well, and adopting some of Sugar's empathic understanding of and love for Josephine and Daphne. The emotional force of the line comes from the honesty with which Joe advises Sugar about men, specifically himself, the central man in both their lives: "*no* guy is worth it." It is the first time in the film that Joe has not felt that, as a man, he *is* worth it. This is scarcely an indication of "masculinity . . . for good."

A more fascinating and perverse evasion comes from Marjorie Garber. Although it radiates an entirely different degree of liberal sophistication, Garber's explanation nevertheless constitutes a firm denial of Osgood's male sexual object:

> Osgood's rejoinder, "Nobody's perfect," has become a cliche in the criticism of transvestite theater, but this does not mean that Osgood looks forward to life with Jerry. On the contrary, he blissfully contemplates life with Daphne, whose metamorphic name suggests her nature. To think that Daphne will cease to exist because Jerry has

described her situation is to wish away cross-dressing and transvestism as if they had no power in the present.[60]

It is interesting that Garber, who uses the terms "cross-dressing" and "transvestism" more or less interchangeably throughout her book, here distinguishes between them, however unclearly. Otherwise, Garber is right on *almost* all counts. The sheer continuity of Osgood's responses throughout the interchange suggests that he does look forward to life with the image and body of the person he has grown to love. But Garber still misses the ringing point. True, Daphne and Jerry are now one and the same. On the surface, they are ambiguous. Anatomically, though, they're *male*. Let's face it: there are two hidden penises behind this hilarious final joke; Osgood has one, and so does Jerry/Daphne. And true to form in Anglo-American culture, theirs is a love that dare not speak its name. Not on screen, not in criticism.

Saying it in a veiled way, however—in fact, all but shouted here on the big screen in 1959—is another matter entirely. When Osgood, referring to Jerry/Daphne's future wedding dress, offers, "We can have it altered," Jerry replies *emphatically*: "Oh no you don't!" But as always, Osgood's grin persists, not only undeterred but now more or less driven by the barely suppressed knowledge of what his lover has to offer.

Osgood's final declaration is openly gay, there's no question about that. The line is meaningless otherwise. Osgood's comfort with the idea of having sex with Jerry couldn't be more specific; that's precisely what provoked hysterical laughter in 1959 and continues to provoke it today, though in a somewhat less hysterical fashion. Yet it is fascinating to look back on twenty-five years of film criticism and see, first, an overarching denial of the sheer *gayness* of "Nobody's perfect," followed in recent years by a springing leap over the notion of categorical gay desire toward an embrace of androgyny, the category-free transgender category that exists as pure abstraction and thus has the great appeal of enabling critics to enjoy the benefits of gay liberation without actually having to deal with homosexual acts. It's worth repeating: this is in striking contrast to the film itself, which ends by declaring what has been left (barely) unspoken—namely, that the sexual trajectory of

Osgood's relationship with Jerry leads inexorably toward a dreaded/desired homosexual act. If Hollywood could play with it, why is it so impossible for cultural critics to come to terms with the naturally affirmative comedy represented by two penises in love?

Of course, this is a culturally radical affirmation. And *of course* it goes beyond simple male-male sex in exactly the way Garber and others describe. But by specifically denoting the open, unapologetic desire of one man for another, the line further intensifies the film's disruptive quality, particularly in terms of the culture out of which it arose. Indeed, even in psychiatric circles—perhaps particularly in those circles—the essential psychic androgyny described by Freud was itself surplus-repressed by cultural discourse in the 1950s, and it was radical for Wilder to play upon it in this film. I have focused on various moments in which it burst forth in comedies of the period, but one should never forget that these moments were the exceptions, not the rule.

Cross-dressing necessarily opens up what Garber sees as the radical "space" and "power" of transgender, and this film's conclusion keeps that space and power very much alive. Moreover, Jerry insists not merely that he is a male but that males are *only* males, and it's this strait cultural notion that Osgood is willing to forgive. *Some Like It Hot* is finally about the kind of emotional androgyny that American culture has tended to deny, oftentimes viciously: Sugar is a nearly suicidal drunk because she is abused by a society that makes her powerless; Joe finds himself increasingly frustrated with the masculine role he must play; Jerry discovers that Osgood is a fine catch only to be told that he is sick to think so, and he consequently ends up longing for death.

Wilder closes this film with a character reverting back to the kind of simple-minded "security" the film has done nothing but denounce. "I'm a man!" Jerry demands. But as this is exactly the kind of limitation he and Joe have learned to overcome, Osgood's final response is right on the humanistic mark: he forgives him, though his big, wide, contented grin indicates that he fully intends to enjoy him physically for exactly what he is. Even for heterosexual audiences of the 1950s, this ending must have provided a jolt of pleasurable reality, the comical acknowledgment of a repressed truth; for today's heterosexuals, the ending offers an equally liberating disavowal of sexual categories. But for gay people, then and now, this is one of *a handful* of Hollywood representations that offer the kind of positive identification that heterosexuals take for granted. Heterosexual clinches, which conventionally clinch literally tens of thousands of movies, are thus rarely of landmark social value; the straight world doesn't have to fight to preserve them as cultural milestones. Ultimately, it comes down to this: to claim that "Nobody's perfect" is not specifically about gay sexuality is to steal what precious little mainstream cultural participation gay men and lesbians can claim for ourselves. Somehow it doesn't seem fair.

Discontent: From *Some Like It Hot* to *Psycho*

Throughout the 1950s, Billy Wilder periodically gave voice to dangerous sexual ideas, but even if his films hadn't been so commercially and artistically successful, he would still come across in retrospect as downright heroic. But even Wilder's stance toward the mores of his adopted culture wasn't always as overtly challenging. Neither *Sabrina* (1954) nor *Love in the Afternoon* attacks its repressive cultural context as sharply as the four films discussed here. *Sabrina* and *Love in the Afternoon* look back to the more gracious cinema of Ernst Lubitsch; Wilder's other comedies look ahead to a period when the dust of the fifties would finally settle, when sexual interdictions in the cinema would break down even further. The sixties allowed Wilder to become even more overtly biting in his critiques, with comedies about wormy men and suicidal women (*The Apartment*, 1960), corporate imperialism and the Berlin Wall (*One, Two, Three*, 1961), prostitution (*Irma la Douce*, 1963), adultery (*Kiss Me, Stupid*, 1964—the most corrosive comedy of his career), and insurance fraud (*The Fortune Cookie*, 1966). These are all comedies for the culturally discontented.

Throughout the 1950s, the world Wilder represented on film never ceased to dwell on either the act or the idea of dying. Only one other director was more famously obsessed with death. Wilder's vision of America may have been peculiar, but Alfred Hitchcock's was even more so. In 1955, when Hitchcock made *The Trouble with Harry*, the second of the two straight-out comedies of his career (the other being 1941's *Mr. and Mrs. Smith*), he surveyed the American landscape and saw a society blithely enveloped by its own contradictions, a people fraught with suppressed hysteria, and a cultural unconscious that had become wildly aware of its own mortality. In a sense, the emotional turmoil underlying the American fifties reached an explicit crisis on screen in 1960, one year after *Some Like It Hot*, when Hitchcock directed his own cross-dressing film. As Brandon French puts it: "*Some Like It Hot* and *Psycho* represent in microcosm the opposing poles of cultural feeling about the revolution in sex roles that was fomenting throughout the '50s and which erupted in the '60s."[61]

But as William Paul points out in his book *Laughing/Screaming*, the two responses share a certain antirepressive psychological dynamic. It isn't so much that *Some Like It Hot* and *Psycho* represent opposite poles of the culture. Rather they elucidate, each in its own hysterical fashion, the irrepressible knowledge of an otherwise clamped sexuality. It's not just conflicting feelings about "sex roles" that these films tap into. It is sexual desire itself—*not* the tailored adult form, but the remains of an unruly, precodified drive which psychic maturation always serves to civilize at great mental cost and which the excessive constraints of the 1950s—Marcuse's surplus repression—served to repress and enrage to the point of delirium: liberating glee in Wilder's film, murderous psychosis in Hitchcock's.

Hitchcock's films usually have a sense of humor, even when they are most unnerving. In fact, in certain ways *The Trouble with Harry* is less "funny" than *Psycho*. But oddly enough, one of the most perverse aspects of *The Trouble with Harry* is that this droll comedy is set in the cheeriest and most vibrant of locations: a crisp Technicolor autumn in virginal, pastoral Vermont. Like the season in which it takes place, this film's colors seem so bright because its purpose is so mortifying.

three

UNREST IN PEACE: HITCHCOCK'S FIFTIES HUMOR

Death as Sex Farce: *The Trouble with Harry*

Selling Harry

"So horribly sad. How is it I feel like laughing?" This more or less universal line, spoken by an unnamed agent in *North by Northwest* (1959), occurs in the scene immediately following Cary Grant/Roger Thornhill's escape from the United Nations, where he has just pulled a bloody knife out of the back of the suddenly dead Mr. Townsend and said, in utter innocence, "I didn't have anything to do with this." Roger Thornhill's trouble *is* sad, and it's also hilarious. *The Trouble with Harry* (1955) isn't nearly as funny, but the same split response applies.

The Trouble with Harry follows in the black comic tradition of Capra's *Arsenic and Old Lace* (1944) and Chaplin's *Monsieur Verdoux* (1947). Maiden sisters who happily murder men is a potent topic, but Capra is too good-natured to allow *Arsenic and Old Lace* to engage fully with its own ghastliness and misanthropy, and as a result the film's humor rarely rises above cuteness. *Monsieur Verdoux*, a comedy about wife killing, is more successful, because Chaplin doesn't try to pull big laughs out of the misogynistic material. The occasional chuckle provoked by *Monsieur Verdoux* stands in marked contrast to the derisive laughter sparked by the Breen Office's response to Chaplin's script; Chaplin quotes the censors in his autobiography:

> Please rephrase Lydia's line, 'Well, forget about him and come to bed,' to read, 'and go to bed.' We presume that this whole section will be played in such a way as to avoid any feeling that Verdoux and Lydia [one of Verdoux's wives] are about to indulge in marital privileges. . . . There should be no showing of, or suggestion of, toilets in the bathroom.[1]

Almost ten years later, Alfred Hitchcock was faced with a similar conflict between legislated taste and irrepressible knowledge, the clamp civilization exerts on the bodily facts of humanity. For Hitchcock, burial doesn't work unless and until the body is granted its due. Interred, exhumed, interred, exhumed—Harry, like certain ideas, refused to stay buried in 1955. The film's eponymous hero, appearing on screen only after his abrupt demise, causes the residents of a quaint American town a lot of grief, but not in the proper sense of the word. Harry's trouble is that he refuses to perform his social role as dead body: to represent one's worst fear (Freud in his later years would have said one's deepest wish) in a dignified and acceptable fashion (which is to say to disappear underground).[2] One reason he cannot do so is that the New Englanders who surround him have invested his lifeless body with a frightening degree of their own repressed sexuality, an unseemly but strangely popular way to treat a cadaver in Hitchcock's Vermont countryside.

Alfred Hitchcock directed two feature films in 1955, *To Catch a Thief* and *The Trouble with Harry*. Their relative slightness may stem as much from their context in Hitchcock's career as from their individual weaknesses; he made them between two more complicated and satisfying films, *Rear Window* (1954) and *The Man Who Knew Too Much* (1956). Critical evaluations aside, these bracketing films fit securely into the suspense genre while *Thief* and *Harry* do not, and they are also more intricate in structure and theme. *Harry*, on the other hand, is a comedy of manners, and as such it is particularly lacking in suspense. Its failure to conform to Hitchcock's reputation has contributed in no small measure to its critical rejection.

Throughout the 1950s, Hitchcock combined comic moments with the more sober conventions of psychological drama, often in the form and manners of women: Marion Lorne's daffy performance as Bruno's mother in *Strangers on a Train* (1951); Thelma Ritter's deadpanned dialogue in *Rear Window*; the farcical portrait of Carlotta (Kim Novak) that Barbara Bel Geddes' Midge uses to ridicule both Scottie's (James Stewart) attraction to Carlotta/Madeleine as well as her own face in *Vertigo* (1958); and Jesse Royce Landis's indefatigably lighthearted mother in *North by Northwest*, who turns Cary Grant's plea for help into an extended and dismissive gag.

These comic moments notwithstanding, Hitchcock hadn't directed an out-and-out comedy since the screwball *Mr. and Mrs. Smith* (1941), a solid commercial hit that for some reason has tended to mystify most of Hitchcock's critical defenders. *Harry*, equally mystifying, is more or less classical in terms of its comic resolution, the end of the narrative being concurrent with sexual coupling. And for anyone willing to accept the film's satire of the puritanical side of the fifties as being even moderately accurate, *The Trouble with Harry* is worth a second look as a study of sex, death, and repression in small town America.

Critics may have willfully ignored the film, but it would not be fair to say that contemporary audiences did so. *The Trouble with Harry* cannot by any stretch of the imagination be considered commercially representative of fifties comedies. It didn't even make *Variety*'s list of films earning $1,000,000 or more in rentals and is, therefore, the only film in this study that failed to find its social vision even mildly ratified by commercial success. But *Harry*'s box-office failure is more complicated than blunt figures (or their absence) might suggest. Figures for film grosses are difficult to determine. *Variety* employs its own complex system of estimation, but during this period the paper did not provide a weekly chart of estimates, as it does now. *Harry* didn't make the end-of-year list, and it's impossible to estimate from *Variety*'s reported figures for individual theaters how much or how little money the film really made. In any case, Paramount employed a limited-release strategy that confined the film to first-run exhibition in large cities, and without national distribution in second- or third-run theaters *The Trouble with Harry* never reached full audience potential. If *Variety's* random accounts are correct, though, the film did rather well in metropolitan first-run theaters, with box-office receipts for cities like San Francisco, Toronto, and other major markets receiving consistently enthusiastic blurbs. In the case of New York's Paris Theater, the film greatly exceeded Paramount's expectations, and it was held over for an extended run.[3]

Given the film's quirkiness, Paramount may have had good reason to forego a wide release, but the studio's distribution strategy made its apparent lack of confidence a self-fulfilling prophecy. In other words, the film's booking at the Paris Theater in New York, together with the fact that it never went beyond first-run theaters in large cities, suggests that Paramount saw *Harry* as something of an art house film and therefore distributed it in the way that, say, British comedies would have been handled. Having done so, and having seen the film succeed within those limited terms, Paramount fulfilled its own prediction that the film was more of an art house film than one of general commercial interest. In any event, there is little reason to believe *Harry* could have matched the commercial success of Hitchcock's other films of the 1950s. Paramount's pessimism notwithstanding, *The Trouble with Harry* is a far richer, more complicated film than even Hitchcock's most ardent defenders have so far been willing to acknowledge, and its place in fifties comedy is rather more important than it may at first appear to be.

At this point in this study, it is safe to say that a pronounced and persistent strain of fifties comedy grew out of a matrix of themes and moods: sexual repression, harsh social constraints in an era of economic plenty, emotional despair at a time of political complacency, psychological fragmentation, and a deep-seated morbidity that contrasts with the mood of simple-minded optimism that later decades have ascribed to the period. In film criticism, typically, the era's most death-oriented visions have been socially disarmed by critical interest in two particular directors' personal obsessions; by describing both

Wilder and Hitchcock as idiosyncratically morbid, film critics steer these directors' representations of life away from the social conditions that made these visions possible and meaningful. Wilder's and Hitchcock's comic morbidity is certainly idiosyncratic to the extent that few other directors, writers, or artists maintained such a refined and tireless interest in death, but their refinement of the topic scarcely corrals their films' contents back into the narrow confines of two individuals' views of the world. Hitchcock and Wilder may have had unusually strong creative responses to questions of death and dying, and they may have characterized American society in terms of their own repressions and fears, but in film after film (and in Hitchcock's case, television show after television show), they successfully presented their obsessions with death as mass entertainment, a topic for gratification and amusement on a vast social and cultural scale.

Life in Two-Dimensions

Morbid cartoonishness, which *The Trouble with Harry* all but takes for granted as an artistic ploy, also found expression in the work of two other contemporary comic artists, Ernie Kovacs and Charles Addams. Kovacs' comic style was unusually anarchic, especially for a television star, and the objects of his humor were varied, but one of his characters assumes an attitude of everyday ghastliness that calls Hitchcock to mind. "Auntie Gruesome," a hideous crone with facial scars, retold classic children's tales in her own special style—a kind of kaffe-klatch monologue delivered in a dungeon. Carried away by mundane details and digressions, the nightmarish Auntie (Kovacs in drag) would usually run out of time and fail to finish the story. Auntie Gruesome's comic gimmick was her matter-of-factness; the tales were often frightening, as was the teller, yet both took on an attitude of seen-it-all-before banality.

Addams's morbidity is even more to the point as far as Hitchcock is concerned. Addams work appeared regularly in the *New Yorker* through the 1940s and 1950s as well as in compilation volumes, and his morbid sensibility often took on domestic overtones. Addams actually entered Hitchcock's art in the form of a joke: in *North by Northwest*, when Thornhill comes upon his new lover and protector (Eva Marie Saint) sitting together with his potential killers, Vandamm and Leonard (James Mason and Martin Landau), he remarks, "The three of you together—that's a picture only Charles Addams could draw." But Addams and Hitchcock share more than a single line of dialogue. For instance, (at least) two of Addams's cartoons are Hitch-cockian in their sense of contemporary domesticity, community values, social interactions, and women's literal liberation. In the first, from 1952, a woman is seated in her living room, her feet up on a footstool. She is leaning back in her chair, talking on the phone, smiling broadly and holding a gun in her hand. Lying on the floor beneath her, a pair of trousered legs (presumably those of her husband) are visible in the lower left, as the woman blithely remarks, "Nothing much, Agnes. What's new with you?" The second cartoon, from 1954, takes place in a radio studio. Two men sit at a table, and one of them reads into a microphone: "I have a question from a lady in Astoria. She wants to know the best method for removing blood stains from a broadloom rug."[4] (As an aside, looking back to *Monkey Business* and the comedy of scientific progress, Addams produced a 1953 cartoon—one year after that film's release—which shows scientists running terrified out a laboratory door as giant white rats rip through their cages and begin to break the lab apart. A scientist on the phone says, "Sanders speaking. Stop all production of XP15, recall all shipments, wire every doctor in the country, and *hurry!*")

Baudelaire was hyperbolic when he declared that "caricatures often constitute the most faithful mirror of life," but there can be no doubt that a strain of cartoonishly exaggerated grisliness ran through the 1950s, mirroring as well as responding to the social and sexual anxieties of the period.[5] Witness Vincent Price, who was almost as much a comedian as a figure of horror. Charles Addams fell squarely on the side of comedy, but the blend was much the same. In these two cartoons, Addams finds humor and horror in the social nature of modern communication: the telephone and the radio link women matter-of-factly to the world outside the home. But in both cases, the household is the locus of murderous impulses directed specifically against husbands, explicitly in the former cartoon, implicitly in the latter. The pleasure of both cartoons lies in dissolving the women's superficial conformity by exposing, through caricature, their fundamental—one might even say radical—discontent. And in each case, Addams seizes on the sheer *ordinariness* of these violent wishes. "Nothing much, Agnes," says his heroine, and Addams assumes that she isn't alone.

Equally workaday in its treatment of a murdered male, *The Trouble with Harry* begins simply. In the film's credit sequence, drawn by high-end cartoonist Saul Steinberg, the camera tracks laterally along a flat landscape made up of bizarre, sticklike trees with geometrical branches outlined in various colors. A silly-looking bird appears, then more birds, and all are drawn as mere outlines with no attempt to flesh them out representationally. These minimalist details lend a childish, reductive quality to the landscape. Steinberg denotes the ground, for example, by a simple straight line. He gives some of the birds smiling mouths (curved lines on their beaks), and he doodles the fantastically designed foliage rather than depicting it with recognizable limbs and leaves.

As the camera tracks right, it reveals more birds of various sizes, all facing attentively toward the right of the screen, where suddenly an enormous shoe looms onto the image. The shoe, seen in profile, is followed by a leg, a torso, and finally an immense head with a blank and foolish expression on its face. Like the birds, the figure has a line denoting its mouth, but unlike the circular eyes on the fowl, the man has a single curved line to serve as a closed eye. The camera stops when the cartoon cadaver fills the image, its horizontal aspect emphasizing the extended width of the VistaVision screen. It is at this moment that Hitchcock's directorial credit appears.

The complexity of this literally sketched representation belies the simplicity of the represented forms. Art historian and theorist E. H. Gombrich makes some very bold claims for Steinberg, most notably that "there is perhaps no artist alive who knows more about the philosophy of representation."[6] Gombrich argues that Steinberg's work incessantly leads the viewer back to questions of seeing and interpreting, an argument that takes on a particular resonance in this case since film critics have often made similar claims for Hitchcock.[7] But as Gombrich points out, as much as one sees in the ink of Steinberg's linear caricatures the dual acts of drawing and perceiving, one must also look at the pathetic faces he has drawn, the mock tragedy he expresses: "Try as we may, what we see is not just ink. The little man who cancels himself remains pathetic and intriguing."[8] The same holds true for Hitchcock, especially in this film. *The Trouble with Harry* isn't especially preoccupied with the issue of perception, at least not in comparison to *Rear Window* and *Vertigo*. And without the distracting convolutions of perceptual play, the comic pathos of the subject—namely small town life and death—comes to light all the more clearly.

Setting the stage for the caricatured Americana that Hitchcock effects with live human beings, Steinberg's cartoon vision of nature in the credits sequence is both juvenile and grotesque, as if drawn by a disturbed child. It exudes an element of corruption that distorts what might otherwise be a kindergartener's view of a landscape. The harshness of the trees, partially outlined in colors not generally associated with foliage (blues and purples) as well as autumnal yellows and oranges, suggests a natural setting seen through an unnatural point of view. Branches become scribbles, leaves colored outlines. The birds, in turn, are rudely personified creatures smiling eerily at a human corpse, a sardonic but oddly literal rendering of the cartoonish creature Harry will become.

Staying Put

The corpse culminates the tracking shot, and by accompanying the revelation of death by a cessation of movement, Hitchcock introduces a leitmotif which, like the sequence's representational flatness, reappears throughout the film. Morbid, perverse, and relatively limited in psychological detail, the film continually plays upon Harry's immobility for comic effect. Other than uttering a single line of dialogue, Harry does nothing in the film but *lie* there.

The original source material, a novel by J. Trevor Story, resembles the film in comic tone as well as in plot structure. Most of the central characters make the transition from page to screen with little violence done to them, and in the course of reading the book one finds not only most of the plot but actual lines of dialogue as well. Story's novel, like Hitchcock's film, takes a deadpanned approach to the imminent but never fully realized sexual drives of a group of people who are weirdly if indirectly aroused by the presence of a corpse. But to see the subtle shifts of meaning between novel and film, it is important to understand that, in contrast to the film, the novel is purely British. In the novel the action takes place on a huge estate which encompasses the village and all the surrounding countryside. In transposing the action from the milieu of landed gentry to that of democratic Vermont, Hitchcock dispensed with the gentry as well as the whole subplot concerning its representative, a character named Mark Douglas, whose stupendous sex drive is so potent that it virtually governs the terrain. Mark Douglas made it as far as the first draft of the screenplay but was cut out by the time of the final shooting script. To get the flavor of what was cut, consider this bit of dialogue between Douglas and a character named Mrs. D'Arcy, who are heading into the woods for a quickie when they come upon a hobo lying down next to Harry. "If there's anything I don't like it's a tramp!," says Mrs. D'Arcy, to which Douglas replies, "Me, too. Unless it has skirts."[9] In Story's novel the townsfolk—all British—are implicitly affected by Douglas's raging libido. In the film, only the Captain (Edmund Gwenn) is English whereas everyone else is American, and it is only the dead body that spurs them obliquely into action. From a perverse British novel about English sexual repression, Hitchcock fashioned an equally perverse American film about characters who are, if anything, even more repressed.

The Trouble with Harry lacks the visual flair of Hitchcock's other fifties films, but *Harry*'s central spectacle is Harry himself—which is to say, a comically immobile artifact. Hitchcock introduces Harry visually through two compositionally striking shots: a forward tracking shot (taken from the height of a standing human being) of the dead body lying on the ground with its head toward the camera, and a shot of Harry taken at nearly ground level, his two feet looming on screen as exaggeratedly as the cartoon corpse's feet and forming a frame-within-a-frame for a small child, Arnie (Jerry Mathers), who peers down at the body. These shots are the shocking conclusion to the film's lyrical opening scene, in which the bright autumn colors of a rural town are recorded in a series of long shots of a church and the surrounding landscape. Church bells are peeling, the richly saturated Technicolor leaves are at their idyllic prime, and a figure, seen first in extreme long shot, walks through the meadow. Hitchcock cuts progressively closer to reveal the figure as being that of a boy carrying a firearm.

The weapon turns out to be a toy (the shooting script describes it with contemporary flair as a "disintegrator ray gun, with the atomic booster and radioactive catalytic supercharger"), but the sequence still moves toward a discomfiting revelation of the violence underlying this pastoral landscape.[10] Arnie hears three shots, and he throws himself down on the ground like a trained soldier, never releasing his gun from a firing position. We assume the little boy has gotten his combat training from TV, and his automatic physical response, like the gunshots, intensifies one's sense of lyricism gone awry. As Arnie lies on the ground, he hears a man's voice say, "Okay, I know how to handle your type." Being precocious and fearless (after all, he has his gun), Arnie runs in the direction of the voice and discovers Harry's body. The entire sequence, lasting only a matter of minutes, moves from an evocation of rural simplicity to a young boy's blunt discovery of a corpse.

When Arnie finally reaches Harry's body, Hitchcock first uses a moving camera to represent the boy's forward motion, with Harry's prone body contrasting markedly with the camera's mobility, then uses a compositionally severe shot taken from the vicinity of Harry's feet to intensify the sense of Harry' new but eternal inertia. Harry's feet, now unable to act as a means of transportation, may now exist only as reminders of past motion. No longer serving a real function, they begin to serve a metaphorical one as Hitchcock repeatedly uses them as a synechdoche for Harry as a whole. When the local painter Sam (John Forsythe) begins to sketch a landscape, he finds himself drawing a pair of feet sticking out from a bush. When the central characters get together at the end of the day to clean Harry's clothes of the dirt of three separate burials, Hitchcock records Harry's presence in the scene by way of the shadow of his feet on the wall. When the bathroom door suddenly swings open near the end, Harry turns up in the bathtub with only his feet visible. His shoes, removed from his body by the hobo, become the sheriff's only tangible evidence of Harry's existence aside from Sam's sketch. (Prior to this theft, the hobo—we'd call him homeless now—wears pieces of frayed burlap wrapped around his feet; this harsh bit of costuming dampens any audience distaste at the act of stealing from a dead man.) And when the hobo removes the shoes, Hitchcock lends Harry's feet a whimsical touch by having him wear blue socks with bright red tips.

Hitchcock's attention to the stiff's feet comes from two separate but related areas. An expression of Harry's immobility, the feet are made comical by virtue of their uselessness, but they are also treated less self-evidently as a key element in the pervasive displacement of sexual energy that underlies each of the central characters' progression through the film. While this visual joke initially fits Henri Bergson's thesis on the relation of laughter to the audience's recognition of the mechanical aspects of the human body, the joke stands on the fact that the dead human body is metonymically reduced to feet: while the rest of Harry's corpse lies flat, his feet stick up in the air. No matter where Harry is, no matter where the camera is placed, his feet are invariably pointing upward, standing at priapic attention. Hitchcock's repetition of this point underscores not only the timeless rigidity to which Harry is condemned but also his role as a perversely sexual memento mori.

Performance Anxiety

The real "trouble" with Harry becomes, through this visual displacement, much richer than a simple inability to remain buried. As his wife Jen (Shirley MacLaine) reveals, Harry was unable to consummate the marriage on their wedding night. She describes herself as having waited by the light of a full moon, dressed in her best night-ie, for Harry to show up. "He never came in," she flatly declares to Sam, who will later propose marriage to her. Equally suggestive is Harry's identity as Jen's brother-in-law, the brother of her first hus-band who, she says with amusing vagueness, "got killed." Harry, being "noble," felt that it was his duty to marry Jen, following the biblical exhortation to brothers in similar situations. Unfortunately, Harry's horoscope on the day of their wedding told him "not to start any new project that day. It could never be finished."

Oddly enough, the biblical passage in question (Deut. 25:5–10) includes a specific punishment for men who fail to perform the sex-ual duties of a dead husband's brother: "Then shall his brother's wife come unto him in the presence of the elders, and loose his shoe from off his foot, and spit in his face. . . . And his name shall be called in Israel, The house of him who hath his shoe loosed."[11]

Despite Harry's abandonment of Jen and the metaphorical impo-tence it suggests, Jen claims that Harry continued to pester her through the years, trying to woo her back, and that he had shown up at her door that particular morning. When he became too persistent, she says, she hit him over the head and left him to stagger into the hills. Later, Miss Gravely (Mildred Natwick) reveals that Harry, in his delirium, attacked her, pulled her into the bushes (from which she escaped), pulled her in again, and was finally subdued only after she hit him over the head with the heel of her shoe.

In this way, Harry's "trouble" is not simply his failure to behave as a proper corpse but more deeply his failure as a heterosexual male to perform sexually and (in a related failure) his refusal to respect women's integrity and refrain from raping them. Though the word is never used, his identity as a rapist is an important element in his sys-tematic denigration, for Hitchcock assumes (correctly I think) that no one in the audience would extend much sympathy to the corpse of a rapist. His killing is thereby justified, at least on the level of audi-ence response.

The attempted rapist's single line of dialogue becomes more mean-ingful in retrospect, and his self-declared knowledge of how "to han-dle" women like Miss Gravely takes on a different cast. What had seemed to be the voice of a male murderer speaking from a position of control ultimately turns out to have been spoken by a dazed sex offender in a moment of desperation. The gunshots that had been associated with him and the power they imply are now revealed to be completely unrelated to him. While the scenario of Miss Gravely murdering Harry will itself be undercut by the doctor's Production Code–worthy declaration that Harry really died of heart failure, one must also bear in mind that this physician has been seen to trip twice over Harry's prone body without noticing that Harry is dead. In any case, Hitchcock turns the revelation of Miss Gravely's self-protective violence into a resolutely positive moment, and Harry's death signals another character's triumph.

The gunshots, meanwhile, cease to be evidence of violence and become instead a roundabout expression of virility. Of the Captain's three shots, the first hits a beer can and the second a "No Hunting" sign put up by local lawman Calvin Wiggs, but the third hits a rabbit. The Captain's initial alarm at the circumstantial evidence pointing to him as Harry's murderer gives way to relief and joy when Arnie turns up with a dead rabbit, but it's the child who makes the connection between dead rabbits and his mother's soon-to-be husband. Arnie first displays the rabbit to Sam on his mother's front porch. In addition to his marked nonchalance in the presence of this animal corpse—Arnie enters swinging the rabbit by its ear—he asks Sam two leading questions: "How do rabbits get to be born?" and "How come you never came over to visit me before?" Sam answers the first question evasively ("The same way elephants do"), but he's more direct in his second response: "I didn't know you had such a pretty mother, Arnie." Arnie replies, with typically perverse logic, by linking sex and violence: "You think she's pretty, you should see my sling shot."

Arnie, who has first confronted death that morning, is now completely at ease with it, and with this ease comes the association of death and sexual energy. Jen tells him, when looking down at Harry's corpse, that Harry is in "a deep, wonderful sleep." (One irony of Jen's description is that she finally sees him "asleep," since they have, as husband and wife, never slept together.) Jen's nocturnal metaphor has an effect on her son: from a dead rabbit to thoughts of baby rabbits (with an implicit reference to the old pregnancy test), from baby rabbits to thoughts of his mother's new suitor, Arnie condenses Harry, the rabbit, procreation, and his mother's potential lover, with a final reference to Harry's head wound courtesy of Arnie's attractive sling shot.

The child makes these transitions as smoothly and swiftly as he proceeds from his house to the house of Miss Gravely, who is entertaining the Captain on what might be called their first date. Before Arnie arrives, the Captain comments upon the nice, big size of the tea cup from which he is drinking. Although we have seen Miss Gravely purchase this cup earlier in the day, she now claims that the cup had belonged to her father and that nobody had used it since he died, a bit of historical revisionism that only intensifies the cup's strangely phallic quality. The Captain, in a graceful attempt to skim over Miss Gravely's morbid comment, expresses the hope that her father died a peaceful death, to which she replies, "He was caught in a threshing machine." Able to lie about the origin of the cup, Miss Gravely nonetheless blurts out this horrible detail much to the Captain's dismay, but the uncomfortable jolt this nascent courtship has just received is cut mercifully short by Arnie, who arrives with the rabbit. "What do you call it?" asks Miss Gravely. "Dead," replies Arnie.

No Trouble at All

While both of the corpses (the rabbit and Harry) carry explicit connotations of sexuality along with the obviously denoted images of death, the apparent sexual anxieties that produce this metaphorical connection between man and animal find their expression not in the form of the characters' psychologies, as they often do in Hitchcock's suspense films, but in the milieu in which the characters live. It is through Hitchcock's perverse depiction of American society, rather than through his characters' individuated psyches, that neurosis expresses itself. The blitheness with which the central characters join in regarding Harry and his murder, the comic tone resulting from this distant, ironic point of view, coupled with the relative shallow-ness of these characters—the whole town shares the same perverse psychology.

The consequent flatness of characterization did not escape Eric Rohmer and Claude Chabrol, who write:

> Of all Hitchcock's works, this one undoubtedly has the raciest dia-logue, the most scandalous situations, and the most (with the excep-tion of *Lifeboat*) misanthropic point of view. Deliberately negative, it shows us the obverse of the coin without indicating to us, as else-where, that it *is* only the obverse; it even lacks the idea of fascination, of vertigo, or of danger. It is the film in which the characters are most lacking in flesh and in which they always behave like marionettes. It should also be said that it is pure *comedy*.[12]

Rohmer and Chabrol appreciate the film's conceit without acknowl-edging the shift of emphasis from individual to communal neurosis, from character to social environment. The social world of *The Trou-ble with Harry* metonymically takes on the characteristics of a nervous disorder: repression so widespread that literally everyone shares it; "the obverse" not standing in relation to the normal; the *world* being perverse, not just the individuals who live in it. By transferring neu-rosis from character to community, Hitchcock makes each succeed-ing shot of the bright, picturesque autumn landscape increasingly ironic, since the intense, color-saturated beauty only serves to mask an underlying illness.

Why this strategy is necessarily "misanthropic" is a point that Rohmer and Chabrol don't address, though they imply that the dis-tanced, ironic treatment of character found in both *The Trouble with Harry* and *Lifeboat* (1943), in which characters are literally cast adrift and left to founder, is a way for the author to punish his characters and therefore to reveal his contempt for them. And yet the dead Harry is so clearly the focus of Hitchcock's scorn, humor, and fear that he can scarcely be accused of holding the others in greater con-tempt. Indeed, Calvin Wiggs, the film's only living villain—the agent of law enforcement—is so unthreatening a figure that he seems relatively benign. Incidentally, Calvin Wiggs (called Calvin Coolidge Wiggs in the script) does not exist in the novel; in Story's version, the Wiggy character (played by Mildred Dunnock in the film) has no son, let alone one with such a moralistic name, and there is no policeman at all.

Rohmer and Chabrol are correct in noting that the world of *The Trouble with Harry*, more fantasy than reality, does pursue its artistic goals at the expense of well-rounded portrayals of individuals, but it also takes the peculiarly social perspective of etiquette. When Miss Gravely comes upon the Captain dragging Harry's corpse into the bushes, for instance, she remarks, seemingly casually, "What seems to be the trouble, Captain?" This line, which Hitchcock himself described as "the spirit of the whole story,"[13] takes as its point of departure a social interaction—a greeting. A woman comes upon a man she knows, and she addresses him. Here, unlike most encounters, one of the parties is engaged in an act that is not only illegal but repulsive, not to mention tense (the Captain's guilt over killing Harry, his fear of discovery, and his self-perceived failure as a human being, as noted in his wistful but psychoanalytically violent observation that "Mother always said I'd come to a bad end"). But Miss Gravely's question, and the tone in which she delivers it, takes none of this into account, and neither does the Captain's calm in the face of calamity. Miss Gravely in particular proceeds as if nothing out of the ordinary was happening, as if "the trouble" (made even more relative by the use of the word "seems") is so mundane that it requires little vocal inflection and no elaboration. Her apparent unflappability is overstated and comical—as is the Captain's physical position. Stooped over and initially facing away from the camera, Captain Wiles is forced to look back over his shoulder, caught in the act, his appellative having failed him. Compare both the blocking and the dialogue with Story's version: "Before Captain Wiles had got half-way to the rhododendron bush with his burden a woman appeared suddenly and miraculously in the middle of the path ahead. The little man . . . did not see his audience until his head was in danger of butting her in the stomach. 'Captain Wiles!' said the woman. . . . 'Yes, ma'am,' he said. The lady looked down at the body. She then looked at the captain's gun, which he had somehow managed to tuck into the top of his trousers. She said: 'Been shooting?'"[14]

Hitchcock's joke carries a second level of meaning which intensifies its humor and complicates the plot. As it turns out, Miss Gravely knows exactly what the trouble is when she asks the question, for she herself has just finished bashing Harry over the head with her shoe. By asking the question, she calmly denies her own culpability by shifting it to the Captain's already burdened shoulders. Feigning ignorance, Miss Gravely primly asks her question in a way that divorces her from the situation and gives her precisely the ironic distance she needs to turn her own guilt into a joke. In a certain sense, all the characters effect precisely this kind of irony, or social sleights of hand, in order to stave off the demoralizing implications of their repressed New England lives.

In the end, of course, Miss Gravely's question is stripped of its irony; as a rapist, Harry deserves what he gets. A parallel situation in dramatic form is George Cukor's *Bhowani Junction* (1956), in which heroine Victoria (Ava Gardner), an Anglo-Indian, is attacked in a deserted railway yard by her British superior officer. She beats him over the head with a railway spike, killing him, and is subsequently called a "heroine of the new India." Nevertheless, unlike *The Trouble with Harry*, *Bhowani Junction* goes on to use this justifiable act of self-defense as a psychological weapon against the heroine, and the dramatic action leads to the discovery of her "crime," a nervous breakdown, a confession, and a final (albeit partial) rehabilitation at the hands and heart of a male superior officer. Killing Harry, on the other hand, ends up being no trouble at all.

A World of Signs

Character psychology cannot help but appear in *The Trouble with Harry* in the form of dialogue and action. But in Hitchcock's *treatment* of situations, psychology is suppressed and even evacuated—hence the distant, almost cosmic perspective from which he views the action. Humor and irony, stemming here from flatness of character, are nonetheless linked to sexual tension, for at least part of the coolness of behavior can be traced to the distinct lack of romance in this quaint American hamlet of the 1950s. It is a town made up of individuals—not a single couple exists at the beginning of the film. Two women have already borne children—Jen and Wiggy. Jen's first marriage ended abruptly upon the death of her husband, and her second marriage, to Harry, was never consummated. Wiggy, whose preoccupation with commerce leads her to declare that the thing she wants most in the world is a cash register, gave birth to the equally stolid Calvin. (Elements of this sort tend to make *The Trouble with Harry* seem like a precise allegory of Western culture.) As for everyone else, Miss Gravely is the town's spinster, the Captain has never married, and Sam is such a cipher that no mention is ever made of his past. By the end of the film, two couples have been formed, with the dead Harry acting as something of a combination aphrodisiac and human epitaph that spurs everyone's atrophied sexuality by reminding them of the endless sleep that awaits them.

Each of *Harry*'s characters rejects the proper, eminently civilized attitude toward death that would entail not only informing the authorities but also treating the corpse with respect. And yet in this community of rebels, it is Sam, the painter, who orchestrates much of the action. He provides the Captain with the moral justification for killing Harry by telling him that he "fulfilled Harry's destiny" and therefore acted as part of the ongoing life-force. He insists upon cutting Miss Gravely's hair and remaking her artistically into a more youthful, less repressed *belle* for the Captain (who, being a fifties male, requires no change in appearance or attitude). The sale of his paintings becomes the occasion for Sam to demand that he be paid in the form of gifts to his friends, with the gifts becoming the material resolution of each character's dramatic goal. And he acts as the romantic leading man, whose coupling with Jen signals the formation of a new family and whose own payment for his art is revealed in the film's penultimate shot to be a double bed. This detail is quite a change from the novel, in which Sam asks for a bugle.[15]

While Sam paints many, many nonrepresentational artworks—

Wiggy's store and outdoor market are both crammed with Sam's work, most of it fairly dreadful (though the script describes him as "an extremely talented painter")—one might say that the medium in which Sam works most successfully as an artist is the community in which he lives. If the town is his canvas, his role as rebel is more a matter of attitude toward his own civilization than rebellion against middlebrow art. Sam succeeds in transforming this town in much the same way as he transforms Miss Gravely; what he effects is hardly revolutionary. Still, he enables the other characters to come to terms with Harry, but since Harry is so much a given, the development of the story becomes less a matter of active participation and more a matter of reaction and understanding. In *Rear Window* James Stewart's Jeff actually *does* very little (and is, in fact, virtually immobile), but he undergoes a violent crisis and emerges with a markedly different perception of the world around him. Likewise, the three central characters in Hitchcock's *Rope* (1948), while they surround an omnipresent corpse, function as protagonists because they develop as characters. Here, however, characters tend toward reiteration rather than development, their major activity being the repeated burial and disinterment of a cadaver, the remains of a hero without a future.

Sam's artistic work sets him apart from the others, and Hitchcock plays upon this categorical difference by introducing him outside of Harry's sphere of influence. Sam is the only one of the four central figures to emerge as a character *before* seeing Harry. Much of Sam's action in his introductory scene is devoted to art: singing, discussing his paintings, remaking Miss Gravely, strolling through the hills and beginning to sketch. In fact, he is so preoccupied with art that he fails to notice Harry, despite the lurid and obvious tips of Harry's socks, until after he has drawn Harry's feet as part of the "natural" landscape and *then* only because of their inexplicable presence on the sketch pad. One noteworthy aspect of Sam's art is that it is relentlessly non-representational with two crucial exceptions: the landscape sketch in which Harry's feet appear, and the portrait of Harry's face which Calvin Wiggs uses as evidence. In the first instance, Hitchcock prepares the spectator for Sam's selective but unobservant viewpoint by presenting a long shot of the landscape with Harry's red-tipped feet being glaringly evident, only to follow through with a full shot of Sam as he begins to draw and an insert shot of the sketch pad with Sam's hand in the act of drawing. Simply put, Sam does not notice the obvious, whereas Arnie, Jen, the Captain, Miss Gravely, and the audience react to it immediately. Sam's world does not admit the fact of death until it is forced to, and then only by way of its representation, not its corporal reality.

Incidentally, Sam's art calls to mind Stephen Heath's observation regarding the painting toward which inspector Benson gazes ("lost," as Heath memorably puts it, "in a kind of fascinated panic") in *Suspicion* (1941).[16] For Heath, that resolutely modern artwork both defines and skews the narrative space of the film. But the painting in *Suspicion* is tangential; Sam's paintings in *The Trouble with Harry* are central. If Benson's painting opens a rift in the narrative of *Suspicion*, Sam's art breaks *Harry* open into a yawning gulf, a disturbance of epic proportions that represents nothing less than the rumbling unconscious out of which *Harry*'s sexual symbols fly. That these symbols do not entirely add up to a coherent, stable whole is to the film's credit, at least as far as their unconscious origins are concerned.

Harry's existence must be proven to the lugubrious Calvin Wiggs in the form of a representational portrait—Calvin has no eye for art—and it is likewise through art that Harry is figuratively brought back to life when Sam quick-handedly opens the portrait's eyes in front of Calvin. The relief from the threat of death that Sam effects through this sleight of hand thus becomes a momentary comic resolution to the mortal dread that pervades Hitchcock's world, a prefiguring of Barbara Harris's wink in the penultimate shot of *Family Plot* (1976). Harry's metaphorical resurrection provides the means by which the four live characters are able to couple. Through Sam's art, they recognize the victory, however, temporary, of life over death, and through the return of Harry's shoes the order of civilization is restored. Given the priapism of his feet, Harry's shoes are now more like fig leaves.

As a young male as well as an artist, Sam has the power to open Harry's eyes, but it is the Captain, whose apparent celibacy has as much to do with age as with the suppression of desire by sublimation, who thinks to steal Harry's shoes from Calvin's car. He thus makes off with the sexual symbol that runs throughout the film, and by so doing reasserts his own virility. It's especially noteworthy that while the two women act to further the goal of resolving the "trouble" with Harry, it is the two men who in this scene have the power to manipulate the symbols to their own advantage. Indeed, the 1950s was characterized by a heightened awareness of symbols and their power. Freudian symbols abound, of course, but cultural interest in symbology extended beyond interior psychology to the social plane as well. A. C. Spectorsky's 1954 study of life and turmoil beyond the suburbs, *The Exurbanites*, is one of the decade's more sobering self-chronicles, with statistics on alcoholism and nervous disorders backing up the author's contention that a wave of profound discontent was sweeping across the centers of power and influence in America. In particular, Spectorsky characterizes the typical exurbanite male as a professional "symbol manipulator": a writer, editor, illustrator, photographer, film or television professional, or advertising executive. The exurbanite commutes into a city to do his job, and on this level any analogy between Spectorsky's subject and Sam, the film's artist, falls apart. Nevertheless, it is suggestive that Spectorsky insists on a correlation between the ability to manipulate symbols and the neuroses of the manipulators, which "exist over and above the endemic malaises of the era," which Spectorsky of course takes for granted.[17] In *The Trouble with Harry*, Hitchcock is more interested in these endemic malaises than in Sam's psychology, but the way he focuses Sam's character on symbolic manipulation is of a piece with Spectorsky's characterization of the era and its "endemic malaises."

An Empty Closet

Rohmer and Chabrol are only partially correct to declare that *The Trouble with Harry* lacks "danger." While Hitchcock invests no sense of fear or revulsion in Harry's body, while his corpse is never frightening, there is one sequence in which Hitchcock gives a living character a healthy scare: the Captain, seated in Jen's living room, gets a shock when the closet door suddenly swings open and reveals its own emptiness. For the Captain, whose age makes it possible for him to refer to his predicted "bad end" without being accused of undue hyperbole regarding the future, the opening of the door not only foreshadows his own looming grave. More disturbingly, it provides a glimpse into the unconscious space of death and desire around which he and the other characters must skirt. Later, in the film's only suspenseful sequence (the one in which Calvin Wiggs arrives at Jen's house and demands to know the whereabouts of Harry), Hitchcock blocks the scene in such a way that Sam, leaning up against the closet door, appears to be preventing Calvin from looking inside, presumably because Harry's body has been hidden there. When Sam moves aside and the door opens, the sight of a similar empty space serves to give the audience a small fright, but Hitchcock then turns the tables by making Harry turn up ludicrously in the bathtub.

From fear to humor, from nothingness to low farce, this sequence proposes a comic vision in which laughter replaces horror. While the omnipresence of Harry's body makes death inescapable, the four central characters come to understand that the finite quality of their lives virtually demands a conscious sexual resolution. They replace Harry's body on the hillside, stage the scene so that Arnie will rediscover it, and close off the narrative with the promise of marriage and sexual activity. With death so pervasive, romance blooms. How could it not, with so many feet in the grave?

Critic Slavoj Zizek, in a provocative Lacanian reading of the film, sees in Harry's final burial the *symbolic* resolution of an original trauma. For Zizek, "'The Trouble with Harry' consists in the fact that his body is present without being dead on the symbolic level."[18] Harry's final burial constitutes what Zizek calls a settling of accounts. Zizek's apprehension of the film's psychoanalytic structure is brilliant, but like much Lacanian criticism it remains curiously detached from psychoanalytic practice—the labored working through that not only animates an analysis but provides its raison d'être. In other words, Zizek leaps from primal event (Harry's death) to communal cure (Harry's final burial) with little interest in the intervening film, and the process by which the cure is effected goes virtually unremarked. In fact, the analytic *work* of the film is literally hard work—the painstaking, repetitive burial and unearthing of the object of everyone's anxiety, a process that, like the talking cure itself, leads eventually to a symbolic restaging of the original traumatic event. Like psychoanalysis, this repetition engenders—through labored telling and retelling—an unflinching familiarity with one's nauseating past, an acceptance of what would otherwise be sickeningly unspoken. Hitchcock is so smooth about this working through that one may miss the point entirely; so matter-of-fact does he become about the cadaver's whereabouts that the deeper nature of the Harry-in-the-bathtub joke may be lost. Plainly put, we must not forget or repress the fact that these characters have not only dug up a corpse but stripped and bathed it, examined its already-decaying flesh from head to toe, washed and ironed its filthy clothes, and regroomed it for a proper final burial. Like a successful psychoanalysis, little about Harry is left uninspected, and by the end of the film a naked dead body in a bathtub has lost its power to disturb.

Yet the cure remains imperfect. This is, after all, a Hitchcock film. The sexual coupling at the film's end is troubled, uneasy. As the two couples watch Arnie rediscover Harry's corpse, Sam—who is to become this child's stepfather—gives voice to his new paternal attitude: "Beat it, you little creep! I mean, hurry home, son." As is often the case, Hitchcock's joke is on the family unit, the fundamentally unstable grouping that inevitably leads to emotional disaster. Classical comedy may end with the formation of a new family, but for Hitchcock, the real humor lies in the revelation of inherent instability in this new order—the well-known fact that must remain unspoken for society to continue: it doesn't work.

The Trouble with Harry is a comic nightmare, a pleasurable exposure of distress. Though it may be a critical transgression to explain a film by way of what *isn't* in it, *Harry*'s comic point may nevertheless be illustrated by a series of small events that do not appear in the final version. In the script's first draft, the four main characters return from Harry's last unearthing to find Arnie at home with a squirt gun and a glass of milk. He immediately squirts his prospective father with the milk and, later, squirts Harry, saying, as Harry had said earlier, "I know how to take care of your type." Dr. Greenbow, witnessing this event, laughs and says, "This is the first nightmare I've had in years!" whereupon Sam responds, "The bit you'll enjoy most when you wake up is where the little boy squirted milk at the corpse."[19] Motherhood, fatherhood, death, regeneration, and comedy: all are brought into a bizarre clump of meaning in this passage. Through this comic business, Arnie's first appearance in the film is clarified: it is he who, on the level of interpreted dreams, has shot Harry with his ray gun in a kind of motivating Oedipal joke that drives the film. And the comedy concludes with appropriate sexual confusion, given Hitchcock's characteristic refusal to heal the wounds he opens: Arnie shoots his new father, too—this time (figuratively) with his own mother's milk, the progenitor of his own sexual fluid.

In the film itself, this impressive condensation exists only as a sort of missing punchline. The shooting-milk bit is eliminated, and the doctor merely stumbles distractedly away, muttering something about a nightmare. But strangely, although the substance of the joke is lost, Jen seems to get it anyway: at the end of the disrupted scene, she thinks to herself a moment . . . and giggles. Perhaps this is because she went to the movies before her own film started and saw a Hollywood comedy—*You're Never Too Young*, the Lewis and Martin film, also from 1955, in which Jerry and Dean play with a squirt gun full of milk. In a later scene in that film, Jerry (playing a man who is playing a little boy) is confronted with a real gun—and presumably a real man in the form of its owner, played by looming Raymond Burr. Little Jerry squirms in his seat and explains, with a particularly nasal twang, "*My* gun shoots *milk*." Two instances of squirt-gun-wielding, milk-shooting boys in a single year may not constitute a cultural trend, but it does give one pause.

A Domestic Interlude: "Lamb to the Slaughter"

A Happy Cop-Killing

Although *The Trouble with Harry* was Alfred Hitchcock's only feature film comedy in the 1950s, the wealth of humor in his work suggests that he, too, found something terribly funny about the era. Hitchcock's particular morbidity may have been idiosyncratic, but the habit he shared with Billy Wilder of seizing upon images of corruption, anxiety, and paranoid dissatisfaction and playing them for laughs was by no means divorced from history. And at least as much as Wilder did, Hitchcock played to the crowd. Unlike most other Hollywood directors, Hitchcock involved himself in television production, thus further capitalizing on the pleasures of an audience deeply amused by images of death and terror. With *Alfred Hitchcock Presents*, which premiered in 1955, Hitchcock became an enormously popular television personality in his own right, introducing and concluding each frightening tale with droll commentaries and deadpan jokes. Every show began with comedy. After all, Hitchcock introduced each episode by literally walking into his own caricature.

Hitchcock directed a total of fifteen episodes of *Alfred Hitchcock Presents* before the decade ended. Distinctions between decades are nowhere more artificial than with Hitchcock's work, since the horrors of *Psycho* are firmly bound to the refined repressions of the preceding decade.[20] Psycho wasn't just a shocking departure from the conventions of the suspense film; it was also a culmination of sorts—a perfect example of the vicious return of the repressed.

One of the *Alfred Hitchcock Presents* episodes is signal to fifties comedy. It's an unusually grotesque half hour of American television focusing on adultery, rage, and guilt-free murder, and it ends in exhilarating laughter: the immortal "Lamb to the Slaughter" episode, in which Barbara Bel Geddes beats her husband to death with a frozen leg of lamb, roasts it, and serves it up to the hungry detectives who come to the house to investigate. As horrifying as it may seem, the tale is pure comedy.

First aired on April 13, 1958, the program begins like every other episode within a frame of artifice and direct authorial address as Hitchcock introduces another glimpse of bourgeois life, this time by standing behind a shopping cart in a sparsely decorated grocery store set. A policeman is writing out a ticket "for blocking the aisles during rush hour." The mood of the frame, like most of the episodes themselves, is characterized by ordinariness disrupted by something bizarre, an event that throws the everyday into question. On one level, Hitchcock's personal fear of the police defines the overtly anti-cop attitude of the action, but this representation of law also suggests a kind of greater social unease. It was a particularly contemporary fear in this era of strict social codes, when enforced regulation invaded beyond reasonable bounds. Here, when the dramatic action of the program (which was written by Roald Dahl based on his own story) begins in a plainly furnished, exceedingly typical middle-class home, the invasive presence of social authority becomes explicit when Barbara Bel Geddes, as Mary, the homemaker, greets her policeman husband at the door. The husband (Allan Lane) is in full dress uniform, with a policeman's great coat exaggerating his already dominating physical presence, while Mary is a model of meek servitude. Obsequious to the point of absolute self-effacement, Mary is also pregnant: an instant self-parody of the ideal fifties wife.

Following not only the overriding sense of "normality" that governs the life of this household but also a general assumption of leisure-time needs, Mary's husband heads straight to the bar to fix himself a drink. He then tells Mary that he's in love with another woman and wants a divorce. Mary, stunned, her world cut out from under her, cannot bear the devastating dual announcement of her husband's infidelity and the new independence he has thrust upon her, and in response, she falls into a kind of domestic stupor and insists that she fix his dinner.

The Raw and the Cooked

As with *The Trouble with Harry*, the visual style of "Lamb to the Slaughter" is understated, but three crucial tracking shots precisely define Mary's heroism. After she retrieves a whole leg of lamb from the freezer in the garage and unwraps it in the kitchen, Mary, in medium shot, begins to walk toward her husband. The camera tracks with her, aligning itself with her movements. (As Jean-Luc Godard put it, every tracking shot is a moral statement.) In the beginning of the shot, the lamb's whereabouts are unclear, but as the shot progresses the camera pulls back very slightly to reveal that she is holding something at waist level. By the time she reaches her husband, the camera has pulled back far enough to reveal both characters in a three-quarter shot as Mary swings the lamb over her head like a club and brings it down on her husband's skull with blunt and brutal force. Hitchcock cuts immediately after the moment of impact (the dull but loud thud acting as an aural bridge) to a shot of the policeman-husband collapsing on the floor, but since for Hitchcock this man represents nothing of emotional or even physical value at this point, the director wastes no time on him and cuts quickly back to Mary in a parallel tracking shot that leads her straight back to the oven, where she begins methodically to cook.

Even with the sense that Mary is not acting entirely consciously at this point, the sequence is reminiscent of Addams's "Nothing much, Agnes" cartoon in that the drab routinization of women's lives is seen as being so pervasive that it continues even after the source of their oppression has been eliminated. Playing out their accepted social role even after murdering their husbands, both Mary and Agnes's lackadaisical friend continue to maintain a domestic facade after they violently destroy the domesticity itself. But unlike her literally caricatured counterpart, Mary is not frozen in time and space and therefore quickly begins to calculate the consequences. She calls a friend and declines a dinner invitation; she tells the friend that she's going to be making dinner for her husband; and then, leaving her husband's corpse to grow cold on the floor, she calmly goes shopping.

Hitchcock uses the rest of the episode to set up a climactic tracking shot of Mary laughing at the joke she has played on her social circumstances. Detectives—her husband's friends—arrive to investigate the murder she has reported upon arriving home from the store, and in the ensuing dramatic action Mary once again plays the model wife, this time fully consciously and with supreme irony. She dutifully answers their questions (with lies), she offers to make coffee for them, and she finally invites them to dine on roast leg of lamb: "Give some to the others, too. They must be absolutely famished by this time. Ask them all in, why don't you, and give them a nice hot meal. It's very good meat, I promise you that," she says in close-up, smiling.

Hitchcock then cuts to lamb bones on a plate, and as the hungry men polish off yet another classic American meal prepared by a servile but happy woman, he cuts to a long shot of Mary, in the center of the frame, seated against the wall. The camera begins to track forward. Mary, not smiling, is staring straight ahead as the men discuss the absence of the murder weapon, but just as the camera reaches her, one of the men says, "For all we know, it might be right under our noses." Mary smiles, then laughs merrily, looking directly at the camera.

"Well, that's the way the old meatball bounces," Hitchcock concludes from his authorial position in the frame, and he proceeds to provide what passes for Mary's comeuppance—in the episode proper, she does indeed get away with murder—by saying that she went on to try the same thing with her second husband but failed because he had neglected to plug in the freezer, thereby leaving Mary stuck with soft meat. Gliding swiftly over the obscenity of this joke (by making another one), Hitchcock then announces, "Speaking of plugs, that is precisely what our sponsor wants to do with his product."

If these retrospective impressions of the 1950s are correct, the decade witnessed a meteoric rise in material consciousness: things to buy, devices to own, items to acquire. Televisions themselves were particularly important products in an era that often seemed to define itself as a vast marketplace in which emotional and spiritual well-being could be bought and sold along with everything else. By the time Hitchcock exits the "Lamb to the Slaughter" episode by pushing his grocery cart off the TV screen, he has created a vision of bourgeois domestic life in which a heroine avenges her subjugation by grabbing a consumable item, wielding it like a mace, and with it smashing the head of her upstanding public servant husband. What's remarkable about the episode is not only its dramatic clarity and intellectual coherence but also the fact that the director didn't even bother to bury its rebelliousness in the subtext. The episode's comic subversion is brazen, obvious, and gleefully unapologetic.

In the way it directly uses laughter to attack the myth of middle-class normality, "Lamb to the Slaughter" provides an effective transition to one of the least appreciated comic sensibilities in the fifties, the boldface Frank Tashlin. A lurid terrain of hysteria and sexual maladjustment, Tashlin's America is a land in which material excess can never be too excessive and anxieties never too shrill. His world is the world of Jerry Lewis, Jayne Mansfield, Great Danes who drive cars, and poodles who dress like movie stars. Like Hitchcock's televised lesson in how to prepare the perfect dinner, Tashlin's cinematic catechisms on United States history and civilization are not for the squeamish or fainthearted. One looks and listens at his or her own risk, for in the distorting mirror Tashlin holds up to the 1950s, America and Americans tend to look a great deal more grotesque than we might otherwise wish.

four

LIVING LOONEY TUNES:
THE ART OF FRANK TASHLIN

Imitation of Life: Tashlin's Comic Mode

Rocking, screaming Little Richard, banging the keyboard and pushing his vocal chords to the limit, is blasting out of the speakers behind
the extrawide CinemaScope screen as Jayne Mansfield, dressed in a
ludicrously form-fitting outfit, is strolling happily down a quiet street.
A paper boy, no older than nine, is staring directly at her buttocks and
whistling lewdly as she walks away, but the child's wolfish response is
nothing compared to the surreal effect Jayne has on the next three
males she meets. First, she emerges from behind a parked ice truck
and walks across the huge expanse of the screen, but the ice man,
when he sees her, cannot move a muscle. All his energy goes into
watching her in disbelief and awe, and he becomes so excited that the
ice block he's holding melts instantly into a gush of water that flows
with a splash onto the street. In the next shot, a milkman holding a
milk bottle at chest level comes out the door of a brownstone. He
looks down at the sidewalk, staring, immobile, as Jayne approaches
from the left. She walks up the stairs in the center of the image (the
camera is now on sidewalk level) and, as she goes inside, the camera
tracks forward just in time for the milk to shoot in uncontrollable
spurts out of the top of the bottle. Jayne is now inside the brown-

stone. All she does is climb the stairs, but the tenant on the first floor is overcome with flabbergasted desire. He is kneeling on the floor, trying to pick up his milk delivery, but after seeing Jayne's legs moving behind the spindles of the banister, his eyeglasses shatter in cartoon fissures that extend out from his pupils, making him look like he's just gone nuts.

This sequence, orchestrated by former cartoonist and prolific humorist Frank Tashlin in *The Girl Can't Help It* (1956), is a certain strain of fifties comedy distilled to its essence: satire, celebration, sex farce, color ("by Deluxe"), the enormous breadth of a CinemaScope screen, and all to the sex-ridden and energetic tune of rock 'n' roll. The "looney tunes" reference in the title of this chapter should be taken literally. Tashlin worked intermittently through the 1930s and 1940s as animator, writer, and director on Warner Bros.'s Looney Tunes and Merrie Melodies as well as on MGM's Flip the Frog and Disney's Mickey Mouse and Donald Duck series. On a formal level, Tashlin's background in animation, where *anything* can occur as long as it can be drawn, enhanced his acute consciousness of color design as well as his tendency to bend the physical laws of planet Earth at will. And as far as his comic characters' actions are concerned, it is not an exaggeration to say that they are generally closer to the performance style of Daffy Duck than Cary Grant.

A major stylistic influence on both Jean-Luc Godard and Jerry Lewis, Tashlin directed his first film in 1950 and made a total of twelve before the decade ended. Tashlin directed ten more films through the 1960s, but it was in the 1950s that he found his artistic voice—which is just to say that the peculiar style of garish but tasteful art direction, cartoonish characters, and collapsing nerves and narrative structures favored by fifties audiences fit right in with Tashlin's sense of humor.

Tashlin made more feature films in the fifties than any other director discussed in this study, including the busy Alfred Hitchcock. Moreover, Tashlin exclusively directed comedies. Wilder moved in and out of melodrama and action-adventure, Hawks abandoned comedy for the Egyptian epic and the western, and Hitchcock, though each of his films has a certain comic undertone, directed only one comedy. Yet Tashlin remains largely unknown outside a small circle of film buffs and scholars (and music video directors: the Rolling Stones' "She Was Hot" video draws heavily on *The Girl Can't Help It*). Even in this very limited society his reputation is not at all secure.

I will focus on only three of Tashlin's films here: *Artists and Models* (1955), *The Girl Can't Help It*, and *Will Success Spoil Rock Hunter?* (1957). This restriction is for practical reasons, and it's frankly arbitrary. There is just too much going on in any Tashlin film to treat it in any less detail than the other films discussed in this book. In addition, reducing the field to three brings Tashlin into balance with his contemporaries. I chose these particular films because I find them to be especially funny, not only artistically but also in their cultural context. *Rock-a-Bye Baby* (1958), which features not only a series of nervous gags with a maternal Jerry Lewis but also a pristine, all-white suburban house destroyed by Lewis and profuse amounts of soot in a matter of minutes is certainly a worthy and enjoyable film, as are *Son of Paleface* (1952) and *The Lieutenant Wore Skirts* (1955). Tashlin's Bing Crosby heartwarmer, *Say One for Me* (1959), on the other hand, leans a bit too close to *Going My Way* (1944) for comfort; it doesn't have much bite. To my mind only *Hollywood or Bust* (1956) measures as highly as the three discussed here, but because of the very subject of that film—the extreme artificiality of the United States and its populace—to include it here would almost be overkill. *Of course* a Lewis and Martin film called *Hollywood or Bust* presents a ludicrous vision of American life and culture. I chose to focus on the other three because they strike me as more unexpected in their raucous apprehension of the fifties through other areas of popular culture—*Artists and Models* and comic books, *The Girl Can't Help It* and rock 'n' roll, and *Will Success Spoil Rock Hunter?* and advertising.

It's too bad Tashlin's films aren't better known. Two blocking mechanisms have gotten in the way. First, although Tashlin's extremist humor parallels the rise of rock 'n' roll in its abrasive and loud obsession with sex, subsequent decades of American culture seem to admire this aspect of fifties art only in musical form. The idea of rude but affirmative sexuality on film screens tends to conflict dramatically with critical preconceptions about film comedy of the 1950s, and rather than accommodating opinion to fit fact, critics have tended to do exactly the opposite. A second and perhaps more effective reason for Tashlin's limited reputation is his association with Jerry Lewis, with whom subsequent generations of Americans have had, well, big problems. Why Jerry Lewis, the preeminent comic actor of the 1950s, was so enormously popular at the time and was so violently rejected later will be one of the explicit issues of this chapter, but for the time being I will suggest only that the implications of both Tashlin's and Lewis's work are evidently so disturbing that in Lewis's case they are repudiated outright as being inventions of "the French" while in Tashlin's case they are dismissed, forgotten, or at best seen as the aberrations of a Hollywood decade rather than as a series of its quintessences.

The peculiarity of Tashlin's work is that it unabashedly and even thunderingly proclaims itself as Hollywood product while at the same time deliberately threatening and subverting not only the reactionary moral rhetoric of its era but also the economic and psychological foundations of the civilization that made Hollywood possible to begin with. I use the term *civilization* in its broadest sense. As Gore Vidal has observed, "Although the United States is the best and most perfect of earth's societies and our huddled masses earth's envy, we have yet to create a civilization, as opposed to a way of life."[1] In any event, because films of the 1950s are so often reduced to their grimmest common denominator, it is not surprising that Tashlin has been ignored. To admit Tashlin is to admit popular culture at its most radical. And that just wouldn't seem like the fifties.

Doubled Up: *Artists and Models*

Satire, Celebration, and the Space of Imminence

Three women, two of them posing with huge artist's palettes in front of their apparently naked torsos and the third draped in bright red, begin the credits sequence of *Artists and Models*. Filmed luridly in

Technicolor and VistaVision, the film is about art and spectacle in the modern world of the 1950s, and as such, it treats illusion and costume not just as "themes" but as elements in a kind of perceptual language. The subject of the credits sequence is modern woman, entirely predicated in this vision by her outrageous costume or lack thereof. More models follow, and as they pose alongside the credits they are utterly without identity, save for the glamorous blue or lavender or mustard or red costume they wear. Smiling and looking vacantly at the camera, sometimes giggling, they are themselves essentially featureless as human beings. Even their bodies are nothing but reduplicated versions of an empty ideal, but (or better, *because* of this) they exist as pure artistic spectacle, infinitely malleable because they are without substance and psychology.

One might see these images as witless products of a sexist culture. As Maureen Turim writes in regard to *Gentlemen Prefer Blondes*, "The line which separates celebration from satire in American culture is perniciously thin."[2] But I would argue first that if such a line must be said to exist, *Artists and Models* falls on the side of satire and, second, not only is the line's thinness not pernicious but it may not be a line at all. It seems to me to be more of a gap, a breathing space where pleasure and critique coincide. *Imminent criticism* describes such a space, though both the pleasures and the critiques found in Tashlin tend to be rather more wildly emergent than the word *imminence* suggests.

In any art form, but particularly in popular art, a given representation or set of representations may depict a cultural phenomenon with such crystalline clarity that it becomes itself a type of criticism. When experiencing this art, the spectator or listener can scarcely fail to notice on however conscious a level the real social and political circumstances that inform the representation, even if no overt, fingerpointing criticism is apparent or even intended. In this way, Frank Tashlin's films can be seen as a set of imminent critiques of fifties culture. He wrote no manifesto declaring his worldview; he clearly enjoyed the garish culture he represented; yet one can see in his films the persistent sexual *strains* of that culture.

To cite a more recent example of imminent criticism in popular culture, one of the season finales of the 1980s television series *Dynasty* stands as a model of emergent criticism embedded within the fabric of the culture under scrutiny. The series concerned the tribulations of master capitalist Blake Carrington, his glamorous formerly working-class wife Krystle, his sometimes gay son and romantically ill-fated daughter, and his shrewish and delightfully vicious ex-wife, Alexis, who had an alarming tendency to stub cigarettes out in half-eaten shrimp cocktails and bowls of caviar. (This habit was itself a form of imminent criticism—the cavalier trashing of luxury items by a fear-inspiring woman serving as a kind of vicarious vengeance against the conspicuous consumption of the 1980s.) One season, a late one in the series' life, ended with an elaborate royal wedding between one of the Carringtons' extended family members and a twerpy prince of Moldavia. In this episode, the American marriage fetish combined with a slavish devotion to foreign nobility to produce a gaudy fairy-tale wedding ceremony, which was to culminate the show. But in a shocking climax that served doubly as a flagrant come-on for the following season and a radical imminent criticism of the past, a band of masked terrorists stormed into the wedding chapel and blew every last Carrington away in a torrent of machine-gun fire, leaving what appeared to be their bloody corpses piled on the floor. This image, seen in bird's-eye view, served as the dramatic final shot of the season. Thus, in a few marvelous moments, years of buried resentment toward the ostentatious Carringtons not only surfaced but exploded in a gratifying rage, and it did so in the form of a contemporary American political obsession—obscure foreign terrorists whose maniacal mission it is to destroy our way of life. These anonymous objects of profound national fear thereby found their deeper expression as *wish*, serving to voice not only widespread impatience with a TV series on the skids but also the continually suppressed desire for total economic vengeance on the part of the mass audience against the show's rarefied subjects. This is imminent criticism. Buñuelian in both content and execution—a similar scene occurs in *The Discreet Charm of the Bourgeoisie* (France, 1972)—the *Dynasty* scene is nevertheless embedded firmly in the culture it attacks.

If American culture has turned women's bodies into objectified spectacles, Tashlin takes this phenomenon and pushes it further satirically; at the same time, he celebrates it. Firmly lodged within the tastes and attitudes of the overheated 1950s, these representations of women by their very excess also provide a type of ironic commentary. Tashlin distances his audience from their culture even while immersing them in it. In Tashlin's comedy, as in the *Dynasty* episode, the delight of the moment does not lie in one's ability to stand widely apart from it; full pleasure is found in full immersion. In the case of *Artists and Models* and other breast-obsessed, sexually rambunctious art of the 1950s, it may not be a pleasure limited solely to quaint sexist straight guys. After all, given that the most prominent male in this film is Jerry Lewis, neither gender gets off easy.

Jerry Lewis: Gay Icon from Hell

In *Artists and Models*, the film proper (this concept is often problematic if not downright untenable with Tashlin) begins with a shot of an enormous pair of female lips in the process of being painted, and the camera cranes back to reveal Dean Martin busily painting what turns out to be a billboard advertising "Trim Maid Cigarettes." In a characteristic blurring of the line between star and character, reality and representation, Tashlin has Martin's character cheerfully humming the song Martin himself has just been singing in the credits sequence. Martin and Lewis were quite familiar figures in the 1950s. By 1955 they had made thirteen films in the six years of their joint screen career. They were among the most successful stars of the period. If one had to pin their popularity down even further, they were among the four most successful screen comedians at the time—Bob Hope and Danny Kaye being the others. Paramount Pictures had originally signed them to a lucrative contract for seven films in five years at $100,000 per film. This was followed by more contracts worth even more money. In 1959, three years after Lewis went solo, he signed a fourteen-picture, $10 million deal with Paramount.[3] Because of the current cultural aversion to Jerry Lewis, it is particularly worth stressing his stardom and commercial success. Today's college students, who know without a doubt that Lewis is admired in France, are amazed to learn that he was ever popular here. In 1993 dollars Lewis's 1959 deal would be worth about $55,000,000.

Martin and Lewis played regularly in nightclubs in New York and Las Vegas. They appeared often on TV in *The Colgate Comedy Hour*. And like any other film performers of their stature, their stardom had molded and defined their personas to the fairly precise point at which they were not only instantly recognizable but recognized specifically in terms of the relationship they regularly promoted. Martin and Lewis were understood and enjoyed for maintaining themselves as a couple, the nature of which hardly changed from film to film: Martin as the suave singer/straight man/love interest, and Lewis as the lunatic, radically uncentered center of attention. Film critic and Jerry aficionado Scott Bukatman perceptively describes the duo's fundamental split in masculine type and image as being essential to its construction; he quotes Lewis, who claims creative credit for the team-up: "I have an idea of making a team out of the handsomest guy in the world and a monkey."[4] As a male-male comedy team, Martin and Lewis were novel in this regard. But their antecedent is found in the screwball comedy couple, who (like Cary Grant and Katharine Hepburn in *Bringing Up Baby* or Henry Fonda and Barbara Stanwyck in *The Lady Eve*) appear to have nothing in common but who are clearly meant for each other. For better or worse, Martin and Lewis were updated screwball partners—that is, until they broke up after making *Pardners* (1956) in an acrimonious split that rivaled any celebrity divorce in amplitude and passion.

In all their movies Martin and Lewis are bound to each other as strongly and as continually as, say, the Marx Brothers or Burns and Allen. But instead of a filial or marital bond, Lewis and Martin and their respective characters maintain their union from film to film on the basis of friendship at the very least and, as Lewis repeatedly declares in his autobiography, "love." Like the equally homophilic Laurel and Hardy, Martin and Lewis play the sexual side of buddyism for dangerous comic effect, turning a kind of vicarious homosexual panic on the part of audiences into pleasure by way of nervous laughter. For Laurel and Hardy, the most extreme instance of this panic is the jaw-dropping sequence in *Their First Mistake* (1932), when Stan and Ollie climb into bed together and Ollie nurses a baby from what appears to be his own breast. (It's more of a letdown than a relief to discover moments later that there's a milk bottle hidden inside his shirt.) But while explicit eruptions like this are infrequent with Laurel and Hardy (though the tension is usually there), they are absolutely *conventional* with Martin and Lewis.

Notice, for example, that Jerry and Dean hit Hollywood in time for a cycle of screwball comedy remakes. William Wellman's *Nothing Sacred* (1937) became Norman Taurog's *Living It Up* (1954), Billy Wilder's *The Major and the Minor* (1942) became Taurog's *You're Never Too Young* (1955); and after Lewis went solo, Preston Sturges' *The Miracle of Morgan's Creek* (1944) became Tashlin's *Rock-a-Bye Baby*. In each of these cases Lewis took what had been the female role. Not all romantic comedies are screwball, but every screwball comedy is romantic in its own tense way, and Lewis and Martin's updates are no exception. But Lewis was already playing the girl in parody form even before these explicit contemporary revisions of classic romantic comedies were made. The romance between them is always there, and it is always suppressed by an imperative heterosexuality that asserts itself, often in a ridiculously unconvincing manner, in the form of brute convention, namely Martin's female love interest. Jerry's periodic female love interests, meanwhile, are usually off the map.

Consider George Marshall's 3-D Technicolor extravaganza, *Money from Home* (1953). Marshall is a director who is credited with over four hundred movies in his career. It is unlikely that he had the time, let alone the talent, to put a personal stamp on any of them. He worked with what he was handed. And here is what he was handed with *Money from Home*:

Adapted from a Damon Runyon story, Martin plays "Honey Talk," a Runyonesque small-time gambler who has to fix a horse race to save his life, and Lewis plays Virgil, a decidedly un-Runyonesque hysteric. Within twenty minutes of the credits sequence Jerry/Virgil has gotten himself into a dress—a flaming red Arabian number with innumerable gauzy veils. Almost immediately—in fact, as if in response—he gets jabbed in the butt with a hot shish kebab skewer with the meat still on it. Soon after—again, as if in direct response to the skewer—he's performing the dance of the seven veils for the pleasure of a tubby sultan who proceeds to advance on Jerry with a lascivious grin. To his great credit, Marshall, who is usually a stylistic washout, captures this moment with a point-of-view close-up, in glorious 3-D, of the potentate's overheated face protruding into the audience.

The fun doesn't stop there. When Dean chides him for causing a ruckus with the sultan, Jerry responds with a kind of frigid guilt: "What was I supposed to do? I wasn't even married to him!" The two men escape from the train, still dressed in their Arabian outfits (Martin is in one, too, though of course his is masculine). Needing to find a ride, Jerry prefigures three of his subsequent films by turning to screwball comedy for inspiration: he does a marvelous parody of Claudette Colbert's hitchhiking scene from *It Happened One Night* (1934), plucking up his diaphanous gown to arouse the oncoming driver while Martin (like Gable) hides out of view. The driver, played by Richard Hayden, falls for it *and has to be told* that Jerry is in fact a male. Later, while Dean's female love interest (Marjie Millar) is off somewhere fulfilling a narrative obligation, Jerry takes on the identity of the Hayden character. He knows he can assume the role because, as he recalls, he had played *Romeo and Juliet* in summer theater—as Juliet. By the time he dances with Dean in one later scene and declares that he is "in love with" the male veterinarian for whom he works in another, Jerry's sexual project has long since taken on the character of a compulsion.

As my discussions of various other protogay moments have shown, Jerry's compulsion did not arise in a cultural vacuum. Scott Bukatman nicely describes how Lewis's whole career has been largely involved with acting out (if not working through) his own warped masculinity, but how did he get this way and why was he so popular? As much as one might like to deny it, this loony male neurotic was hatched by American culture. For example, *Money from Home* appeared three years after a British anthropologist (cited by historian

Stephen J. Whitfield in his study of Cold War culture) found that "the overriding fear of every American parent" was that a son would become a "sissie," by which is obviously meant more than a propensity to play with dolls.[5] Should that dreaded development occur and the "sissie" grow to full adulthood without committing suicide, psychiatry offered the hand, or claw, of hope. Moralistically subverting the very essence of Freudian theory, American analysts responded to Freud's radical view of the nuclear family as the *cause* of mental illness by perversely insisting that the traditional American family, with its painfully limited sexual and gender roles and concomitant sense of overarching repression, was the *cure*. As part of this pseudonormative tyranny, psychiatrists held out to the adult "sissie" the promise of heterosexual conversion through analysis.[6] And when that didn't work, and it rarely if ever did, there were always electroshock and aversion "therapies" designed to obliterate the offending sissieness by force. In fact, in 1953, the year *Money from Home* was released, the psychiatric community's violent assault on gay people reached a crescendo of sorts when the former director of psychiatry at Bellevue Hospital suggested in the *Journal of Social Hygiene* that "therapeutic castration" was a "valid subject for research" into the treatment and, one supposes, ultimate cure of homosexuality in the male.[7] Into this world, and out from it, leaps Jerry Lewis.

Lewis's compulsive sexuality is one of the era's most obviously *guilty* pleasures. The 1950s, unlike the 1920s and 1930s when Laurel and Hardy were fooling around, were obsessed with homosexuality—not only the horror of actual sex acts between adults of the same gender but also the *potential* for such acts, the sense of terrifying imminence that high school guidance counselors learned to pin down with the fascinatingly open-ended label "latent homosexual." In a spastic and frenzied effort to identify, diagnose, and eliminate an ordinary fact of human behavior—let alone a fundamental element of every human psyche—American culture repressed itself to the point of Jerry Lewis.

As outlandish laughingstock, Lewis was well equipped to play these anxiety-filled protogay characters who in other genres (had they been allowed to exist) would have been the focus of fear and scorn.

But comedy, particularly the extremely broad farce of Jerry Lewis, turned fear into loud delight. As Bukatman describes, Lewis's linguistic incoherence invokes "the position of the nineteenth-century female hysteric." And by taking on this persona, Lewis "acts out his own ambivalence toward an inscribed and proscribed position (masculinity)."[8] Bukatman is right on the mark, but one must hasten to add that this ambivalence was not purely personal to Jerry Lewis in the postwar era, nor was generalized masculinity the proscribed position. The explicit proscription was homosexuality, and it was voiced in especially shrill tones through government purges, psychiatric treatments, and Lewis's sexual comedy. By incarnating the kind of subversive homosexual desire that could not be overtly expressed let alone fulfilled (hence its sheer repetition), and by doubly subverting this desire by making it seem, as Lewis's character puts it in *Artists and Models*, "retarded," Lewis could express the (for lack of a better word) homoeroticism that could no longer be denied on screen but could scarcely be stated forthrightly in this era of officially sanctioned gay-bashing. And while this moronic and obnoxious persona will never be one of the gay movement's shining lights, Jerry Lewis is nonetheless a remarkable figure in its history, a jester in a court of sexual panic who, by the force and amplitude of his inanity, could get away with gleefully stretching if not entirely flouting one of the culture's most pervasive sexual interdictions. He is the hysterical manifestation of his culture's failed repression—imminent sexual criticism incarnate. To look at Lewis today is to remind ourselves too uncomfortably of who we were and what made us hysterical. His current reputation is not at all surprising.

Split Personalities

Because Jerry and Dean were one of the most popular couples in the United States in the early and middle 1950s, Martin's appearance in the first shot of *Artists and Models* makes Lewis's almost a fait accompli. Sure enough Martin, as "Rick," rather clinically sticks his head inside the bright red gaping lips of the billboard and finds Lewis, or

"Eugene Fullstack" as he is called here, who is casually leaning against the inside wall reading "Bat Lady" comic books with a panicky but fascinated look on his face. "It looks like the Bat Lady's gonna blow one of the Rat Man's heads off!" he notes with continuing clinical eloquence. This is in itself a repetition, albeit a much more psychologically complex one, of the duo's very first moments in the movies. Seconds after Martin is introduced as a sidewalk-stand juice jerk in George Marshall's *My Friend Irma* (1949), he calls through a hole in the wall to "Seymour" and out pops the head of fellow juicer Jerry. (In studying the Martin and Lewis oeuvre, one could no doubt do a lengthy analysis of orifices alone.)

Eugene's Rat Man is not to be confused with Freud's famous patient Ernst Lanzer, who is known in the annals of psychoanalysis as the Rat Man. Freud's Rat Man was an obsessional neurotic who, while in the military, became abjectly terrified by a superior officer's tale of an Asian punishment involving rats. Criminals, the Rat Man's captain told him, were tied down on their stomachs, a bucket of rats were set loose on their buttocks, and the rats (this of course is what most upset the Rat Man) would burrow into the criminals' anuses. Having heard this already disturbing story, the Rat Man to his even greater distress found himself imagining the same thing happening to his father and girlfriend; from the simultaneous horror and pleasure this fantasy evoked sprang the Rat Man's obsessional neurosis.

Obviously, Ernst's sexually charged fantasy life was somewhat different from Eugene Fullstack's. On the one hand, Eugene immediately appreciates his identification with the rodent protagonist. He has no problem seeing himself as a rat, whereas Ernst needed intensive psychoanalysis to help him understand that what appeared to be horrifying rodent-villains were in fact expressive of his own deeper wishes and were therefore representations of himself. On the other hand, Ernst was cured.

Jean-Louis Comolli and Robert Benayoun, two of the most articulate of the nearly 56 million French men and women who are generally thought to be caught up in mass adoration of Jerry Lewis, have each noticed the consistency with which Lewis's characters fragment into doubles and/or distorted aspects of themselves.[9] As Jerry's playing of not only his own but Richard Hayden's role in *Money from Home* demonstrates, this splitting of one character into two predates Tashlin as far as direction is concerned. This is a Lewis device; Jerry claims to have collaborated on most of his scripts and can be considered his own auteur.[10] In Marshall's *Scared Stiff* (1953), for instance, Lewis walks past a mirror and out pops another version of Lewis, one who speaks with an even dumber inflection as he leans out of the mirror and addresses his twin; the two Lewises then proceed to have an entire conversation with themselves in which the mirror image gives the "real" Jerry helpful advice. Lewis's most striking use of doubling came a decade later in *The Nutty Professor* (1963), in which the babbling, bungling hero finds his Jekyll-and-Hyde partner in the form of the unctuous Buddy Love, who bears a hilarious resemblance in aura if not in body to his former partner Dean Martin, but here Lewis's duplicity is much more subtle, less a concern of the story than of what passes for the character's mental state.

On the picayune level, it's worth noting that in *Artists and Models*, the Rat Man in whose plight Eugene vicariously revels has (at least) two heads. But less minutely, here's how Eugene enthusiastically describes his dreams, which take the same cartoon-horror form as the "Bat Lady" comics: "My subconscious was battling against my conscious, and the basic intelligence of my mind wouldn't allow myself to comprehend some of the problems that were forethought prior to sleeping." Lewis's is a personality that ceaselessly unravels; its most consistent aspect is the constant dissolution to which it subjects itself. Evidently, and for whatever reason, audiences of the 1950s took great pleasure in such imminent mental crumbling, for they paid to see it over and over and over again. Jerry Lewis is the embodiment of fifties hysteria in its most clinical form: the jerking movements of his body; his grotesque tics and facial contortions; his abrasive nasal gibbering; all of which, owing to the extraordinary popularity of Lewis's comedies, may not only be seen as powerful expressions of an underlying social insanity but a pleasurable response to the pressures that provoked them.

Hysteria and Representation

Psychologist Jules Janet describes the process of undoubling (*dédou-blement*, the term often employed by Comolli, Benayoun, and the rest of "the French" in regard to Lewis) as lying at the foundation of hysteria: "The second personality, always concealed behind the first, the stronger as the latter is weaker, takes advantage of the least chance to overcome it and show itself in full light."[11]

It may not be enough to cite one or two instances of doubling and fragmentation in Jerry Lewis's movies as evidence of hysteria on the mass level of culture. But the repetition of the device, coupled with the nature of Lewis's screen persona as a whole as well as with his enormous popularity, suggests something on the order of a fixed idea on the part of both star and society. And while a complete diagnosis of the hysteria's root causes is obviously a topic too broad for this particular study of fifties film comedies, it is intriguing nonetheless to conceive the relationship of Lewis's comedy to history in terms of psychological mechanics. As Pierre Janet writes:

> The various symptoms of hysteria are not spontaneous manifestations, idiopathic of the disease, but are in close connection with the provocative trauma. The most common accidents of hysteria . . . should be interpreted in the same way as the accidents of traumatic hysteria—namely, by the persistency of an idea or dream. The relation between the provocative idea and the accident may be more or less direct, but it exists always.[12]

Tashlin never offered an etiology of cultural hysteria. He was a film director, not an anthropologist. But in his work one can see certain clues: in the billboard scene of *Artists and Models* Tashlin sets up a 1955 America constituted almost entirely by artifice and violently distorted sexuality. Tensions not only emerge, they explode—or, more precisely, they've *already* exploded and Tashlin is simply shoving his audience in medias res. The billboard, treated as a bizarre distortion of human desire, takes oral gratification to an extreme when the "trim maid" whose huge mouth serves as the focal point of the advertisement is shown to be a mechanical apparatus. Inside the mouth, where Eugene is reading about how the Bat Lady is about to rip a man's head off, is a smoke-making machine designed to bring the ghastly female to life as a Titanic smoker-consumer.

Woman as cigarette, woman as cartoon terror, woman as lurid and larger-than-life facade, woman as blowing machine—everything but woman as human. Little wonder that disaster ensues almost instantly. The mechanical woman, like the bride of Frankenstein, wreaks a horrible revenge on her creators/subjects: first she sucks up all of Eugene's "Bat Lady" comic books and then she sucks up Eugene. Upon emerging from the mechanical throat, he coughs into the contraption and tiny puffs come out of the enormous orifice, making him seem even more puny and pathetic. Then, more devastatingly, the monstrous woman spits out hundreds of chewed-up "Bat Lady" pages and sends them cascading onto the street, where two of the fifties' more impressive cultural figures—an ad executive and a cop— are standing. Forced to witness the chaos that a personality like Eugene Fullstack has made of a good campaign and a quiet street, these two icons are soon to be doused with *brilliant* splashes of red, yellow, and white paint when Eugene kicks the paint cans off the scaffold. As though they were aimed on purpose, the cans hit them squarely on their heads, and Tashlin concludes the sequence by cutting to a very high-angle long shot of the street, now transformed into a tableau vivant Jackson Pollack.

The visual splendor of this sequence alone ought to be enough to convince even the most resolutely anti-Lewis critics that *Artists and Models* is an extraordinarily complex and daring work of art. But what Godard learned from Tashlin is what gives this work its power, namely the interweaving of the beauty of the representation with its underlying meaning(s). In *Pierrot le Fou* (France, 1965), Ferdinand (Jean-Paul Belmondo) paints his face bright blue prior to committing suicide, and he does so for no other reason than the *look* of it, which at that point in a film about how art invades life is a pretty good reason. Similarly, Tashlin constructs scenes in *Artists and*

Models not with an eye toward character motivation per se but rather toward motivating the means of the representation itself. Just as Godard disrupts the ongoing crime plot of *Pierrot le Fou* with a musical comedy number featuring dancing extras who suddenly appear on an idyllic beach and just as suddenly disappear never to return again, so Tashlin dwells visually on details like the colors of the paint (especially as they are rendered in Technicolor) and the workings of the smoke contraption to further the development not of the characters but of the artistic self-awareness behind them. The film is, among other things, about its own construction.

British film theorists Claire Johnston and Paul Willemen, writing in the early 1970s, congratulated "the avant-garde nature of Tashlin's practice of filmic writing" in which "reality is deconstructed, re-activated and re-produced."[13] Although reality has necessarily been deconstructed, reactivated and reproduced on film since Méliès—and the Lumières, for that matter—Johnston and Willemen correctly cite Tashlin's "modernity" as being the result of the process through which Tashlin represents the fifties and not just the vision of the fifties he represents. But Tashlin's art is indisputably that of Hollywood, not the avant-garde, and it would seem even from Johnston's and Willemen's own discussion of Tashlin that it took avant-garde theorists almost twenty years to figure out what a major Hollywood director knew in 1955—namely, that the pleasure of the text lies at least in part in the ready perception of its construction.

The Author's Voices

Voice-over narration specifically addressed the fact of form throughout the era both in the cinema and the theater: a talking Oscar in *Susan Slept Here* (1954); an unseen but familiar voice in *The Solid Gold Cadillac* (1956), Fred Allen in the play, George Burns in the film;[14] Wilder's three narrators; an authorial Damon Runyon figure in the beginning of *Money from Home*; one of the main characters in *My Friend Irma*, and so forth. And in all cases the voices effectively present the audience with versions of reality that declare themselves by their very nature to be mediated, structured, and controlled. Such announcements do not only come at the beginning: in the final shot of *Rear Window* (1954) the window blinds descend as if they were a theatrical curtain, and "printed" on the center blind are the words "Paramount Pictures."* In *The Solid Gold Cadillac* director Richard Quine abruptly shifts from black and white to color for the final two shots of the eponymous car in an ending that turns the fairy-tale kingdom gimmick of the original play into the fantasyland of the cinema.

Even in a low-budget product like Monogram Pictures' *Jiggs and Maggie Out West* (1950), based on the newspaper feature "Bringing Up Father" by George McManus, consciousness of form provides not only a comic conclusion but an entire worldview. There the stubby hero and his beanpole wife (played by real-life actors), having spent the film searching for gold in "Jackass Junction, Nevada," find the formally buried treasure in the form of their real author, cartoonist McManus, who sits behind a drawing board telling his startled fictional creations things like "I wanted to see how you'd act in western surroundings" and "Don't worry, Maggie. *I'm* your gold, and you and Jiggs are mine."

Such self-aware moments do not always contribute positively to the film, nor is such self-awareness always formally strategic. Immediately after the sweet, delicate end of George Cukor's dark romantic comedy, *The Marrying Kind* (1952), a shot of actor Aldo Ray bursts onto the screen with the words, "You have just seen our new personality, Aldo Ray. Please watch for his next picture."

Tashlin's interest in revealing the filmmaking process, in emphatically demonstrating the *activity* of writing, composing, performing, editing, and projecting film, is really then a condensation of the era's awareness of form rather than a departure from it, a historical development of classical Hollywood cinema and not a rejection or distortion of it. If you can get beyond the exclusive academic *hauteur* of the

---

* Universal Pictures, which now owns the right to the film, saw fit to cut this final shot from the prints and video tapes currently in release, leaving *Rear Window* without either its self-enclosed symmetry—the first shot is of the blinds going up—or its final self-referential joke.

language, Stephen Heath's comments in *The Nouveau Roman*, quoted by Johnston and Willemen, accurately describes the work Tashlin performed for American corporations (namely, Fox and Paramount): "A text opens in and from that complex formation of modes of articulation that gives, as it were, the theater of its activity, a series of settings always already there as its very possibility."[15]

Images

The overlapping of the ostensible story of artists and models with *Artists and Models*, the way in which the film turns in on itself, is most forcefully expressed by way of doubling and repetition. Bessie (Shirley MacLaine) really is the Bat Lady of the comics (or rather, she is the model for the Bat Lady). Eugene's dreams, sparked by the comics, are then expressed as comical dreams, which Rick writes down and turns back into comics. The big musical number, "Artists and Models," is performed on a stage in front of an audience (this film has not, until that point, been a backstage musical—it turns into one completely arbitrarily, like the beach sequence in *Pierrot le Fou*). And a costumed woman at the "Artists and Models Ball," where the finale takes place, has dressed her legs up as twin women with matching faces and skirts.

A related preoccupation of Tashlin's is the role and nature of images: ad campaigns, comic books, television, and of course the movies. In each case, the effect of the image is twofold. Images bear meaning in their content, but they also project meaning through their form, and it is on this level that Tashlin's compulsive criticism of television is sharpest. (In addition to *Artists and Models*, Tashlin ridicules TV in *Susan Slept Here, The Girl Can't Help It, Will Success Spoil Rock Hunter?*, and *Rock-A-Bye Baby*.) Unlike comic books and billboards, which may (and in Tashlin's world always do) have a graphic beauty that accompanies their puerile giddiness, television is small-scale, banal, and unattractive in image quality. Obviously it's gotten better since Tashlin's day, but in the 1950s, when Technicolor and widescreen processes yielded gigantic images with supersaturated colors, TV looked all the more impoverished to the eye. In *The Girl Can't Help It* and, more riotously, in *Will Success Spoil Rock Hunter?*, Tashlin ridicules the video image mercilessly by comparing its tiny screen size to the enormity of CinemaScope. Here, he also uses it as a comic foil for VistaVision, but more importantly as another excuse to redouble the experience of his characters, to fuse reality and image together so farcically that their differences become all the more clear. In the middle of the film, Eugene appears on a talk show devoted to the subject of denouncing comic books just after Rick has landed a lucrative job drawing them. Rick, on the sidewalk, watches as his friend speaks "to him" from the tiny screen. "I realize that that is why I am now a little retarded," Eugene says apropos his hobby. As with every instance of video-within-a-film in Tashlin's work, the world on TV is even more wretched and stilted than the world of the film.

Consider as contrast the very different message of what may be the most culturally gripping fusion of fiction and reality in the fifties. On January 19, 1953, a day before General Eisenhower's inauguration as president, a mammoth 68.8 per cent of the country's televisions were tuned in as the fictional Lucy Ricardo "gave birth" to Little Ricky on the very day Lucille Ball gave birth to Desi Arnaz, Jr. Whereas Tashlin's strategy forces a confrontation between what's real and what's false, the message of *I Love Lucy* was that the two were one and the same.[16]

The Paucity of Realism

Comics and cartoons, like movies, simply *look* better to Tashlin's eye than the real world does, probably because they allow for an intensity of expression denied by dull veracity. For Tashlin such visual intensity is mirrored by physical violence. Robert Mundy, writing on *Artists and Models*, notes the high-pitched violence on which the comics (as represented by the Bat Lady and Zuba) depend. George Winslow, the deep-voiced child from *Gentlemen Prefer Blondes* (and here billed as "George 'Foghorn' Winslow"), laconically states his opinion of the Bat Lady to her publisher, Murdock: "She stinks. No blood. I like blood." In a strange linking of sex and violence, Bessie asks the boy, "What can I do to entertain you?" "Not a thing," he drolly responds—"You're too old for me, mophead." "Foghorn" Winslow then asks, "Is this a dagger?" and promptly hurls it directly at Eugene. Rick's success is built on violence; he becomes the author of the wildly successful "Zuba" series, based of course on his roommate's dreams, and he tells Murdock, "A couple more issues and you and I'll make them forget Hitler." But Mundy's conclusion is odd, not to mention oddly incomplete: "Tashlin is very serious in his concern for the effects of horror comics."[17] Tashlin's repeated use of violence as jokes, however, qualifies whatever "serious" intent he may have had. If there is a commentary value to be found in this deathless series of violent jokes, it is that such violence may be grotesque but it is terribly thrilling and pleasurable nonetheless, especially to the children of the happy bourgeoisie of the mid-1950s as well as to Tashlin himself.

Rather than offering a moral critique as such, Tashlin as entertainment creator uses violence as a source of humor and pleasure for his audience—a state of pleasurable immersion in the culture under critique. For instance, when Eugene discusses the effect of comics on TV, he tells the story of a "five year old trying to stuff his grandmother in the trunk compartment of a car." This, to Eugene, is appalling for the simple reason that "any five year old should know he's not old enough to drive a car." To get the joke, one must fall into the gap that both separates and subsumes celebration and satire and, in so doing, assume multiple points of view, a sort of aesthetic schizophrenia. The critique—that American culture is obsessed with violence—must blend with one's full participation in that culture. And indeed, the fantastic image of the kid stuffing grandma in the trunk is very funny.

This is a dangerous space, insofar as far as any entertainment can be considered dangerous. As Robert Warshow declared in 1954, comedy and comic books can be acts of cultural terrorism: "It should be said that the E.C. comics do in fact display a certain imaginative flair. *Mad* and *Panic* are devoted to a wild, undisciplined machine-gun attack on American popular culture, creating an atmosphere of nagging hilarity something like the clowning of Jerry Lewis."[18]

Dreams, Secret Formulas, and National Security

Dreams, comics, and movies provide Tashlin with the cultural references he needs to undermine stability, whether it's that of an individual character, an artistic medium, an audience member, or the country at large. Part of this attack depends on psychology. Once again, popularized psychoanalysis appears like Freud in a clown suit as the source of jokes as well as their brunt. For example, the dreamwork at which Eugene toils may be as reductive and two dimensional as a comic book, but then so is his intriguing relationship with Rick. The panicky but ultimately liberating laughter this cartoonish relationship is designed to provoke results from the simultaneous suppression and exposure of a dirty little secret. In their first domestic scene together, Eugene, wearing an apron, receives some harsh news from his friend when Rick, tired of the rut he's in, declares, "Look, junior, divorce is the only way out. We've been together too long—ever since we were tenderfeet in the kangaroo patrol. You get custody of the beans and Bat Lady." Sullen, Eugene stands in the doorway watching as Rick packs, but when Rick relents and begins to take his clothes back out of the suitcase, Eugene smiles and sniffles. Their marriage has been saved, but not without trauma.

This tension calls to mind the real Jerry Lewis discussing the "complete emotional breakdown" he suffered when he and Dean split up: "After the breakup, I asked Patti [then Mrs. Lewis] why she'd never said anything about Dean, and she told me that Dean was like a second wife to me and that she had no right to speak against him. Isn't that something?"[19]

Back in the film, later that night, Eugene has a powerfully upsetting dream in the bedroom he shares with Rick. Like any good couple of the 1950s, Rick and Eugene sleep in twin beds. Eugene's is covered with Bat Lady comic books. Fitfully asleep, Eugene sits up, still dreaming, then screams and throws the books in the air:

Vincent the Vulture! Defender of truth and liberty and member of the Audubon Society! He is half boy, half man, half bird, with feathers growing out of every pore. [Vincent is fleeing from] Zuba! Zuba the Magnificent! Vincent is very aware that behind those inviting red lips, behind those purple boudoir eyes, and behind that cleaving cleavage is a diabolical soul! Zuba is trying to extract from Vincent his secret formula.

The nightmares of the adult American male, characterized here as a pure grotesque, are suffused with such overtly sexual images that no explanation is necessary for them—neither here nor in theaters of the time. (As Pierre Janet notes in regard to hysteria, "the simplest somnambulism should be considered as identical with [the] great phenomena of double existence, which are sometimes so manifest. It is always the result, the manifestation, of an undoubling (dédoublement) of the personality.")[20] After all, Eugene's description of the hellish Zuba fits just as well for any number of the era's sultry femmes fatales: Joan Collins in the Howard Hawks–William Faulkner *Land of the Pharoahs* (1955), Marilyn Monroe in Henry Hathaway's *Niagara* (1952), Dorothy Malone in Sirk's *Written on the Wind* (1956), Mamie Van Doren in Albert Zugsmith's and Jack Arnold's *High School Confidential* (1958), Jan Sterling in Wilder's *Ace in the Hole* (1951), and others. Scores of voluptuously evil women stalked the decade's dramas, and Eugene's cartoon creation is nothing more than a comical version of the devil dames with whom audiences were already familiar.

Here, though, comedy is the vehicle for critical commentary on the potent if pathetic conventional scenario of monster-women bent on extracting "secret formulas" from upstanding males like Vincent/Eugene/Jerry. Given the era's Cold War paranoia, the spy plot of *Artists and Models* takes on an air of radical farce as top secret rocket fuel becomes positively seminal to the nation's security. In 1954 the threat of communism wasn't abstract. The Rosenbergs had been executed only one year earlier, the state having decided that these two New York Jews had passed along secret formulas to the Soviets. As a partial consequence, Russians spies were thought to have infiltrated every corner of American society. As Stephen J. Whitfield notes, a popular high school history textbook published in 1954 gave drastic paranoia an oddly matter-of-fact quality:

> Unquestioning party members are found everywhere. Everywhere they are willing to engage in spying, sabotage, and the promotion of unrest on orders from Moscow. Agents of the worldwide Communist conspiracy have been active inside the United States. Some of them have been trusted officials of the State Department, regularly furnishing information to Russia. Others have passed on atomic secrets; still others have even represented the United States at the UN.[21]

Obviously, these "atomic secrets" were seen as essential to the country's strength and survival. And in a bizarre way the American military took on the psychocultural trappings of the nation's testicles, with secret atomic formulas serving as our precious bodily fluids. American political hygiene dictated that our juices had to be protected at all costs, an ideological association that *Dr. Strangelove* brought out into the bright light of ridicule in 1964. Still, *Artists and Models* shows how close this was to the surface ten years earlier, when Congress was feverishly passing the Communist Control Act of 1954 and the Loss of Citizenship Act, both of which built on previous legislation toward the ultimate goal of curtailing, confining, and ultimately expelling any recalcitrant, infectious formula-stealers from the body politic. By robbing the nation of the potent secrets of our firepower, communist spies threatened to sap our very masculinity. In this context, the simultaneous national obsession with homosexuality seems even more clinical.

And Tashlin's response seems especially funny. The New York Jew who serves as the Soviets' unwitting conduit for military secrets is Jerry Lewis, and in the role of Sonia, the devious Soviet spy, he casts . . . Eva Gabor? Never one of the fifties' most convincing actresses, Eva Gabor becomes in Tashlin's world the *reductio ad ridiculum* of the era's strategic and sexual threats. Idiotic and unbelievable, Lewis and Gabor are thus all the more appropriate as reflections of the Cold

War's neurotic projections. Tashlin's farcical depiction of the era's consuming political problems prefigures in (more or less) human form the hilariously withering cartoon representation of the Soviet menace offered at the very end of the decade by animator Jay Ward in his prime-time TV series *Rocky and His Friends*. We take this show for granted today, but as a cultural measurement of the 1950s it couldn't be more graphic. Look at the world depicted by Bullwinkle et al. when the show premiered in November 1959. In *Rocky* the Soviet spies Boris Badenov and his dramatic wife Natasha are of course wildly and ineluctably incompetent in their devious struggle against, as Boris always puts it, "squirrel and moose." From a formal literary perspective, the notion of narrative closure gives way almost entirely in *Rocky* as the four central characters engage in an endless series of disconnected, generally pointless incidents involving precious "mooseberries" and other items of critical value. But what gives the cartoon its ludicrous punch is the fact that the all-American Rocky is *barely* more capable than Boris and Natasha, while the equally all-American Bullwinkle is an outright imbecile. In *Artists and Models* neither side comes off any better. In Tashlin's vision, the very survival of the planet lies in the maladroit hands of Jerry Lewis and Eva Gabor. Perhaps one could read this as the most extreme case of paranoia in all Cold War cinema, but I see it as being more comically subversive, a way of ridiculing rather than reinforcing the international status quo.

Beyond Belief

Vincent/Eugene/Jerry is so full of psychic contradiction that the sum of his parts—child, adult, and fowl—vastly exceeds his whole. Rick forcibly removes the sleeping Eugene from the bedroom after his outburst and puts him on the fire escape, where he is awakened by a loud discussion upstairs. When he goes up to investigate, he discovers Shirley MacLaine dressed as the Bat Lady, the model for Dorothy Malone's Abigail Parker, the Bat Lady's creator. (Tashlin has already revealed this to the audience in a weird tilt shot beginning with a close-up of a pair of women's legs clothed alluringly in dark stockings and black shoes and ending with a close-up of a bat-masked female head.) Needless to say, when Eugene knocks on the door and the Bat Lady answers, he is thrown into a tailspin: he flees down the stairs and promptly runs into the wrong apartment. An obese woman is asleep, and he nearly smothers her in his excitement before she retaliates violently and sends him screaming: "The Bat Lady scared me and I ran into the Fat Lady!" he babbles in terror to Rick, thus culminating an incident that has as its primary purpose the pleasing verbal inanity of the line. As Robert Mundy writes, "Is there another director who would show a Bat Lady and a Fat Lady . . . just so a character can confuse them verbally?" On that score, later in the film Rick runs after Eugene and Sonia, who are both costumed. Rick says to a cabbie: "Did a bat and a fat rat come out?" The cabbie, nonplused, replies: "They just left in that foreign job."[22]

Tashlin's is the comedy of patent implausibility. Eugene mimes the lighting of two candles, and they instantly light—but not in the order he mimed them. Eugene craves steak, so a steak drops out of the sky. When Tashlin wishes to express the extreme popularity of Rick's art (Eugene's nightmares), he cuts to a baby in a carriage: the baby is "reading" a Vincent the Vulture comic book, holding it up with his tiny hands. In *Marry Me Again* (1953), one of Tashlin's early films and thus one his more restrained efforts, someone drops an airplane breakfast tray on the head of a passenger and the food lands in the precise shape of a face—two fried-egg eyes and a smiling bacon mouth. In each case, wish fulfillment brings gratification where none would be possible otherwise—a fitting aestheticization of Tashlin's moral purpose as a comedian. In the 1950s a full-scale political, cultural, and sexual revolution was impossible; options were limited. This narrowing of terms enabled a mainstream Hollywood director like Tashlin, a man who had absolutely no interest in revolution, to work the space of imminence to brilliant comic advantage.

In *Artists and Models* the most extreme case of Tashlin's comic hedonism may be the film's narrative structure, wherein the big "Artists and Models" production number coincides perfectly—and foolishly—with the end of the film. Eugene and Rick are (for no reason at all) the stars of the show, and they do an elaborate routine on a stage shaped like a palette with paint represented by large piles of colorful material. As they sing and do shtick, Rick approaches the red pile, which conceals a female model who stands up dressed in a red gown. When Eugene attempts the same trick with the violet pile, nothing happens—it's simply a pile of cloth. Rick goes for the blue pile and finds a woman; Eugene attacks the yellow pile and finds nothing. The routine continues until Eugene approaches the pink pile, the only one left, and, following the film's logic, finds a monstrosity in the form of a woman who "grows" on stage to be at least seven and a half feet tall.

The performers are in costume, but so is the on-screen audience: this is a masked ball. If this audience functions in a way similar to the nightclub audience in the opening of *Gentlemen Prefer Blondes*, as the film audience's surrogate, Tashlin adds an additional level of irony by having his surrogates wear obvious false fronts. After a short routine in which Rick and Eugene paint various women then paint mustaches on each other, the patchwork spy plot intervenes abruptly and displaces the action for just as long as it takes to resolve itself. Sonia (dressed as the Bat Lady) spirits Eugene (dressed as the rat drawn earlier in the film by Abigail) away to get the secret formula, and in a frenzied series of slapstick routines and perfunctory resolutions, the villainous Soviets are vanquished and the heroes return to a happy and secure America, represented here as a costume ball staged in a theater.

When almost all is said and done as far as the plot is concerned, Eugene pairs with Bessie, Rick pairs with Abigail, and they all run into the limelight and pick up where they left off—*not* in the "Artists and Models" song, which they had abandoned, but in genre expectation. Standing on the stage, they all look to the left of the frame, whereupon Tashlin pans to a church set complete with bells ringing. By the time he pans back (no more than five seconds later), the characters are all decked out in wedding outfits and completing the song with the words, "when you pretend." The whole prenuptial and nuptial ceremony occurs ludicrously and artificially within the spatial and temporal continuity of a single shot, which is to say that Tashlin sees its content—namely, the American marriage fetish and the whole ideological package that goes with it—as plainly stupid. The camera cranes back, through and above the crowd, and everyone cheers as the heroic couples clinch in what may be one of the most triumphantly false endings in Hollywood history, a travesty not just of genre expectations and Hollywood conventions but of the domestic, family-sprouting imperative on which our society, not to mention Hollywood of the 1950s, is often presumed to rest.

The biggest question left unanswered by this paste-up resolution is: what becomes of Eugene's attachment to Rick? It isn't just that Eugene had provided Rick with a prototypical fifties home, complete with magical steak and candles as well as tension, tears, and the threat of divorce. Rick himself finds a certain comfort and joy in this union. After he lands the comic book job, he tells Eugene and Abigail that he has sold a painting. Rick is on the left, Eugene in the middle, and Abigail on the right as Eugene, beaming with pride and pleasure, leans forward and rests his head lovingly on Rick's chest. Such love is not one-sided, as Rick demonstrates by asking, softly and with genuine warmth, "What is it, curlytop?" Eugene then kisses him gently, saying "That's from Mrs. Muldoon," and immediately kisses him again, saying "And that's from me." Rick accepts Eugene's affection, but approaches Abigail for the corresponding heterosexual moment, effectively cutting Eugene out. But Eugene Fullstack is not so easily rejected. He jumps up between them—very, very close—and as they kiss, he grins broadly in what might be just friendship but, given what we have just witnessed, is more like a vicarious thrill.

Fully aware of this radical aspect to Lewis's screen persona and able to incorporate it into the subversive fabric of the films themselves, Tashlin consistently presents Lewis's anarchic sexual energy as a series of figurative formal treats, moments of pleasure as spontaneous and delightful as a play on words. What else can one make of the shocking instant in their joint bedroom when Eugene, fussing with a fake shirtfront that persists in popping up and smacking him squarely in the face, blurts out to his buddy, "I can't keep this dickie down, Ricky!"

The Girl Can't Help It: Nobody Else Could Either

In a sense, this is a pathetic generation, especially in the great cities because of the effect of nervous tension, synthetic excitement, and noise; but the malady extends into the country districts also, for the air waves transmit tension.

—Norman Vincent Peale (1952)[23]

Tutti frutti, all rooty. Tutti frutti, all rooty. Tutti frutti, all rooty. Tutti frutti, all rooty. Tutti frutti, all rooty. A wop bop a luma, ba lop bam boom.

—Little Richard (1955)

Gorgeous Lifelike Color

In the center of an almost square black-and-white image, the actor Tom Ewell walks toward the camera on an empty stage with musical instruments suspended in the air in the background. He looks directly at the lens and casually addresses the audience:

Ladies and gentlemen, the motion picture you are about to see is a story of music. I play the role of Tom Miller, an agent. A small-time theatrical agent who'd been a, well, you'll see. This motion picture was photographed in the grandeur of CinemaScope and—pardon me.

Ewell takes a step toward the left of the screen and flicks at the air with his index finger and thumb. The image responds like a stagehand and draws itself open to reveal almost half again as much space as there had been. A whole new instrument, a full-size harp, is now visible—dwarfed—on the screen. Ewell moves to the right and repeats the flicking action. The image swings open again and reveals a grand piano.

As I was saying, this motion picture was photographed in the grandeur of CinemaScope and in gorgeous lifelike color by Deluxe. [He notices that this is not the case.] *In gorgeous lifelike color by DeLuxe!*

After he repeats the line, the drab stage is bathed in pink and blue and yellow and lavender, hues that would be difficult if not impossible to find in the natural world. Tashlin cuts to a medium close-up.

Oh, yes. Our story is about music. Not the music of long ago but the music that expresses the culture, the refinement, and the polite grace of the present day.

A jukebox appears on the right. It begins to blast Little Richard's "The Girl Can't Help It" as Ewell, drowned out, mouths the rest of his introductory presentation. The camera tracks forward to the record spinning in the jukebox, and the credits sequence begins as couples dance acrobatically on a huge and empty dance floor.

In her study of the Hollywood musical, Jane Feuer writes:

'Distanciation', 'estrangement', and 'alienation effect' refer to techniques whereby the spectator is lifted out of her transparent identification with the story and forced to concentrate instead on the artifice through which the play or film has been made. To this end Godard will call attention to the very things Hollywood movies seek to cover up. His actors will refer to the fact that they are in a movie; the soundtrack will blare up at inopportune moments; cuts which are 'invisible' in Hollywood movies will jar rather than flow together into a seamless rendering of the story; indeed the story itself will be no more than a series of digressions and allusions."[24]

Yet this opening sequence, like those in *Monkey Business* (1952), *Susan Slept Here*, and *The Seven Year Itch* (1955)—not to mention the ending of *Jiggs and Maggie Out West*—makes Feuer's sweeping generalization about "Hollywood movies" and their suppression of formal operations a little hard to sustain. To be fair, Feuer does have a point. Godard does what she says he does, and many Hollywood films do something else entirely. Hollywood does have a formal code of conduct, and it sometimes seems inviolable. But what sets the Hollywood of the 1950s somewhat apart is the frequency of the violations. As a contemporary director, Frank Tashlin is especially interesting because he disrupts the tradition even while embedding himself in it. One might argue that Hollywood in the fifties could be characterized as a period of late classicism in which conventions turned in on themselves in parallel response to the economic breakdown of the studio system. But like the concept of "late capitalism," that confident seventies' and eighties' film theory chestnut, Hollywood's continuing economic and artistic survival makes the term as well as the idea of "late classicism" impossible. After all, it's upsetting to think that *The Girl Can't Help It* is almost forty years old.

A Moralistic Satire?

The Girl Can't Help It is about music, specifically rock 'n' roll. But like *Monkey Business*, the film has provided strange fodder for critics looking for moral denunciations of popular culture. Raymond Durgnat may have tried to correct the critical commonplace of Tashlin's moralism when he wrote:

> Not that Tashlin is, basically, a satirical moralist, like Sturges or Wilder. He resembles them in some ways, but in others his outlook, like Laurel and Hardy's, is that of ideological innocence, and is all the better for it, emphasizing, as they do, the trials and tribulations of everyday living and feeling. What sometimes seems defective is that dramatic tension, as a result of which the best comedies would be very sad indeed if they weren't very funny instead.[25]

On second thought, perhaps he did not try to correct this impression. In any case, Peter Bogdanovich writes:

As funny as Tashlin's movies are, they also reflect a deep sadness with the condition of the world: his devastating picture of the rock-n-roll age (*The Girl Can't Help It*), Voltarian in its grotesquery, is almost tragic in its purposeful ugliness. All the more so when one realizes how much Tashlin admires beauty.[26]

A more balanced but still righteously indignant view comes from Ian Cameron, who begins by echoing Norman Vincent Peale:

A synthetic world, a world whose artificiality Tashlin does not like. But when Tashlin doesn't like things, instead of attacking them with open hate, he simply finds them funny. There is in his films a dual approach to his subjects. An obvious affection for movies, stars, rock 'n' roll, horror comics, is coupled with a desire to use laughter to prick the bubble of illusion around them. His films are celebrations as much as satires—*The Girl Can't Help It* is a film that debunks rock, but contains seventeen rock numbers, every one of which Tashlin obviously enjoyed enormously.[27]

Historian Charlie Gillett, writing in his monumental history of rock 'n' roll, *The Sound of the City*, sees Tashlin's critique on altogether different and, to my mind, more accurate terms:

The Girl Can't Help It . . . was unusual both in its remarkable collection of several of the best rock 'n' roll singers—Gene Vincent, Little Richard, Fats Domino, and Eddie Cochran—and its strong story, witty in the situations involving Jayne Mansfield and Tom Ewell, realistic in its portrayal of the bitter competition between coin machine operators. . . . In this film at least, the sensuous possibilities of rock and roll, though comically handled, were more directly expressed than they had been, for obvious reasons, on community radio stations.[28]

At stake here is a conception not just of Tashlin and his opinion of rock 'n' roll but of the satirical foundation of his art, its critical capacity as well as the thrust of its entertainment. What remains lacking in the few essays that have been written about Tashlin's films are discussions of how they operate as feature-length Hollywood movies. It was on this level, after all, that they were conceived, produced, experienced, and enjoyed at the time. As paradoxical as it may seem, the wealth of incident, gesture, sound, and visual play in Tashlin's work has resulted in a preoccupation with "themes" and "features" that are said to characterize his entire career from beginning to end; oddly, this tendency occurs in the context of anti-auteurist academic arguments. Where is Frank Tashlin in all of this? And where is his comedy?

Mostly, he's been lost in the shuffle. Johnston and Willemen, for instance, repeatedly use Tashlin as a club with which to beat the auteur theory, which was then being challenged by structural and semiotic criticism. As part of this project, Willemen makes it a point to offer a list of structural "features" instead of the retrograde auteurists' list of "themes." After cutting through the jargon, however, one finds that the two concepts refer more or less to the same thing. Meanwhile, so as not to be a dreaded positivist, Willemen calls his essay "no more than a working hypothesis, a way of approaching Tashlin's work which might prove fruitful if elaborated further." Alas, before anyone had much chance to proceed, Johnston and Willemen (together with Phil Hardy) went on only a few years later to appreciate the contradiction of their own anti–author author studies, declaring: "Auteurist studies, linked to the grouping of a series of films merely because they were made by one and the same director, were deeply implicated in the theory of meaning founded on the assumption of the existence of a transcendental ego, as described most clearly by Julia Kristeva."[29]

Thus, within the space of three years, Willemen made his own proposal vis-à-vis Tashlin impossible, and the name of Frank Tashlin was heard virtually no more in film studies. I would like to revisit Johnson and Willemen's originally illuminating ideas about Tashlin, to leave the question of the transcendental ego to others, and to look instead, however positivistically, at *The Girl Can't Help It*.

Self-Alienation and Aesthetic Pleasure

In *The Girl Can't Help It*, the first postcredits shot—one can scarcely call it the "film proper," since the credits are thoroughly embedded in the story as well as the manner in which the story is told—is of a man playing a saxophone while writhing on the floor of a nightclub. In the second shot, Ewell is drinking at the bar. A logical progression, one could argue, but it's not the logic of cause and effect as much as that of effect and effect. As seen in the credits sequence, the world of 1956 is one of acute self-awareness, visual excitement, sexual energy, and profound alienation—the dancing couples are lost in a vast sea of beautiful vacuous space. This emptiness might be seen to have provoked the music rather than the other way around, but Tashlin treats it instead as a preexisting condition of American culture. Here in the bar, Tom Miller does not appear to be drinking because of the rise of wild and unchained musical energy. Rather, the frenzy of the musician and the alcoholism of the agent appear to be part of a general cultural malaise, the difference being that the musician's response is public and creative whereas Miller's is private and destructive. The two are equally self-absorbed.

In the following sequence, Miller meets "Fats" Marty Murdock (Edmond O'Brien), the gangster who will convince the down-and-heading-out agent to turn his girlfriend Jerri Jordan (Jayne Mansfield) into a star. Drinking once again appears as second nature to Miller, and Murdock actually refers to it as the source of the collapse of Miller's career. But Tashlin quickly interrupts the ostensible narrative with a farcical film-within-a-film: Fats's home movies, the story of his life in conventional newsreel form complete with equally conventional voice-over narration—shots of a more youthful Fats; shots of slot machines being smashed; shots of Fats dancing wildly with attractive women and grinning raunchily at the camera as the narrator explains, "Slim Murdock puts on weight making whoopee with European bathing beauties. Nice goin', Fats!"

Aside from Fats's excessive physical actions, not to mention his excessive physique, the newsreel sequence's comedy lies in the fact that Fats, who has presumably *lived* this life, finds it perfectly and accurately expressed by a parody newsreel. The filming of shots, the editing of these shots, and their aural captioning—none of the processes involved in filmmaking seems to have distorted anything, at least not from the point of view of their subject. Fats accepts it all as being completely truthful, so much so that he then takes over the narrator's role: "I got lonely for my native land. You know, 'Breathes 'dere a man with soul so dead . . .'" On film, Fats returns to the States ("My lawyer says its okay to come home. I don't know 'til I come back my lawyer's been disbarred"), and the first narrator resumes: "Atlanta Penitentiary—the future home of Fats Murdock." Shifting gears, Fats becomes a film critic: "Now comes the sad part," says Fats. "A big man once, now just another number." Tashlin cuts to the real Fats, not in the newsreel but in the room; he's in tears, the lights come up, and the sequence is over.

Having first structured his life as documentary, Fats then turns it into melodrama complete with "the sad part" at the conventionally proper moment. Artifice, specifically that of Hollywood filmmaking, has so thoroughly suffused this vision of American life that it is no longer possible to distinguish between fact and fiction, or more precisely it's no longer possible for this particular character—a disreputable gangster—to make the distinction. As is often the case in Tashlin's work, one can see in the populace of fictional America the psychological consequences of the America Tashlin satirizes. In this light, as it reflects off of Fats's movie screen, Tashlin calls to mind Walter Benjamin, who wrote: "Mankind, which in Homer's time was an object of contemplation for the Olympian gods, now is one for itself. Its self-alienation has reached such a degree that it can experience its own destruction as an aesthetic pleasure of the first order."[30] There are, admittedly, basic differences in their points of reference. Benjamin is referring to fascism with a capital F, namely Nazism, whereas, of course, Tashlin is referring to America in the 1950s. To this extent, Tashlin really is a bit of a moralist. But unlike the rest of us, he enjoys the infractions his characters inflict on his ethical code.

Jayne Mansfield: The Making of a Star

Already having transformed himself into a movie star with his own personal print of his life on file for evening viewing, Fats's wish for the idealism stardom represents—combined with the same entrepreneurial spirit that landed him in the Atlanta Penitentiary—drives him to an obsessive desire to make his girlfriend famous. Miller explains that not everyone is eligible for stardom and promotion, that there must be a basis of talent on which to build. As he graciously declines Murdock's offer, a sliding door opens behind him to reveal Jayne Mansfield packed into an extremely tight white dress with a white fur stole and seemingly hundreds of diamonds. Her zealous platinum hair is styled in an elaborate, rigid series of curls that cascade onto her shoulders. She is leaning against the door frame, posing and staring blankly.

Miller turns to leave, and Tashlin cuts on the action to a shot taken over Jayne's shoulder: he gasps violently when he confronts this superhuman creation, and the drink he holds shakes uncontrollably in his hand. Like the billboard in *Artists and Models*, this fabulous woman is an object of terror, a source of male paralysis. But here, instead of elaborating on the figure's artificiality, Tashlin pins the crudeness of the representation specifically on the two men. Miller, in a panic, says "Rome wasn't built in a day," to which Fats crudely responds, "She ain't Rome. What we're talkin' about is already built." Jayne, in the background, then looks down at the floor in an unmistakable gesture of humiliation that undercuts the base joke as Miller says, "No argument."

With an abrupt cut, Tashlin moves from Jayne's introduction as Jerri Jordan, a self-parody of Mansfield's already parodic image, to a shot of an unnamed rock 'n' roll band in the middle of singing a song with the repeated lyrics, "You're my idea of love." Miller is at a club celebrating his new client, alone, and when the band moves into "Ain't Gonna Cry No More," he dances with the cigarette vendor and does so with such vigor that he collapses—only to dance his way back up to a standing position.

"You're my idea of love": from Grable to Monroe to Mansfield, the forties and fifties moved from a fantastically homespun and thoroughly unironic image of blonde idealization to an image vacillating between innocence and complicity and finally to the mind-boggling self-consciousness of Mansfield, to whom legend has assigned an IQ of 165. It was a myth nurtured, though certainly not born, on the desk of Fox's publicity chief Harry Brand, who claimed among other things that Jayne had been a child prodigy on the violin; had been coached by three ballet masters; was an accomplished swimmer, diver, skater, and horsewoman; spoke Spanish and German; and was within one semester's work of a B.A. Jayne was a publicist's dream. She built her career on a solid foundation of inane hype in which "glamour art" publicity played a hefty role. As she herself put it, "I have only turned down two requests for such publicity—once when I was asked to be Miss Roquefort Cheese of 1954, and another for Miss Pain Allayer. These two did nothing to me." At one point, after she became a star, she even went so far as to license a $5.98 flesh-toned vinyl "Jayne Mansfield Hot Water Bottle" modeled in the shape of Jayne herself and supposedly built to scale at one-third to one.

Mansfield's professional career didn't begin with parodying Monroe. Both women's images arose almost concurrently out of the same breast-fixated historical circumstances, though Marilyn beat Jayne onto the screen by several years. Monroe had moved rather quickly into acting, while Jayne spent the early- to mid-fifties chasing those "glamour art" jobs. But Mansfield did become a stage and screen star specifically as a Monroe parody in George Axelrod's Broadway hit, *Will Success Spoil Rock Hunter?* She had come to Axelrod's attention via the RKO film *Underwater* (1955). Jayne played no role in that movie. She did, however, appear widely in the film's publicity. RKO arranged a novel press junket to Silver Springs, Florida, where *Underwater*, starring Jane Russell, was screened underwater for more than 150 journalists. Flown to Florida on TWA (which happened to be owned by Howard Hughes, who also owned RKO), these game movie reviewers were outfitted in Jantzen swimsuits and Timex waterproof watches and given oxygen courtesy of Aqua Lungs borrowed from the Air Force. Sensing kindred spirits among all the trademarked products, Jayne crashed the event.

At the time, she was a complete unknown as an actress; as *Variety* put it, "How she got on the junket from L.A. nobody knows, but she proved worth her weight in cheesecake to the affair." Once again, the supposed buoyancy of bosoms provided a comedy theme for the critics: "It was generally agreed by the press that the aqualung was as redundant in her case as in Miss Russell's." A flood of publicity photos of Jayne dressed in a bright red swimsuit ensued. Axelrod saw (at least) one of them and cast her as Rita Marlowe in *Rock Hunter. Variety*, in reporting the *Underwater* story, had already called Jayne "a road company Marilyn Monroe." And unfortunately, "Marlowe" is too close to "Monroe" to ignore, however much one wants to.[31]

Monroe herself was a double image to the extent of her own self-awareness, but Mansfield was nothing if not a walking commentary on femininity and marketing in the fifties. Monroe could play the *fausse-naïve* whereas Mansfield was strictly and brazenly *fausse*: the pink Cadillac; the Miss Florida Grapefruit crown; the highly publicized marriage to Mickey Hargitay, former Mr. Universe. Calculation and exploitation were the tools of Mansfield's trade, and the moment of Jerri's simultaneous introduction and humiliation gives them a clear emotional rationale.

The Big Threat: Rock 'n' Roll Breasts

Not every lyric in *The Girl Can't Help It* refers as specifically as "you've my idea of love" to the events of the story, but the songs generally offer some degree of oblique commentary through their lyrics, and they *always* do through the style of the music itself. From the blunt message of the title song and its positive restatement, "She's Got It" (both by Little Richard), to the Treniers' "Rockin' Is Our Business" (played in a recording studio owned by a crime boss) and the Chuckles' "Lollipop Lies" ("She's got sugar-lipped kisses / and cherry-dipped charms / She's a cinnamon sinner / selling lollipop lies"—sung as Jerri bumps and grinds her way to the ladies room), musical numbers reiterate dramatic tensions. And since most of these tensions result from the heroine's extraordinary sexual authority, the power not of an interior psychology but of the image's veneer, the film incorporates the sexual energy of rock 'n' roll into its own "political" agenda. With the possible exception of Julie London's "Cry Me a River"—the only song to refer to Miller's pre-Jerri past—this artistic stance openly celebrates what Charlie Gillett calls the "three main grounds for mistrust and complaint" on the part of the music industry and the general public about the rise of rock 'n' roll: "rock 'n' roll songs had too much sexuality (or, if not that, vulgarity), . . . attitudes in them seemed to defy authority, and . . . the singers either were Negroes or sounded like Negroes."[32]

Threat—to sexual propriety, to the racist status quo, to authority in general—is the film's ongoing project, and "musical comedy" in a most literal sense is its ammunition. Without trying to mimic Bosley Crowther discussing Jane Russell, one could say that "The Girl Can't Help It" sequence is nothing if not a deliberate frontal assault. Jayne's breasts may be objects of desire, but she uses them as weapons, defeating men by rendering them as helpless as nursing babies. Moreover, the precocious paper boy, prepubescent but no less a part of his culture, is an acute image of presexuality distorted by the social expectations of gender. Like the George Winslow character in *Gentlemen Prefer Blondes*, this boy is a parody of adulthood in which the behavioral paradigms of the heterosexual male are seen as seedy, transparent in their goals and pathetic in their execution. When the real adult males appear, they are positively paralyzed by the threat Jerri embodies; the child, at least, retains the capacity for pleasure and action. The ice man, the milk man, and the tenant, in contrast, become physically catatonic in Jerri's presence, and their inability to respond to the threat she so effortlessly radiates causes such massive energy overloads that the physical laws of nature become inoperative. Ice melts, milk gushes, glasses shatter—all because of the incarnate appearance of the era's buxom and hair-dressed ideal. If vulgarity means sexual explicitness, this sequence is thoroughly and proudly vulgar. With the black and sexually outrageous Little Richard screaming the words, Jerri's theme song becomes the militant anthem of a sexual and racial invasion into the previously quiet territory of white bourgeois domestic-ity. Ordinary heterosexual white men, disarmed by the very sight of her, wind up as buffoons defeated by frustration and ridiculed by the laws of nature itself.

She comes, she is seen, and she conquers: this world is in such a state of imminent collapse that even the most passive of her respons-es, being viewed, is enough to shatter the illusion of a stable reality. Laura Mulvey makes the following assertion in her short but influen-tial essay on woman as spectacle:

> There are three different looks associated with cinema: that of the camera as it records the pro-filmic event, that of the audience as it watches the final product, and that of the characters at each other within the screen illusion. The conventions of narrative film deny the first two and subordinate them to the third, the conscious aim being always to eliminate intrusive camera presence and prevent a distancing awareness in the audience.[33]

Here, Jerri Jordan is explicitly the fetishized figure of woman, so dis-ruptive an image that it destroys whatever meager illusion of reality the film has maintained until this point. As a Hollywood narrative film that ceaselessly plays upon Hollywood conventions (of comedy, music, performance, costume, art direction, camera placement, light-ing, editing, and narrative structure), *The Girl Can't Help It* adds a fifties flavor to Mulvey's insistence that "the first blow against the monolithic accumulation of traditional film conventions" was "taken by radical film-makers," a roster to which the name of Twentieth Century-Fox must now be added.

But beyond this appreciation of what constitutes radical filmmak-ing, Mulvey's argument doesn't hold as far as *The Girl Can't Help It* is concerned. The image of woman (in this case, the profoundly potent image of Jayne Mansfield) may suggest "a threat of castration and hence unpleasure," as Mulvey argues, but this image's power scarcely stops there. The men she conquers do not appear to be experiencing "unpleasure"; in fact, they are held tight in a paralysis of *overpleasure*.

Their circuits have been blown; that's the joke. More accurate and suggestive in describing the ambivalence of this joy/terror punch is Gaylyn Studlar, who sees the image of woman provoking both gratification and threat, a double stimulus inherent to the dream screen:

> The pleasures of cinema are, in many respects, infantile ones. They start with the pre-Oedipal pleasures of the dream screen. . . . In 1946, [Bertram] Lewin introduced the idea that all dreamers, whether aware of it or not, project their dreams upon a blank screen, a dream screen, that represents the maternal breast, the first site of falling asleep into dream. In the very act of naming his discovery, Lewin readily admitted that the similarities between film and the dream screen phenomenon were not lost on him. He theorized that in dream the sleeper's loss of ego boundaries resembles the experience of the nursing child who imagines an undifferentiated sense of 'fusion with the breast.' Ego boundaries are lost as the sleeper identifies with the breast/screen on which dreams are projected.[34]

Studlar stresses that she is not "attempting to reduce cinematic pleasure to one developmental stage or to purely unconscious functioning."[35] By the same token, I am not trying to reduce Studlar's argument to its application to Jayne Mansfield and other big-breasted movie stars. But there is without a doubt a certain snug and hilarious fit between Studlar's image of audiences held pleasurably in a kind of rapt bondage by a controlling female image on the one hand and the figure of Jayne Mansfield on the other, especially as she stupefies three men simply by walking across the screen. Violently regressed, these poor men are dispatched to a state of pure, helpless, paralyzed *want*. Sexual desire, overheated by virtue of the endemic repression of the era, explodes in a gush as the men gaze at Jayne. If Studlar is correct, the sequence is exemplary as evidence of the pleasurable blurring of ego boundaries in the cinema, not only for the three subject/victims but also for the film's audience as well. Just as babies enjoy a psychic fusion with the mother as they nurse, so do the limitations of adult object relationships melt away under the authority of the screen's images in general and the image of Mansfield's breasts in particular. Following this psychological model, the men not only want Jayne sexually; they want *to be* Jayne sexually, presexually, at any phase sexually. Perhaps so do we all.

Discrediting the World

As Studlar argues, the sight of a woman on screen—especially such a commanding woman—can be in itself not only a masochistic act but an act of rebellious intervention: "The restoration of the dream screen in the structure of the cinematic apparatus permits identificatory pleasures that are particularly important to the male spectator who is encouraged by the patriarchy to 'outrun' identification with the maternal body."[36] Taking a different approach to reach a similarly disruptive goal, Salvador Dali, in a 1930 volume coincidentally titled *La Femme Visible*, announced the rise of what he called the "paranoiac-critical method," later described by Andre Breton: "I believe the moment is at hand when, by a paranoiac and active advance of the mind, it will be possible (simultaneously with automism and other passive states) to systematize confusion and thus to help to discredit completely the world of reality."[37] As Breton and Dali both described it, surrealism was an effort to intervene, to disrupt, and to change. Paranoia was the means:

Paranoia: Delirium of interpretation bearing a systematic structure.

Paranoiac-critical activity: Spontaneous method of "*irrational knowledge*," based on the critical and systematic objectification of delirious associations and interpretations.[38]

Tashlin's fusion of surrealistic outrage and Hollywood cinema attracted the attention of the "militant surrealists" on the editorial board of the French journal *Positif*. These critics saw Tashlin's comedy as bearing the legacy of surrealism, so it is hardly surprising that they responded so enthusiastically to Jerry Lewis as well.[39] The very explicitness of Tashlin's and Lewis's jokes, their movement toward delirium and lunacy as well as their obsessive concern with male paranoia: these are some of the reasons "the French" admire Lewis and Tashlin. The rationale for their enthusiasm seems to me to be not only defensible but undeniable as a legitimate aesthetic criterion. But what gives *The Girl Can't Help It* its cultural foresightedness is its apprehension of rock 'n' roll as a kind of surrealistic device, the musical version of automatic writing. With one fairly minor nominal substitution, "The Girl Can't Help It" fits Jean Arp's description of the genesis of automatic poetry as it comes "straight out of [Little Richard's] bowels or out of any other of his organs that has accumulated reserves."[40] By repeating phrases in a tone verging on hysteria, Little Richard provides an aural counterpart to the fluids and fissures of the image; as Charlie Gillett describes him, "Little Richard was one of very few singers who became more expressive with meaningless sounds and disconnected phrases and images than he was with properly constructed songs."[41]

A Quest for Success

To the tune of Little Richard and his accumulated reserves, Jerri's incendiary parade leads her straight to Tom Miller's apartment, where she muses on her inability to control her own excessive image. In an echo of her traversing the CinemaScope frame—the "simple" movement with which she commands the image and destroys three spectators—Tashlin has her cross the width of the kitchen and simultaneously send Miller into nervous collapse. Once she crosses, she effectively possesses not only the room but Miller as well; this action signals their eventual union. But as she quickly demonstrates, Jerri's Barnumesque facade masks another parody-ideal: cleaning, organizing, cooking, and serving breakfast, Jerri turns out to be a model fifties housewife. "I'm domestic," she efficiently explains. As she presents Miller with a perfect meal, Tashlin pushes the representational conflict to an extreme by repeatedly framing Jerri from the neck down. Her enormous breasts literally become her crowning attributes as she discusses her irritation with society's preconceptions: "I just want to be a wife—have kids," she declares, smiling phonily in the general direction of the camera, and then Tashlin cuts off her head: "But everyone figures me for a sexpot! No one thinks I'm equipped for motherhood."

The Girl Can't Help It is nothing if not a quest for success as defined by the era's set of expectations: stardom, money, marriage, and babies. Everyone gets what he or she wants by the end, but satire verging on brittle sarcasm rules in Tashlin's depiction of the means by which they achieve gratification. Sexual in content, martial in strategy and execution, "Operation Powder Room"—Miller's name for the repeated promenades to the toilet with which Jerri commandeers the interest of club owners—begins with Little Richard once again providing a musical accompaniment, but here he is physically present as the main act of the first nightclub. "I'm ready to rock 'n' roll," the deliriously effeminate Richard yells and sings, and like Jerri/Jayne his performance hinges on boldface artificiality: even before the last note dies away, he takes a long step away from the microphone and bows in a theatrically insincere gesture of thanks for the applause.

"Operation Powder Room" continues to the tune of "She's Got It" with Jerri throwing her hips violently outward in order to facilitate left and right turns as she zig-zags her way to the bathroom. In the precision of her movements and the gusto with which she follows orders, she's an exemplary soldier in a campaign of sexual and commercial intimidation. Miller tells her that if a club owner addresses her, she is to reply, "Ask my agent," and when the first one arrives and presents her with a series of questions, he receives but one predictable answer. Given the self-conscious world of entertainment in 1956, his response is natural: "She's a comedienne, eh?"

Jerri is now well on her way to igniting the music industry, and Tashlin cuts to rocker Eddie Fontaine paradoxically singing a song called "Cool It Baby," though the "baby" in question is anything but cool, being a sex object with an orally gratifying trait that would make any straight teenage boy drool: "I love your eyes / I love your lips / 'taste even better than potato chips." In the next club Jerri once again finds her own career as consumer product, specifically as human junk food, mirrored by rock 'n' roll as the Chuckles sing about a woman's "sugar-lipped kisses and cherry-dipped charms." After these two lewd musical numbers, Abbey Lincoln's gospel-based "Spread the Word" adds a sacrilegious element to Jerri's crusade by demanding the kind of parodic honesty Jerri is presumably delivering: "Spread the word / spread the gospel / spread the truth / it must be heard!" (By the way, Lincoln is at that moment wearing one of Marilyn Monroe's lurid red gowns from *Gentlemen Prefer Blondes*.)[42]

In this final club Jerri herself reveals an awareness of the military nature of her evening's activity. As she marches across the room, an owner rushes up to her:

Owner: Can I be of any service to you?

Jerri (*shocked*): Please! I'm going to the powder room! (*She gasps, then confides*) Oh—that was an ad lib. Sorry. "Ask my agent!" (*She salutes*) Bye bye!

Visual Breakdown

Until this point, Tashlin has revealed remarkably little about the hero of the film other than his alcoholic despair and career failure. But when Miller returns to his home after this evening of calculation and Svengali-like opportunism, he finds himself haunted by a famous recording star. His aching, masochistic desire for an ideal female image causes the figure of Julie London to superimpose itself in every room of his house. London is first on a record singing her hit song, "Cry Me a River," but as Miller reaches for the ubiquitous bottle of liquor in the kitchen, he looks up to see London seated at his dinette set. She is posing in a red evening gown and singing directly to him. He clutches his head in fear and pain and rushes out, only to confront

London in the living room, dressed now in elegant pants and jewels. He roars into the kitchen—she greets him in a fur stole and strapless orange dress. He staggers into the bedroom—bathed in pink light, she's draped across the bed in a pale negligee. He runs out the door and backs his way toward the camera as London, now in a green gown and mink wrap, leans on the mantle and continues coolly to sing. Now immersed in agony and madness, Miller is forced to escape from his own apartment, and as he starts down the outside stairs he finds: Julie London, first on the landing in a white blouse and pink skirt, and then, more terrifyingly, blocking his exit in a quasi-bridal white chiffon number with a big fabric bouquet at the waist. She turns, goes down the stairs, looks back to deliver the final curse ("cry me a river / cry me a river / I cried a river over you . . .") and fades away. With such a bravura delivery on the part of this fantastic object of desire, Miller has no choice: he breaks down and cries, his head in his hands, and the sequence is concluded.

Like both Abbey Lincoln and Jayne Mansfield, Julie London cannot be *simply* represented. In all three cases the female performer's image is broken down into constituent elements. With Abbey Lincoln, it's reflection, voice, and body; with London, it's voice, body, and costume, all of which coalesce into a male masochist's dream. London's hit song, after all, is one of female triumph and revenge against earlier male cruelty, with lyrics like "Now you say you love me / Well, just to prove you do / You can cry me a river . . . I cried a river over you." Moreover, Tashlin warps brute realism in terms of character veracity by having Julie London—the real Julie London—appear as the former lover of the fictional Tom Miller, the agent who supposedly managed her career prior to her commercial success with "Cry Me a River" on the (real) Liberty label in 1955, success that the fictional Miller foisted upon the now-fictional London, who only wanted to be a wife and mother.

Like the models in *Artists and Models*, women are on graphic display in *The Girl Can't Help It*, and although Tashlin capitalizes on the spectacle of women, satire throws the spectacle if not the capital into question. There is a sequence in *Hollywood or Bust* that eloquently expresses Tashlin's idea of female farce: on their way to Hollywood,

Lewis and Martin and a Great Dane named Mr. Bascom drive (at one point, the dog takes the wheel) through a flawlessly pastoral American landscape, a Technicolor idyll that begins the moment they exit the George Washington Bridge. Verdant hills, healthy fields, tasteful farms, a flaming red Chrysler New Yorker convertible with no other cars on the road . . . The United States is perfect and they sing a happy song. A beautiful farmgirl dressed in calico poses and waves as they drive by. Another one pitches hay while wearing miniculottes. Milkmaids appear, pose, and wave. Women riding tractors, women posed on a split-rail fence, women perched all over a haywagon—all are smiling, waving, and posing, and all are dressed as extras in a road show *Oklahoma*. In other words, the idealism of this travesty landscape, ridiculous in its redundancy, is powerful enough to have generated twenty or thirty equally idealized women to act as human props.

Jerri's costumed body functions in a similarly schizophrenic fashion in that her exaggerated physique transmits two conflicting messages at the same time. On their way to Murdock's mansion in the Hamptons, for instance, Jerri insists that they stop and have a textbook picnic complete with real lemonade ("I didn't use any of that frozen stuff. I squeezed fresh lemons early this morning!"). Dressed in a flaming yellow sun outfit, Jerri enthusiastically declares, "We have lots of time. You get the basket, I'll undress!" She runs behind a spindly tree and pulls off her skirt—to reveal a matching swimsuit bottom. First the titillating declaration, next the ludicrous attempt at shielding the disrobing from the audience's gaze (making it all the more titillating), yet both the declaration and the pathetic censorship of the tree are disarmed and made pointless by the tasteful acceptability of the costume. In *Will Success Spoil Rock Hunter?*, too, Mansfield's character maintains an exaggerated sense of modesty, but since a preoccupation with sex underlies her prudishness, Mansfield's vision of propriety—a broad parody of fifties mores—is complete hypocrisy. Just as she automatically interprets the club owner's pleasant offer of assistance as a vulgar reference to her excretory needs, she unnecessarily calls attention to potential nudity despite its impossibility. Since her body is itself an affront to middlebrow good taste, to have Jayne Mansfield act bourgeois is a stroke of genius.

Politics and Rock 'n' Roll

What with all the sunshine and fresh-squeezed lemonade, Miller must fall in love with Jerri, but the specter of Murdock and his crime-ridden background hangs over their romance. At one point, Miller hears gunshots and immediately assumes that Murdock is shooting him; guilt and paranoia pervade. When they arrive at Murdock's, the host regales Miller with the story of how everyone got "blasted" in the living room in a terrible gangland shootout. "It's a kind of an educational kind of historical kind of place," Murdock says proudly. But it is critical to note, I think, that "Fats" Marty Murdock intimidates not only Jerri Jordan and Tom Miller; he will soon be intimidating the nation's music industry, since his underworld operations give him the alarming power he needs to take over the commercial side of rock 'n' roll. Later, in a scene that might well be read as an updated version of Tony Camonte's rise to power in Hawks's *Scarface* (1932), Murdock supervises the smashing of competitors' jukeboxes and the threatening of bar owners. Film historian Thomas Doherty calls this representation of record-industry corruption "cynical"; rock 'n' roll historian Charlie Gillett on the other hand calls it "realistic."[43] Here, though, he simply humiliates Jerri, who's just trying to make crepe suzettes. Murdock also terrifies Miller who, having heard Murdock's gruesome stories, now hesitates to pursue the romance.

As usual, Miller heads to a bar, and when "Cry Me a River" comes on the jukebox, one expects Julie London redux. This time, however, Jerri fades in—first on a neighboring bar stool, then behind the bar polishing a glass. When the two of them get together in a rehearsal hall (with Gene Vincent in another room singing "Be-Bop-a-Lula") to test Jerri's singing voice, their eventual union is sealed when it's discovered that Jerri's voice breaks light bulbs. Murdock becomes enraged when he hears Jerri triumphantly yell, "I do so stink! I'm telling you I *stink stink stink*!" But when he sees Eddie

Cochran on television singing "Twenty Flight Rock," he discovers that trained singing voices are not necessary for rock 'n' roll stardom and promptly laughs himself into a frenzy.

This, one suspects, is what led Ian Cameron to read *The Girl Can't Help It* as a film that "debunks rock," but the fact is that Murdock's observation is accurate in every way. Little Richard wasn't the only singer to fare best with a series of disconnected shouts and moans. Cochran's main talent was his sharp, rhythmic guitar work, but his vocals had a similar quality; as Gillett describes it, his performance style had a "punk edge," a "pose which captured the teenage bravado that James Dean had been going for in *East of Eden* and *Rebel Without a Cause*."[44] And it is worth mentioning that as Jerri and Miller watch Cochran on television, Jerri's African-American maid appears and, enjoying the music, begins to dance enthusiastically.

Perceiving that a whole new world of musical expression has opened, Murdock reveals that he is himself a songwriter. His song, "Rock Around the Rock Pile" (a parody of Bill Haley's 1955 hit, "Rock Around the Clock"), begins essentially as an awful vamp but transforms itself into a rock 'n' roll tune midway through by following the model of rhythm and blues and varying the melody in a minor key. It's an ideal song for Jerri, who needs only to shift momentarily from being a sexual siren to an aural one. At the recording studio, she sits at the microphone yawning until her part comes up; she shrieks on cue ("when I hear the siren blow / *shriek* / I get 'dose blues") then takes a stroll over to the Fruit-O-Matic to buy a "fresh" apple, which she eats for the rest of the session.

Following the lead of sociologist Edgar Z. Friedenberg, author of *Coming of Age in America*, a 1963 study of the nation's youth culture, critic Thomas Doherty distinguishes between "imperial" and "indigenous" approaches to teenagers in films of the era, particularly the teenpics that serve as the subject of his study. For Doherty, Tashlin is clearly an imperialist with disdain for the colonized teens whose disposable income he harvests through exploitation: Tashlin "displays something less than sensitivity to, respect for, or understanding of the teenage subcultural preference (rock 'n' roll music) that is, in tandem with Jayne Mansfield, one of the film's three main exploitation angles."[45] Doherty may be one of the only film critics ever to make a funny breast joke, but he still misses the mark. Unlike almost all the teenpics he analyzes in his appreciative study of the genre, this one's a comedy—a particularly broad comedy at that. Sensitivity to rock 'n' roll, to women, to men, or to any type of convention is not *this* type of comedy's goal. Doherty complains that some of the performers in *The Girl Can't Help It* (Ray Anthony, Abbey Lincoln, and Julie London) are not rock 'n' rollers and are therefore aimed more at adults than at teenagers, and he resents "Rock Around the Rock Pile" for being a parody of something that apparently shouldn't be parodied. Why rock 'n' roll ought to escape farce is unclear, especially in Frank Tashlin's overwhelmingly farcical world. In these films Tashlin doesn't directly promote or heroicize anything beyond the redemptive freedom afforded by comedy, particularly sex comedy. In some later films (1958's *The Geisha Boy* and *Say One for Me*, for instance), he does treat things straight—at great peril, for it turns out that the only thing he takes seriously is sentimentality. Here, however, Tashlin's interest is in mockery, though he plainly enjoys and upholds the raucous life-force that animates not only rock 'n' roll but his own brand of juvenile humor.

Doherty's discussion of imperial art is both validated and denied by the "Big Chief Running Water" sequence in *Hollywood or Bust*, wherein Jerry and Dino sing: "Get a load of Big Chief Running Water" (medium shot of befeathered Indian sitting under a downpour); "Dig his crazy teenage daughter" (long shot of nubile squaw wearing a sort of Hopi bikini, red high heels, and a lot of mid-fifties Max Factor while performing a lewd go-go dance against a pole); "Man she's the rockin' and a-rollin' best!" Here, Tashlin is literally imperial, viewing Native Americans from the silliest and most obvious of perspectives while seeing rock 'n' roll as a bizarre ritual/spectacle with unmistakably sexual goals.

But these are scarcely mirror-of-life representations. If there is such a thing as imperial comedy, it would seem to me that it would have to uphold the imperial world at the expense of the colonial—in other words, a laughing source pointing at a laughingstock. But Tashlin's comedy is more extensive and indiscriminate. He *likes* extremes. Big Chief Running Water isn't just a funny Indian; he's a parody, not simply of real human beings but also of an already ridiculous cultural convention which film westerns tend to take rather more seriously. The whole film, in fact, parodies Hollywood conventions as Jerry and Dean drive across the nation in a series of ludicrous Hollywood production numbers. In this regard, there is little difference in Tashlin's view between Big Chief Running Water and the white protagonists of the film, between colonial subject and imperial masters. I can't—and won't—speak for Native Americans about how they might view this image, but speaking strictly as an imperialist I must say that I don't find Jerry Lewis, Dean Martin, and Anita Ekberg (the Nordic ideal playing her starlet self, who serves as Lewis's parodic lust interest) to be especially vindicated as images of legitimate cultural supremacy. By the same token, neither are the ridiculous Hollywood musical numbers of *Hollywood or Bust*, nor are Julie London, Fats Murdock, and "adult" sensibilities in *The Girl Can't Help It*.

Working Through, on Tape and Film

Recording sound, manipulating it technologically, and constructing from it a finished product: just as the recording studio sequence provides a demonstration of how records are made, Murdock's sidekick, Mousie (Henry Jones), gives the audience a taste of wiretapping. Murdock has gotten him to tape Jerri's phone conversations with Miller, and as they sadly discuss the impossibility of their relationship, Mousie, with earphones, is moved to tears. When he presents Murdock with the tape and the tape turns out to have been drastically edited so as to remove all traces of love and affection from the conversation, the audience receives a graphic lesson in the art of falsifying history through technology—in other words, the process of filmmaking. It's as specific in its educational goals as it is successful in its comic ones, for Mousie's artifice makes possible the continuation of the relationship. In other words, the essential narrative convention of romantic comedy (namely, romance) continues only because of editing—a series of tailored lies.

The rest of *The Girl Can't Help It* counterposes crime with love as Jerri becomes a star (with a two-page spread in *Variety*) because of Fats's underworld power. Once again, a Tashlin plot resolution finds its way onto a stage as Jerri is scheduled to perform on the same bill with another "Fats"—Fats Domino—and the Platters, who sing "You'll Never, Never Know" as Jerri and Miller, backstage, follow the group's cue and bid each other farewell. When the time comes for Jerri to take center stage, she tells Miller that the song is dedicated to him and, revealing an ever greater degree of calculation, suddenly acquires the ability to sing a lyrical love tune called "It Happens Every Time." Outside, a gun battle is brewing between Fats and his rival, Wheeler, and Fats realizes that his only salvation is to take the stage, where he hammily sings and dances as policemen apprehend Wheeler. Jerri and Miller are backstage in a clinch as Murdock sings, but Tashlin then cuts to a shot of Murdock singing on a TV screen—which compared to the CinemaScope frame is downright minuscule—with Mousie on guitar beside him. He then dissolves to:

. . . yet another stage, the empty one seen in the first shot of the film. "Well, that's the story, ladies and gentlemen," says Tom Ewell. "A story about music." Jayne enters, followed by four brand new children, and adds her own comments: "A story about love, and marriage." Murdock enters, pushing a stroller with an infant inside: "And babysitters." "Sing for us, Uncle Fats!" says a child. "Sing, Uncle Fats!" says another child. "Aw, I dunno," Fats answers. "Ask my agent." "Let them buy your records," Tom Ewell tells his fictive friend.

This ending might have sufficed as far as qualified romantic resolutions are concerned. The central couple—Jayne Mansfield and Tom Ewell—is implausible enough, as is the sudden intrusion of an entire fictional family complete with an uncle/babysitter in the form of an underworld kingpin. All the players are standing on a theatrical stage—*not* the one incorporated into the action of the narrative but the detached and vacuous one that opened the credits sequence. Farce and theater abound, but Tashlin isn't satisfied. He has Tom

Ewell say "So long, everybody" and repeat the flicking gesture with which he expanded the image to CinemaScope width. The couple clinches as blackness intrudes from the sides of the frame.

It is still not quite enough. Fats Marty then steps through the black masking as if it were a curtain, and he runs grinning toward the camera as the blackness closes behind him. "Don't listen to him, folks," the gangster confides. "I'll see ya outside in the lobby when you leave. I sing anything you want. I'm a jim-dandy singer!" Music builds as Fats reaches up to catch a cigar that has been thrown to him—from the audience! He puffs and smirks before the final blackout.

The Living End: *Will Success Spoil Rock Hunter?*

How to Destroy a Broadway Hit

When Tashlin scrapped most of the characters and all of the plot, mood, and comedy style of George Axelrod's Broadway hit *Will Success Spoil Rock Hunter?*, he junked the play's ideological thrust as well. Almost a third of the film takes place before the action of the play begins, and after play and film finally, glancingly, meet on heroine Rita Marlowe's massage table, they immediately part company for good. Rock Hunter, the nebbish protagonist in the Tashlin version, is a minor film actor who in fact doesn't appear except in passing mention in Axelrod's play. Tashlin dispensed with Axelrod's playwright/screenwriter character, his agent character, his masseur character, his secretary character, and even his *central* character (George MacCauley, the hack who sells his soul to the devil in return for riches and fame, is barely a shadow of Tashlin's Rock). Tashlin kept only the Rita Marlowe character, but he transformed her into someone else entirely.

The play, for the most part, is a bitter satire of the film industry, with a powerful agent playing Mephistopheles to a one-time fanzine writer's Faust. Irving LaSalle, the cutely named agent (in his dedication, Axelrod dedicates 10 percent of the play to Irving "Swifty"

Lazar), demands increased percentages of MacCauley's earnings for favors like script deals and Oscars, and eventually he owns Mac-Cauley in toto. Only the last-minute and selfless intervention of the *real* writer Mike (who coincidentally takes the form of a New York–based playwright with a sour view of Hollywood) prevents MacCauley's descent into hell. The play ends with the following interchange between Mike, the playwright, and George, the hack:

Mike: Look, Georgie, we take a plane and we can be in New York tomorrow! In time for the snowstorm! The only thing I need is my clothes. [. . .] I don't need my clothes. The hell with my clothes. I don't need anything. I'm a writer, Georgie, a writer. If you want to be a writer you don't have to wish for it—you just sit down at the typewriter and do it. You know what I mean.

George: I guess so. Actually, the only thing I ever wrote was this one article. I called it "Will Success Spoil Rock Hunter?" Actually, it was quite well received for what it was.[46]

Accompanying Axelrod's insistent satire of the crassness and vulgarity of Hollywood writing and filmmaking is an affirmation of the heroic individual, Mike, who bucks the cynical commercialism and unending conformism seen as constituting the American cinema and returns to the realm of genuine worth, integrity, and talent—the New York theater district, of all places—where intellect and honesty thrive. Mike's heroism is such that he doesn't abandon the painfully mediocre George in the process, and George's moral triumph is his genuine affection for the superficial Rita. As for Rita, Axelrod first has her declare that she is "quitting pictures" to run away with George, but George then spends the last 10 percent of his soul/gross ("the only ten percent that really counts," says Irving) to prevent her from ruining her career, and she happily departs for the studio.[47] The resolution of the film version could hardly be more different.

Tashlin once bluntly admitted that he "tried to get out of using the play" but that "they [Twentieth Century-Fox] had to buy the play to get Mansfield." Tashlin wrote the script in thirteen days, and the film turned out to be his favorite picture.[48]

A Visit to Poodletown

There are a number of elements of *Rock Hunter's* overall design that seem to me to define not only the film's project but the analytical project of this study as well, and they revolve around representations of contemporary notions of success, sex, art, and culture. For clarity's sake, here's a brief summary of the film: Rockwell P. Hunter (Tony Randall), a minor ad copywriter, is desperate to find a gimmick for the Stay-Put Lipstick campaign because his firm may lose the account. When he discovers that his niece April has sneaked out of the house to greet famous film star Rita Marlowe (Jayne Mansfield) at the airport, he gets a brainstorm: sign Rita to endorse Stay-Put. Rita agrees, in return for a reciprocal promise from Rock to pretend to have an affair with her in order to make her ex-boyfriend jealous. As Rita's "Lover Doll," Rock becomes a worldwide celebrity. He is eventually made president of the company, but his real girlfriend Jenny (Betsy Drake) becomes justifiably jealous of Rita, and she breaks off their engagement. Rock realizes that material success is meaningless without self-respect and love, and he, Jenny, and April end up as happy chicken farmers in a fulfillment of Rock's lifelong dream.

Little is to be taken at face value in Tashlin's vision of the late 1950s, and yet everything's value is on its fabulous surface. Consider Rita's dog. Neither a pure metaphor nor a pure metonymy for Rita, Shamroy nonetheless maintains an informative and symbolic relationship with the star. Shamroy's platinum fur already matches Rita's hair, and Tashlin periodically dyes it to match Rita's outfit. When Rita wears blue, Shamroy wears blue. When Rita wears lavender, the dog follows suit. When Rita changes into a polka dot cape, the dog appears with polka dot fur. When Rita emerges from the bath in a towel, the dog reaches an unparalleled level of anthropomorphism by running after her with a towel draped discreetly around its shoulders.

The preciousness of its species, together with the fastidiousness of his or her costumes, makes this poodle a further elaboration of the false elegance and flaming theatricality of its owner. As the possession of a star, the dog is automatically granted luxuries unavailable to most of the film's spectators. Shamroy's lavish lifestyle, therefore, is a satirical focus of envy and entertainment, a ridiculous comment on Mansfield's own ridiculous comment on Hollywood stardom and its excesses. In other words, to borrow Woody Allen's timeless phrase, Shamroy is a travesty of a mockery of a sham.

When, in the flurry of publicity surrounding Rita's love affair with Rock, Shamroy finally reaches the point at which his or her picture appears in the newspaper with the fantastic caption, "Shamroy speaks—Rita's dog approves of Lover Doll," his success story hits its zenith. Fame, material success, an air of artifice and high fashion, the affections of a movie star, and above all national publicity: Shamroy is truly an ideal. But this dog wasn't alone. Shamroy's screen wardrobe provides a handy illustration of the distinction between an appalling cultural reality and the critical function of representation. In the late fifties, the *Saturday Evening Post* ran a story on a Park Avenue boutique for dogs called "Poodletown," which made a lucrative business selling canine bathrobes, raincoats, rain hats, gabardines, suede sport coats, smoking jackets, and "black lace collars and matching hostess aprons—the aprons for the poodles' mistresses." The story tells of how Elizabeth Taylor once pulled up at Poodletown's door in Mike Todd's Rolls Royce and, running amok inside, spent in excess of $600 on a "dazzling array of doggie accessories . . . from pajamas to the sapphire mink coat."[49] Whereas the *Post* story is exemplary of a purely imminent criticism embedded in the cultural fabric, Tashlin's representation of the same phenomenon takes criticism beyond the stage of preconscious imminence by throwing it into the bright DeLuxe Color light of open ridicule. It's not that Tashlin tosses this on screen to make a sour, distanced comment on America's doggie fetish. On the contrary. For Tashlin, to laugh at something is *to connect* with it.

Dirt

Given two of the central, flip-sided obsessions of America in the fifties—enforced domesticity and its simultaneous Freudian under-cutting—the era's sense of good and bad taste couldn't have found a more appropriate site of terror and laughter than the bathroom. On American movie screens, this rank but compelling interest in what goes on behind closed bathroom doors reached a real crisis in 1960 when, in *Psycho*, immediately before being stabbed to death in the shower, Marion Crane (Janet Leigh) throws scraps of paper into the toilet bowl and flushes it. Hitchcock records this action in a high-angle shot of the bowl that was revolutionary in its directness in 1960. Suddenly, after decades of toilet-trained Hollywood discretion, you could look right in there and see the contents swirling. This was extraordinary, as Hitchcock well knew. Norman Bates (Anthony Perkins), seen until that point (and slightly beyond) as a kind of boy-ish, typically maladjusted American male, cannot even bring himself to say the word "bathroom" earlier when he shows Marion her room.

Tashlin has a similar interest in the bathroom as a site of cultural anxiety, but rather than being the place where a psychopath's con-flicting feelings of desire and repulsion find their most violent expres-sion, Tashlin's bathroom is an idiot's paradise. He enjoys bathroom jokes. In *Rock Hunter* choirs of angelic voices rise in praise and ado-ration when Rock, having been promoted on the basis of his fake affair with Rita, receives a key to what is euphemistically called "the executive powder room," as if the all-male executive staff would be likely to powder its collective nose. In *The Girl Can't Help It*, too, Jerri's quest for stardom is given the code name "Operation Powder Room." Tashlin likes the euphemism for the sake of its own built-in failure; because of its dainty foolishness, the expression "powder room" calls attention to the very bodily functions it seeks to deny.

For Rock's first promotion, his friend Rufus (Henry Jones) acts as cheerleader for his initial trip to the gleaming, mirrored chamber (seen only partially through the doorway), grossly bleating "Go, boy, go!" For his second promotion, when Rock leapfrogs to become head of the entire company and is therefore privileged to have his own private bathroom, Tashlin cuts to a close-up of Rock's blissful face, almost in tears, as the angels sing in crescendo, "You've got it made, you've got it made, you've got it made!" Tashlin makes the acquisition of a private bathroom the pinnacle of Rock's achievement; there is nothing more for him to attain. A sublime (*read* sublimated) space, Rock's bathroom is idealized and therefore sacrosanct; Tashlin, unlike Hitchcock, was either unwilling or unable to show the insides. One harkens back to the Breen Office's finger-wagging advice to Charles Chaplin a decade earlier: "There should be no showing of, nor suggestion of, toilets in the bathroom."[50] Tashlin shows Rita in the bathtub covered modestly in bubbles (insofar as Rita/Jayne can do anything modestly), but he never allows the camera to venture inside Rock's private "powder room." In fact, in both of Rock's bathroom promotions, the bathroom door closes on the camera, which remains demurely in the hall. For Rock a private bathroom is the only safe, inviolable place left on earth.

In a world in which the bathroom is an idealized "powder room," language always harbors the potential to offend propriety by saying things it shouldn't. Thus, Rita is always on the lookout for double meanings and ugly connotations. She finds them in the following phrases and words: "going into seclusion," "incorporating," and "endorsement."

Implicitly seeing the lurid sexuality of her image as being beyond reproach by virtue of its self-evident artificiality, Rita is disconcerted by words left open to more damaging interpretations—readings that she herself supplies with little provocation. One odd aspect of her prurient linguistic interests is that the first of the so-called dirty words, "going into seclusion," is a temporary rejection of marriage and society while the second and third are specifically linked to the business world. Rock is at the side of the massage table telling her that his interest lies in "getting your endorsement," and Rita, shocked, responds with "Now don't go talking dirty!" But she is, at that moment, on the phone with her boyfriend, Bobo Branigansky (played by Jayne's real-life husband, muscleman Mickey Hargitay), while at the same time trying to get Rock to play the part of her new lover. She puts him on the phone with Bobo, and he discusses the structure of Rita's corporation: "Miss Marlowe is the titular head of the company," he says, and Rita squeals with delight. Dirt is acceptable and even desirable as long as its function is circumscribed by intentionality.

Rita is not the only character with an express interest in dirt. In a series of parody television commercials which serves as the film's credits sequence, a woman describes the impressive power of "Wow," the new detergent with "fallout, the exclusively patented ingredient." As she speaks, suds from "Wow" rise menacingly behind her and threaten to consume the kitchen. In the final commercial, a housewife looks directly at the camera and begins her discussion of a new washing machine with, "If you're like me and have six dirty children and a big filthy husband . . ." The machine is then so powerful and eager to clean the mess that America has made of itself that it pulls the woman in head first.

Tashlin's interest in the idea of cleanliness as a bourgeois fetish parallels that of his contemporary, Roland Barthes, whose *Mythologies* was published the same year *Rock Hunter* was released. Writing on "Soap Powders and Detergents," Barthes proposed a "contrast [between] the psycho-analysis of purifying fluids (chlorinated, for example) with that of soap-powders (Lux, Persil) or that of detergents (Omo)" and made the following observation: "Products based on chlorine and ammonia are without doubt the representatives of a kind of absolute fire, a saviour but a blind one. Powders, on the contrary, are selective, they push, they drive dirt through the texture of the object, their function is keeping public order not making war."[51]

Rita's linguistic censorship, like the euphemism "powder room" and the detergent "Wow," follows the second of the two models; always in need of keeping the essential structure of her ongoing performance intact but at the same time having to beware of encroaching impurities, Rita cleanses her speech to fit her pristine image no matter how contradictory the end result may be. As she announces to the press, "I have no romance. All my lovers and I are just friends."

Barthes also notes the luxury function of suds, and his comments apply equally well to Rita's and Shamroy's bubble bath: "To begin with, it appears to lack any usefulness. . . . Foam can even be the sign of a certain spirituality, inasmuch as the spirit has the reputation of being able to make something out of nothing, a large surface of effects out of a small volume of causes."[52] Rita happens to possess a certain body shape and appearance, and because of this she amasses a fortune; Shamroy belongs to a star, and because of this he amasses a fortune. In both cases, the effect vastly exceeds the cause and is, therefore, already a mark of success. To have these two excesses cleansing themselves in an excess of bubbles is, obviously, the height of fifties luxury.

Troubled: Love, Marriage, and Mental Cases

Clearly, people are under tremendous pressure in this world. Three characters (all women) have, had, or seek psychiatric treatment in *Rock Hunter*: the teenage daughter of Rock's friend Rufus; Vi, Rita's confidante/dresser (Joan Blondell); and Rita herself. Rufus describes his daughter as "a perfectly normal juvenile delinquent until she had a breakdown. Rock 'n' roll got to her. Now I take her to a psychiatrist." The violent intrusion of exciting, sex-driven music into Rufus's suburban home seems to have had its effect. Vi has been driven mad by unfulfilled desire, which she describes in conventional fifties fashion while pouring a tumbler full of whiskey with a shot glass of soda. And Rita admits that she too had wanted to enter psychoanalysis but that "in Hollywood they're so busy with producers you can't even get an appointment." A few scenes later, Rock inadvertently reveals what might be discussed on a Hollywood couch when he describes his extraordinary celebrity: "A Hollywood producer wants me to star in a remake of *Love Me Tender*—with me playing all the parts! Imagine me as Debra Paget!"

Vi at least cites a specific personal reason for psychiatric problems. Rufus's daughter and Rita, on the other hand, have more amorphous causes that have to do with crises involving financial and material success, not to mention the omnipresence and simultaneous absence of sex. The girl lives in a large and well-kept house and she drives her own sports car, while Rita lives in even grander surroundings and drives an even larger car. Yet something about these comfortable existences drives both characters into a psychiatrist's office. They simply can't take it any more. In all three cases, comedy is on the periphery as far as psychological insights are concerned. The need for psychotherapy, in contrast, is treated as an unimpeachable given in the modern world.

What about personal satisfaction through love and marriage? Two marriages occur in *Rock Hunter*. One is a complete charade, the other a farce.

For the first marriage, Rita spirits Rock away to Greenwich, Connecticut. On their way, Rita says with no small amount of irritation that she has "probably been snapped at more than any girl in history, except that communist queen—you know . . ." "Catherine the Great?" asks Rock. "She wasn't a communist. She was a czarina." "I don't care what was wrong with her," Rita responds. The point is that Rita is tired of being kissed on film, so much so that after a day at the studio all she can do is "watch my old movies on television." For Rita, love is tiring and irritating and exists only in the form of fiction; so, she pulls up at a Justice of the Peace and pretends to have a wedding. She has arranged for photographers to be present (they jump out of the bushes and storm the JP's house), and she theatrically faints (action seen only in the form of newspaper pictures of the event), thereby postponing the ceremony. In this way, both she and Rock capitalize on marriage as a social imperative while simultaneously dispensing with it as far as its assumed purpose is concerned.

The second marriage, or rather triple marriage, fulfills genre expectation and Hollywood narrative convention at the end of the film by uniting the hero with his true love, "nice Jenny Wells"; the heroine with her true love, George Schmidlapp (riotously played by Groucho Marx); and the secondary characters Vi and Rufus with each other. Mise-en-scène, including Groucho as a love object, is important to the scene, and so is editing: Tashlin introduces the newlyweds by cutting from Rita and George Schmidlapp kissing on a stage—with Schmidlapp wearing a neon sign endorsing Stay-Put

Lipstick on his back—to a flock of chickens. From the chickens Tash-lin cuts to Rock, Jenny, and April tossing chicken feed. This is how he defines marriage and the happiness of conventional endings in a demoralized age.

Double Vision

In addition to floating between pure satire and pure celebration, Tashlin's comedy also hovers in the space between two equally grat-ifying perceptions: first of a unity and then of its destruction. When Henri Bergson writes that laughter is a recognition of human mech-anism, I think that he is also implicitly referring to a double-sided, even two-headed awareness: the coincidence of social reaffirmation and a type of revolt, the need to stand up and the urge to fall down:

> We have seen that the more society improves, the more plastic is the adaptability it obtains from its members; while the greater the ten-dency towards increasing stability below, the more does it force to the surface the disturbing elements inseparable from so vast a bulk; and thus laughter performs a useful function by emphasising the form of these significant undulations.[53]

Likewise, when Freud writes about punning and joking, he claims that pleasure is a dramatic economy of thought—two different mean-ings understood simultaneously in the case of wordplay, and two dif-ferent and conflicting modes of thought in the case of certain jokes—reason and order countermanded by the liberating conceptual terror-ism of nonsense. Freud might as well have been referring directly to Shamroy or Bobo Branigansky when he wrote, "The technique of the nonsensical joke . . . consists, therefore, in presenting something that is stupid and nonsensical, the sense of which lies in the revelation and demonstration of something else that is stupid and nonsensical."[54] It should be clear even from this study not only that fifties comedies saw in double vision the continuation of Hollywood conventions as well as their active self-dissolution but that they appreciated the stupid and nonsensical as ends in themselves. Tashlin's films in particular are an endless chain of stupidity and pleasure designed to liberate, however momentarily, anyone with little enough self-control to laugh.

Tashlin's humor in particular fills the gap between an accepted reality and a shocking surreality, between an ideological ideal and its self-evident and pleasure-inducing collapse. Twentieth Century-Fox films generally begin with a now-famous fanfare that was musically extended in the early fifties to allow time for the CinemaScope logo to follow the Fox trademark. *Will Success Spoil Rock Hunter?* begins with Tony Randall, in the lower left of the screen, seated at a set of drums and instruments, playing all the parts of the expected music. This *immediate* joke—nothing appears on screen before it—calls attention to the artifice of the representation even before the representation has much of a chance to begin, and it does so by upholding the routine even as it breaks it down.

But it also suggests an intrusion of the commonplace into the world of fantasy. Like the great Oz behind the curtain, Randall's introduction smashes the fanfare's illusion of grandiosity and pretension by making an ordinary mortal, dwarfed ridiculously by the CinemaScope screen, responsible for an entire orchestra's worth of sound.

The invasion of the drab continues as Randall introduces himself as "Tony Randall," the star of "the delightful motion picture called" (he looks on a slip of paper for the answer) "*The Girl Can't Help It*— no, we made that!" He looks on another slip and reads "Gertrude, Crestview 5, 1–2 . . ." The film cannot begin because the star cannot remember what it's called; he can only find scraps of paper with the names of yesterday's movies and lovers written on them. Only the appearance of the three actresses in larger-than-life superimposition allows the story to begin: dressed in gowns and furs, they suddenly appear on the right side of the screen and scoldingly chant the title.

In the middle of the film, Tashlin abruptly dissolves from Rock's apartment to a netherworld defined solely by blue light. Intermission music comes on the soundtrack as Tony Randall appears. Addressing the camera, he graciously informs the audience that the intermission exists for the benefit of TV fans who are used to commercials; this will turn out to be, in fact, a commercial for the cinema. The image shrinks from CinemaScope size to television size, from color to black and white. Randall is now on TV; the image can accommodate only his head, which it quickly distorts. The image begins to flip vertically; "snow" appears, first as static, then as real (or rather surreal) snow. The image expands to full size as Randall gives his impersonation of a radio-dramatized version of *Rock Hunter.* "Jenny Wells loves Rocky Hunter. Rocky Hunter loves Jenny Wells. But naughty Rita Marlowe has come between nice Jenny Wells and . . ."

Structured as an intervention that disrupts the progress of the narrative for no other reason than to destroy any remaining illusion of reality, the "commercial break" sequence is as deliberate a satire on the illusion of Hollywood romance as it is an attack on television and radio. The final sequence of the film drives the point home. Dressed in a farmer's outfit complete with a corncob pipe and standing in front of a blue-sequined curtain, Tony Randall, flanked by Jayne Mansfield, Groucho Marx, Joan Blondell, Betsy Drake, Henry Jones, Lili Gentle, and John Williams, preaches the moral lesson of the film in which they have all just appeared, a satirically refracted homily that condenses the decade in a nutshell, with heavy emphasis on the nut: "We've learned that success is just the art of being happy, and being happy is just [the others join in] the living end!"

Like repressed desire in a decade of constricting social demands, a flower in the pot being held by John Williams begins to mutate wildly, the bloom growing taller and taller until it cannot be contained within the frame. Sensing what's really important in this world, the camera tilts up with the hyperactive flower, leaving the characters far below, cut out of the frame, their conventional happiness defying reason, their genre now denying propriety even so much as a place on the screen.

epilogue

THE BIG CARNIVAL

In Vincente Minnelli's *The Long, Long Trailer* (1954), mobile-home-maker Lucille Ball, overwrought with the wealth of scenery at her cross-country doorstep, begins to pick up souvenir boulders in a sentimental effort to insure her memory and guarantee the eternal presence of the past. Quickly, the once-efficient trailer becomes weighted down with solid rock. The driver, traveling salesman/husband Desi Arnaz, demands that she part with the boulders, and she grudgingly obliges. The trailer proceeds up a steep mountain. Near the top, at a cliff, calamity: the trailer ends up dangling off the edge, in part because Lucy has insisted on keeping just one final rock, her favorite rock, the rock that means the most to her.

Socrates, like Lucy, might have benefited from the same lesson. At the end of the *Symposium*, with most of the guests long past caring one way or the other, Socrates drives home the double point that the same person could write both comedy and tragedy, that the foundations of the two arts were essentially identical. But Socrates made just one point too many; his argument failed to move the assembly because by that time even his few remaining friends had fallen asleep.[1]

Lucy's trailer and Socrates' argument both suffered from overkill, excesses that Minnelli and Plato found funny but that produced in the victims—Desi and Aristophanes—a rather different response: anger in the former, slumber in the latter.

At the risk of inciting either fury or boredom, this is the final boulder, the last postulate. No matter how subtle or crude, comedy is by its nature excessive, and in its excess lies its most rebellious pleasure. Comedy saturates whatever it touches with a resonating, empowering sense of physical joy, the belly laughter of a carnival world. "A riot of semiosis," "a spasm of satire": as described by critic Terry Eagleton, comedy is an acute sensation of freedom: "Through this crude cackling of an ambivalently destructive and liberatory laughter emerges the shape of an equally negative and positive phenomenon: utopia."[2] No one doubts that the 1950s were a time of horrific oppression, of rigid personal codification and decisive political censorship embodied by, emanating from, and reflecting off the shiny bald head of President Eisenhower. But even in this period of crushing institutional control, the institutions couldn't crush laughter.

Watching and listening to fifties comedies has shown, if nothing else, that comedy is escapist in the best and most utopian sense of the word. Four different directors, with styles and attitudes that are often perceived in their dissimilarity, all produced comedies that singled out the sensitive issues of the day and made them uniformly ridiculous: pervasive sexual interdictions, the terrors implicit in scientific "progress," the desire to kill one's mate and therefore to be free, the female body and what it represents to patriarchy in protracted decline, the demoralizing hatred of the workplace, and all in the context of mankind's descent from monkeys, who seemed to be burdened with none of civilization's discontents. In the laughter of an imprisoned society was the dreamlike hope of unregulated pleasure, a possibility that often must have felt millions of years away.

Laughing at an oppressive world may seem an impotent gesture. A certain stone-faced moralism, the heritage of the work ethic, would demand constructive action to the exclusion of bodily hedonism and leisure-time fun. But breaking the world down in consciousness is still an act of intervention, a rebellion made all the more remarkable by its involuntary nature. Laughter physically opens up the individual to what the fifties in particular seemed to deny: a crude and vivid awareness of the body and the collective eroticism of social interchange.[3] From the skewed classicism of *Monkey Business* and *Gentlemen Prefer Blondes* through Billy Wilder's gallows humor and Alfred

Hitchcock's subversive morbidity to the shrill CinemaScopic fragmentation of *The Girl Can't Help It* and *Will Success Spoil Rock Hunter?*, film comedies of the 1950s turned a dismal reality into a communal wet dream, a most un-American activity.

Like fun house mirrors, Hollywood movies refract rather than reflect the world that produces them. Their visions of life are delightful distortions of a shifting and polymorphous reality: they hint at it, they play with it, they deny it, and by investing in their audiences this multivocal rendering of human experience, they change it. Films are themselves a type of play, a kind of comedy. The only way to argue against their testimony is to say that they aren't funny, a position so restrictively subjective, so dogmatically personal, as to be amusingly, even hysterically, irrelevant.

notes

Preface

1. Andrew Sarris, *The American Cinema*, p. 55.
2. Sigmund Freud, *Jokes and Their Relation to the Unconscious*, p. 105.

Introduction: Hearing the Laughter

1. Freud, *Jokes and Their Relation to the Unconscious*, p. 90.
2. Alan Stern of the *Boston Phoenix*, quoted in Andrew Sarris, "A Few Kind Words for the Fifties," *Village Voice*, September 14, 1982, p. 47.
3. Advertisement for *The Robe*, *New York Times*, September 14, 1953, p. B4.
4. Nora Sayre, *Running Time*, pp. 140–41.
5. Jerry Lewis, *Jerry Lewis in Person*, p. 196.
6. Ian Cameron, "Frank Tashlin and the New World," p. 65.
7. Martin Mayer, "Television's Lords of Creation," p. 25.
8. Peter Biskind, *Seeing Is Believing*, pp. 262, 340.
9. Douglas T. Miller and Marion Nowak, *The Fifties*, p. 6.
10. John Brooks, *The Great Leap*, p. 141.
11. Richard Hughes and Robert Brewin, *The Tranquilizing of America*, pp. 26–27, 57–81, 175–80.
12. Austin Wehrwein, *New York Times*, August 7, 1959, quoted in Miller and Nowak, *The Fifties*, p. 138.
13. Miller and Nowak, *The Fifties*, p. 138.
14. Miller and Nowak, *The Fifties*, p. 127.
15. Reuel Denney, "Reactors of the Imagination," *Bulletin of the Atomic Scientists* 9 (July 1953), no. 6: 206.
16. Paul S. Boyer, *By the Bomb's Early Light*, pp. 334, 339.
17. Michael Amrine, "What the Atomic Age Has Done to Us," *New York Times Magazine*, August 6, 1950, p. 26.
18. Boyer, *By the Bomb's Early Light*, p. 276, quoting Joseph Barth, *The Art of Staying Sane* (Boston, 1948), pp. 184–85.
19. Boyer, *By the Bomb's Early Light*, pp. 280–81, 340–41, quoting Dorothy Thompson, "Atomic Science and World Organization," *Ladies' Home Journal* (October 1945), p. 128, and Charles Wolfe, "Nuclear Country: The Atomic

Bomb in Country Music," *Journal of Country Music* 7 (January 1978): 18.

20. Mrs. L. F. Van Hagen, "Life in These United States" entry, *Reader's Digest* (October 1952), p. 52.

21. Hal Block, "Hal Block's Inventions for a Better Tomorrow," *Saturday Evening Post* (January 11, 1958), p. 48.

22. John Kobler, "Gangway for the Atomic Garbageman!" *Saturday Evening Post* (January 25, 1958), pp. 36, 73.

23. "Crazy," *Oxford English Dictionary*, 1961 edition.

24. Eric Partridge, *A Dictionary of Slang*; Harold Wentworth and Stuart Berg Flexner, *A Dictionary of American Slang*; and *A Supplement to the Oxford English Dictionary*, 1972 edition.

25. Miller and Nowak, *The Fifties*, p. 35.

26. Charlie Gillett, *The Sound of the City*, p. 3.

27. Gillett, *The Sound of the City*, pp. 1–118.

28. David Reisman, "Listening to Popular Music," *American Quarterly* 2 (Winter 1950): 359–71.

29. Ann Charters, *Kerouac*, p. 133.

30. Jack Kerouac, *On the Road*, p. 42.

31. Herbert Marcuse, *Eros and Civilization*, p. 37.

32. Marcuse, *Eros and Civilization*, p. 39 (emphasis in original), quoting Ernest Schachtel, "On Memory and Childhood Amnesia," in Patrick Mullahy, ed., *A Study of Interpersonal Relations* (New York: Hermitage Press, 1950), p. 24.

33. Gillett, *The Sound of the City,* p. 58.

34. Ralph M. Newman, "Screamin' Jay Hawkins," *Bim Bam Boom* 2 (September 1972): 35.

35. Victor Navasky, *Naming Names*, p. 345.

36. Navasky, *Naming Names*, p. 350.

37. Larry Ceplair and Steven Englund, *The Inquisition in Hollywood*, p. xiii.

38. Stephen J. Whitfield, *The Culture of the Cold War*, p. 10.

39. J. Laplanche and J.-B. Pontalis, *The Language of Psychoanalysis*, p. 195; Pierre Janet, *The Mental State of Hystericals*, 486–88.

40. Laplanche and Pontalis, *The Language of Psychoanalysis*, p. 194.

41. Krin Gabbard and Glen O. Gabbard, *Psychiatry and the Cinema*, pp. 81–114.

42. Janet Walker, "Hollywood, Freud, and the Representation of Women," p. 142.

43. Sigmund Freud, "'Civilized' Sexual Morality and Modern Nervousness," p. 29.

44. Sayre, *Running Time*, p. 101.

45. Phillip Rieff, *The Triumph of the Therapeutic*, pp. 54–58.

46. Frank S. Nugent, "All About Joe," *Collier's* (March 24, 1951), p. 68.

47. Laurie Henshaw, *Melody Maker* (England), February 4, 1952, quoted in Gillett, *The Sound of the City*, pp. 6–7.

48. Molly Haskell, *From Reverence to Rape*, p. 56.

49. Stefan Kanfer, *A Journal of the Plague Years*, p. 82.

50. Ezra Goodman, *The Fifty-year Decline and Fall of Hollywood*, p. 425.

51. *Film Daily Yearbook* (1960), p. 103.

52. Paul Clark, former State Department Office of Security, employee, in Greta Schiller's documentary film *Before Stonewall* (1985); "List of Security Separations." *New York Times*, January 4, 1955, p. 14; Miller and Nowak, *The Fifties*, pp. 401–18; Biskind, *Seeing is Believing*, p. 328.

53. Freud, *Jokes and Their Relation to the Unconscious*, pp. 16–17.

54. Freud, *Jokes and Their Relation to the Unconscious*, p. 101.

55. Freud, *Jokes and Their Relation to the Unconscious*, p. 103 (emphasis in original).

56. Jane and Michael Stern, *The Encyclopedia of Bad Taste*, pp. 58–59.

57. Unnamed critic quoted in Richard M. Langworth, ed., *1957 Cars*, p. 42.

58. Quoted in Marjorie Garber, *Vested Interests*, p. 233.

59. Tashlin, quoted in Peter Bogdanovich, "Frank Tashlin: An Interview and an Appreciation," p. 57.

60. Laplanche and Pontalis, *The Language of Psychoanalysis*, p. 124.

61. Philip Wylie, quoted in Michael Rogin, *Ronald Reagan, the Movie*, p. 242.

62. Rogin, *Ronald Reagan, the Movie*, p. 236.

63. Rogin, *Ronald Reagan, the Movie*, p. 240.

64. Marcuse, *Eros and Civilization*, p. 19.

1. Howard Hawks and the Comedy of Frustration

1. Eric Barnouw, *Tube of Plenty*, pp. 145–48.

2. Barnouw, *Tube of Plenty*, p. 148.

3. Thomas M. Pryor, *New York Times*, November 11, 1949, p. 31.

4. Robin Wood, *Howard Hawks*, pp. 176–77.

5. Wood, *Howard Hawks*, p. 177.

6. Wood, *Howard Hawks*, p. 83; John Belton, *Cinema Stylists*, p. 269.

7. Sarris, *The American Cinema*, p. 55.

8. Jacques Becker, Jacques Rivette, and François Truffaut. "Entretien avec Howard Hawks," *Cahiers du Cinéma* 56 (February 1956): 9.

9. Peter Wollen, *Signs and Meaning in the Cinema*, pp. 85–86.

10. Raymond Durgnat, *The Crazy Mirror*, p. 214.

11. Durgnat, *The Crazy Mirror*, p. 224.

12. Wood, *Howard Hawks*, p. 81.

13. Wood, *Howard Hawks*, p. 79–80.

14. Gerald Mast, *Howard Hawks, Storyteller*, pp. 166, 161.

15. Mast, *Howard Hawks, Storyteller*, p. 161. Mast cites the script of *Monkey Business* (titled "Darling I Am Growing Younger"), in the collection of the Papers of Howard W. Hawks, the Harold B. Lee Library of Brigham Young University (Box 7, Folders 6 and 7).

16. Leland Poague, *Howard Hawks*, p. 80.

17. Belton, *Cinema Stylists*, p. 275.

18. Richard Dyer, *Stars*, p. 36.

19. Freud, *Jokes and Their Relation to the Unconscious*, p. 236.

20. Freud, *Jokes and Their Relation to the Unconscious*, p. 236.

21. Peter Bogdanovich, *The Cinema of Howard Hawks*, p. 32.

22. Wood, *Howard Hawks*, p. 171.

23. Maureen Turim, "Gentlemen Consume Blondes," *Wide Angle* 1 (1979): 56.

24. Bosley Crowther, review of *Las Vegas Story*, *New York Times*, January 31, 1952, p. 37; review of *Son of Paleface*, *New York Times*, October 2, 1952, p. 32; review of *Gentlemen Prefer Blondes*, *New York Times*, July 16, 1953, p. 17.

25. Pauline Kael, *5001 Nights at the Movies*, p. 441; Biskind, *Seeing Is Believing*, p. 293.

26. Haskell, *From Reverence to Rape*, p. 105.

27. Turim, "Gentlemen Consume Blondes," pp. 56–57.

28. Lucie Arbuthnot and Gail Seneca, "Pre-Text and Text in *Gentlemen Prefer Blondes*," *Film Reader* 5 (1982): 17–21.

29. See P. Cook and Claire Johnston, "The Place of Women in the Cinema of Raoul Walsh"; and Maureen Turim, "Designing Woman: The Emergence of the New Sweetheart Line," *Wide Angle* 6 (1984): 4–11.

30. Jonathan Rosenbaum, "Gold Diggers of 1953," *Sight and Sound* 5 (Winter 1984/85): 45.

31. Rosenbaum, "Gold Diggers of 1953," p. 45.

32. Gaylyn Studlar, *In the Realm of Pleasure*, p. 15.

33. Studlar, *In the Realm of Pleasure*, p. 18.

34. Studlar, *In the Realm of Pleasure*, pp. 29–30.

35. David Chierichetti, *Hollywood Costume Design*, pp. 125–28.

36. Studlar, *In the Realm of Pleasure*, p. 18.

37. Jane Russell, *Jane Russell: An Autobiography*, p. 58.

38. Arbuthnot and Seneca, "Pre-Text and Text in *Gentlemen Prefer Blondes*," pp. 17–18.

39. Freud, *Jokes and Their Relation to the Unconscious*, pp. 16–27.

40. Anita Loos, *Gentlemen Prefer Blondes/But Gentlemen Marry Brunettes*, pp. 59–60.

41. Wood, *Howard Hawks*, p. 171.

42. Andrew Sarris, "The World of Howard Hawks," p. 60.

43. Mast, *Howard Hawks, Storyteller*, pp. 357–58.

44. Russell, *Jane Russell*, pp. 138–39.

2. Billy Wilder and the American Dream

1. James Agee, *Agee on Film*, p. 415.

2. Brog., review of *Sunset Boulevard*, *Variety*, April 19, 1950, p. 8.

3. Durgnat, *The Crazy Mirror*, p. 215.

4. Milan Kundera, *The Book of Laughter and Forgetting*, pp. 61–62.

5. "Urge Fed License of Film People as Public Morals Aid," *Variety*, March 15,

1950, pp. 1, 63; "Senator Johnson Expected to Modify Certain Facets of Anti-Film Measure," *Variety*, March 22, 1950, p. 4.

6. "Showmanship Selling Seen Requiring More Personnel," *Hollywood Reporter*, March 13, 1950, p. 4.

7. Ronald Reagan, quoted in the *New York Times*, October 30, 1949, sec. 2, p. 4.

8. "Stars' Personals with Own Pix Pay Off Big in the Hinterlands on Publicity," *Variety*, October 11, 1950, pp. 7, 53.

9. "Stars' Personals Pay Off Big," *Variety*, October 11, 1950, pp. 7, 53.

10. "For Whom Are We Making Pictures?" *Variety*, September 27, 1950, p. 3; "Stars' Personals Pay Off Big," *Variety*, October 11, 1950, pp. 7, 53; "'Sunset' Looks to Music Hall Record," *Variety*, September 13, 1950, p. 7.

11. "1929 Swanson Fiasco Is Finally Reviewed as a Museum Piece," *Variety*, July 26, 1950, p. 119.

12. Wood, *Howard Hawks*; Richard Corliss, *Talking Pictures*, pp. 147—48; Peter Wollen, lecture at Columbia University, New York, 1980.

13. Kundera, *The Book of Laughter and Forgetting*, p. 61.

14. Neil Sinyard and Adrian Turner, *Journey Down Sunset Boulevard*, p. 277.

15. Sigmund Freud, "Humor," p. 265.

16. Studlar, *In the Realm of Pleasure*, p. 16, quoting Theodor Reik, *Masochism in Modern Man*, p. 23.

17. Maurice Zolotow, *Billy Wilder in Hollywood*, p. 29.

18. Freud, "Humor," p. 265.

19. Gloria Swanson, *Swanson on Swanson*, pp. 260, 483.

20. Agee, *Agee on Film*, p. 412.

21. Haskell, *From Reverence to Rape*, pp. 246–47.

22. Agee, *Agee on Film*, p. 413.

23. Northrop Frye, *Anatomy of Criticism*, pp. 163–86.

24. Billy Wilder and I.A.L. Diamond. "Dialogue on Film," *American Film*, p. 47.

25. Zolotow, *Billy Wilder in Hollywood*, p. 165.

26. Zolotow, *Billy Wilder in Hollywood*, p. 165.

27. Vladimir Nabokov, *Laughter in the Dark*, p. 292.

28. Frye, *Anatomy of Criticism*, p. 164.

29. Sinyard and Turner, *Journey Down Sunset Boulevard*, p. 140.

30. Garber, *Vested Interests*, p. 16.

31. Richard Plant, *The Pink Triangle*, pp. 148–49, 154, and 113.

32. Whitfield, *The Culture of the Cold War*, p. 43.

33. John D'Emilio, "The Homosexual Menace: The Politics of Sexuality in Cold War America," in D'Emilio, *Making Trouble*, p. 57.

34. Jonathan Ned Katz, *The Gay/Lesbian Almanac*, p. 652 (Katz cites *Newsweek*, October 10, 1949, pp. 52–54).

35. Vito Russo, *The Celluloid Closet*, p. 107.

36. Russo, *The Celluloid Closet*, p. 107.

37. D'Emilio, *Making Trouble*, p. 61.

38. Robert Mundy, "Wilder Reappraised," *Cinema* (October 1969): 19–24 (London)

39. D'Emilio, *Making Trouble*, p. 60.

40. William Paul, *Ernst Lubitsch's American Comedy*, p. 228, quoting Lubitsch in the *New York Times*, March 29, 1942.

41. Oscar Wilde, *The Picture of Dorian Gray*, pp. 234 (ch. 20), 109 (ch. 8), and 105 (ch. 7).

42. Steve Seidman, *The Film Career of Billy Wilder*, p. 36.

43. Axel Madsen, *Billy Wilder*, p. 118.

44. Sinyard and Turner, *Journey Down Sunset Boulevard*, p. 215.

45. Judith Crist, *The Private Eye, the Cowboy, and the Very Naked Girl*, pp. 96–97, quoted in Rebecca Louise Bell-Metereau, *Hollywood Androgeny*, p. 24.

46. Bell-Metereau, *Hollywood Androgeny*, p. 24.

47. Roland Barthes, "Introduction" to *Tricks: A Novel* by Renaud Camus, trans. Richard Howard, p. vii.

48. Brandon French, *On the Verge of Revolt*, p. 152.

49. Bell-Metereau, *Hollywood Androgeny*, p. 56.

50. Bernard F. Dick, *Billy Wilder*, p. 91.

51. Haskell, *From Reverence to Rape*, p. 257.

52. Billy Wilder and I.A.L. Diamond, "Dialogue on Film." *American Film* 1 (July–August 1976): 43.

53. Bell-Metereau, *Hollywood Androgeny*, p. 58.

54. French, *On the Verge of Revolt*, p. 138.

55. Haskell, *From Reverence to Rape*, p. 257.

56. Corliss, *Talking Pictures*, p. 154; Sinyard and Turner, *Journey Down Sunset Boulevard*, p. 222; Dick, *Billy Wilder*, p. 90.

57. Sinyard and Turner, *Journey Down Sunset Boulevard*, p. 225.

58. Dick, *Billy Wilder*, p. 90.

59. Corliss, *Talking Pictures*, p. 153.

60. Garber, *Vested Interests*, p. 7.

61. French, *On the Verge of Revolt*, p. 152.

3. Unrest in Peace: Hitchcock's Fifties Humor

1. Chaplin, Charles. *My Autobiography*, pp. 437–45.

2. Marcuse, *Eros and Civilization*, p. 22.

3. *Variety*, October 1955 through February 1956 and passim.

4. Addams, *Homebodies*, pp. 80 and 7.

5. Charles Baudelaire, "Caricaturists," in Baudelaire, *The Mirror of Art*, p. 154.

6. E. H. Gombrich, *Art and Illusion*, p. 204.

7. See John Belton, *Cinema Stylists*; Laura Mulvey, "Visual Pleasure and Narrative Cinema"; William Rothman, *Hitchcock: The Murderous Gaze*; and Peter Wollen, *Readings and Writings*.

8. E. H. Gombrich, "The Wit of Saul Steinberg," pp. 377–80.

9. John Michael Hayes, *The Trouble with Harry* (first draft, July 27, 1954), p. 24.

10. Hayes, *The Trouble with Harry* (shooting script, September 14, 1954), p. 4.

11. *The New Scofield Reference Bible*, pp. 244–45.

12. Eric Rohmer and Claude Chabrol, *Hitchcock*, p. 137.

13. François Truffaut, *Hitchcock*, p. 169.

14. J. Trevor Story, *The Trouble with Harry*, p. 12.

15. Story, *The Trouble with Harry*, p. 104.

16. Stephen Heath, *Questions of Cinema*, p. 21.

17. A. C. Spectorsky, *The Exurbanites*, pp. 7, 12.

18. Slavoj Zizek, "Hitchcock," trans. Richard Miller. *October* 38 (Fall 1986): 99–100.

19. Hayes, *The Trouble with Harry* (first draft), pp. 151–53.

20. Truffaut, *Hitchcock*, pp. 89, 149.

4. Living Looney Tunes: The Art of Frank Tashlin

1. Gore Vidal, "Immortal Bird," *New York Review of Books*, June 13, 1985, p. 8.

2. Turim, "Gentlemen Consume Blondes," *Wide Angle* 1 (1979): 52.

3. Lewis, *Jerry Lewis in Person*, p. 224.

4. Jerry Lewis, quoted in Scott Bukatman, "Paralysis in Motion: Jerry Lewis's Life as a Man," p. 190.

5. Whitfield, *The Culture of the Cold War*, p. 43.

6. Kenneth Lewes, *The Psychoanalytic Theory of Male Homosexuality*, pp. 140–83.

7. Jonathan Ned Katz, *Gay American History*, pp. 278–27, quoting Karl M. Bowman and Bernice Engle, "The Problem of Homosexuality," *Journal of Social Hygiene* 39 (1953), no. 1: 10–11.

8. Bukatman, "Paralysis in Motion," p. 193.

9. Jean-Louis Comolli, "Chacun son soi," *Cahiers du Cinéma* 197 (Christmas 1967–January 1968): 51–54; Robert Benayoun, *Bonjour, Monsieur Lewis* and Benayoun, "Simple Simon; ou L'anti-James Dean," *Positif* 29 (1958): 18–22; and Robert Benayoun and André S. Labarthe, "En Robert quête d'auteur: Jerry Lewis." *Cahiers du Cinema* 197 (Christmas 1967–January 1968): 27–45.

10. Jerry Lewis, "Dialogue on Film," *American Film* 2 (September 1977): 33–48.

11. Jules Janet, quoted in Pierre Janet, *The Mental State of Hystericals*, p. 495.

12. Janet, *The Mental State of Hystericals*, pp. 495–96.

13. Johnston and Willamen, eds., *Frank Tashlin*, p. 6.

14. Howard Teichmann and George S. Kaufman, *The Solid Gold Cadillac*, p. 3.

15. Heath, quoted in Johnston and Willamen, eds., *Frank Tashlin*, p. 6.

16. Barnouw, *Tube of Plenty*, p. 148.

17. Robert Mundy, "Frank Tashlin: A Tribute," p. 13.

18. Robert Warshow, *The Immediate Experience*, p. 84.

19. Peter Bogdanovich, *Pieces of Time*, p. 72.

20. Janet, *The Mental State of Hystericals*, p. 491.
21. Whitfield, *The Culture of the Cold War*, p. 33, quoting Bragdon and McCutchen's *History of a Free People* (1954).
22. Johnston and Willamen, eds., *Frank Tashlin*, p. 15.
23. Norman Vincent Peale, *The Power of Positive Thinking*, p. 77.
24. Jane Feuer, *The Hollywood Musical*, p. 35.
25. Durgnat, *The Crazy Mirror*, p. 233.
26. Bogdanovich, "Frank Tashlin: An Interview and an Appreciation," p. 59.
27. Ian Cameron, "Frank Tashlin and the New World," in Johnston and Willamen, eds., *Frank Tashlin*, p. 86.
28. Gillett, *The Sound of the City*, pp. 206–207.
29. Claire Johnston, Paul Willamen, and P. Hardy, "Introduction," *Edinburgh Magazine* (1976), p. 3.
30. Walter Benjamin, *Illuminations*, p. 242.
31. "'Janie, Make with the Lungs': Sexsational RKO Cheesecake Dunk," *Variety*, January 11, 1955, pp. 1, 65; Earl Wilson, *The Show Business Nobody Knows*, p. 209; see also Martha Saxton, *Jayne Mansfield and the American Fifties*.
32. Gillett, *The Sound of the City*, p. 17.
33. Mulvey, "Visual Pleasure and Narrative Cinema," p. 214.
34. Studlar, *In the Realm of Pleasure*, pp. 178–79, quoting Lewin, "Sleep, the Mouth, and the Dream Screen," pp. 420–21.
35. Studlar, *In the Realm of Pleasure*, p. 178.
36. Studlar, *In the Realm of Pleasure*, p. 192.
37. André Breton. *What Is Surrealism?*, p. 415.
38. Breton, *What Is Surrealism?*, p. 416.
39. Johnston and Willamen, eds., *Frank Tashlin*, p. 17.
40. Jean Arp, "Abstract Art, Concrete Art," p. 391.
41. Gillett, *The Sound of the City*, p. 86.
42. Julia Rubiner, ed., *Contemporary Musicians* 9:148.
43. Thomas Doherty, *Teenagers and Teenpics*, p. 95; Gillett, *The Sound of the City*, p. 206.
44. Gillett, *The Sound of the City*, pp. 313 and 101.
45. Doherty, *Teenagers and Teenpics*, p. 94.
46. George Axelrod, *Will Success Spoil Rock Hunter?*, p. 73.
47. Axelrod, *Will Success Spoil Rock Hunter?*, pp. 69–70.
48. Bogdanovich, "Frank Tashlin," p. 57.
49. Henry Lacossit, "What a Way to Treat a Dog!" *Saturday Evening Post* (January 4, 1958), pp. 26–27.
50. Chaplin, *My Autobiography*, p. 445.
51. Roland Barthes, *Mythologies*, p. 36.
52. Barthes, *Mythologies*, p. 37.
53. Henri Bergson, "Laughter," p. 189.

54. Freud, *Jokes and Their Relation to the Unconscious*, p. 58.

Epilogue: The Big Carnival

1. Percy Bysshe Shelley, "The Banquet of Plato," pp. 219–20.
2. Terry Eagleton, *Walter Benjamin; or, Towards a Revolutionary Criticism*, p. 145.
3. Eagleton, *Walter Benjamin*, p. 150.

bibliography

Addams, Charles. *Homebodies*. New York: Simon and Schuster, 1954.

Agee, James. Review of *Sunset Boulevard* in *Sight and Sound* (November 1950). Reprinted in *Agee on Film*. New York: McDowell and Obolensky, 1958.

Amrine, Michael. "What the Atomic Age Has Done to Us." *New York Times Magazine*, August 6, 1950, p. 26.

Arbuthnot, Lucie, and Gail Seneca. "Pre-Text and Text in *Gentlemen Prefer Blondes*." *Film Reader* 5 (1982): 17–21.

Arp, Jean. "Abstract Art, Concrete Art." Reprinted in Herschel B. Chipp, ed., *Theories of Modern Art*. Berkeley: University of California Press, 1968.

Axelrod, George. *The Seven Year Itch*. Original typescript on file (Restricted Material #279) at the New York Public Library, Library for the Performing Arts.

——. *Will Success Spoil Rock Hunter?* New York: Samuel French, 1957.

Barnouw, Eric. *A History of Broadcasting in the United States*. 3 vols. New York: Oxford University Press, 1966–1970.

——. *Tube of Plenty*. New York: Oxford University Press, 1982.

Barr, Charles. "CinemaScope: Before and After." *Film Quarterly* 16 (Summer 1963), no. 5: 4–24.

Barthes, Roland. "Introduction." *Tricks: A Novel* by Renaud Camus. Translated by Richard Howard. New York: St. Martin's, 1981.

——. *Mythologies*. Translated by Annette Lavers. New York: Hill and Wang, 1981.

Baudelaire, Charles. *The Mirror of Art: Critical Studies by Baudelaire*. Translated and edited by Jonathan Mayne. London: Phaidon, 1955.

Becker, Jacques, Jacques Rivette, and François Truffaut. "Entretien avec Howard Hawks." *Cahiers du Cinéma* 56 (February 1956): 4–17, 49–53.

Bell-Metereau, Rebecca Louise. *Hollywood Androgeny*. New York: Columbia University Press, 1985.

Belton, John. *Cinema Stylists*. Metuchen, N.J.: Scarecrow Press, 1983.

Benayoun, Robert. *Bonjour, Monsieur Lewis*. Paris, 1972.

——. "Simple Simon; ou, L'anti-James Dean." *Positif* 29 (1958): 18–22.

Benayoun, Robert, and André S. Labarthe. "En Robert quête d'auteur: Jerry Lewis." *Cahiers du Cinéma* 197 (Christmas 1967–January 1968): 27–45.

Benjamin, Walter. *Illuminations*. Edited and introduced by Hannah Arendt. Translated by Harry Zohn. New York: Schocken, 1969.

Bergson, Henri. "Laughter." In Bergson, *Comedy*. Introduction and appendix by Wylie Sypher. Garden City, N.Y.: Doubleday Anchor, 1956.

Bevan, Donald, and Edmund Trzcinski. *Stalag 17*. Original 1951 typescript on file at the New York Public Library, Library for the Performing Arts.

Biskind, Peter. *Seeing Is Believing: How Hollywood Taught Us to Stop Worrying and Love the Fifties*. New York: Pantheon, 1983.

Block, Hal. "Hal Block's Inventions for a Better Tomorrow." *Saturday Evening Post* (January 11, 1958), p. 48.

Bogdanovich, Peter. *The Cinema of Howard Hawks*. New York: Film Library of the Museum of Modern Art, 1962.

——. "Frank Tashlin: An Interview and an Appreciation." In Johnston and Willamen, eds., *Frank Tashlin*. Edinburgh: Edinburgh Film Festival, 1973.

——. *Pieces of Time*. New York: Dell, 1974.

Boyer, Paul S. *By the Bomb's Early Light: American Thought and Culture at the Dawn of the Atomic Age*. New York: Pantheon, 1985.

Breton, André. *What Is Surrealism?* Translated by David Gascoyne. London: Faber and Faber, 1936. Reprinted in Herschel B. Chipp. *Theories of Modern Art*. Berkeley: University of California Press, 1968.

Brion, Patrick. "Biofilmographie de Jerry Lewis." *Cahiers du Cinéma* 197 (Christmas 1967–January 1968): 65–69.

Brog. Review of *Sunset Boulevard*, *Variety*, April 19, 1950, p. 8.

Brooks, John. *The Great Leap*. New York: Harper and Row, 1968.

Bukatman, Scott. "Paralysis in Motion: Jerry Lewis's Life as a Man." In Andrew S. Horton, ed., *Comedy/Cinema/Theory*, pp. 188–205. Berkeley: University of California Press, 1991.

Buscombe, Edward. "The Idea of Genre in the American Cinema." *Screen* 11 (March–April 1970), no. 2: 33–45.

Byars, Jackie. *All That Hollywood Allows: Re-Reading Gender in 1950s Melodrama*. Chapel Hill: University of North Carolina Press, 1991.

Cameron, Ian. "Frank Tashlin and the New World." In Johnston and Willamen, eds., *Frank Tashlin*. Edinburgh: Edinburgh Film Festival, 1973.

Cavell, Stanley. *Pursuits of Happiness: The Hollywood Comedy of Remarriage.* Cambridge: Harvard University Press, 1981.

Ceplair, Larry, and Steven Englund. *The Inquisition in Hollywood.* Berkeley: University of California Press, 1983.

Chaplin, Charles. *My Autobiography.* New York: Simon and Schuster, 1964.

Charters, Ann. *Kerouac: A Biography.* San Francisco: Straight Arrow, 1973.

Chierichetti, David. *Hollywood Costume Design.* New York: Harmony Books, 1976.

Comolli, Jean-Louis. "Chacun son soi." *Cahiers du Cinéma* 197 (Christmas 1967–January 1968): 51–54.

Comolli, Jean-Louis, Jean Narboni, and Bertrand Tavernier. "Entretien avec Howard Hawks." *Cahiers du Cinéma* 192 (July–August 1967): 14–21, 67–68.

Cook, P., and Claire Johnston. "The Place of Women in the Cinema of Raoul Walsh." In P. Hardy, ed., *Raoul Walsh.* Edinburgh: Edinburgh Film Festival, 1974.

Corliss, Richard. *Talking Pictures.* New York: Penguin, 1975.

"Crazy." *Oxford English Dictionary* (1961 edition).

Cremonini, Giorgio. "Jerry Lewis." *Il Castoro Cinema* (December 1979).

Crist, Judith. *The Private Eye, the Cowboy, and the Very Naked Girl.* Chicago: Holt, Rinehart and Winston, 1967.

Crowther, Bosley. Review of *Gentlemen Prefer Blondes. New York Times,* July 16, 1953, p. 17.

——. Review of *The Las Vegas Story. New York Times,* January 31, 1952, p. 37.

——. Review of *Son of Paleface. New York Times,* October 2, 1952, p. 32.

——. Review of *The Trouble with Harry. New York Times,* October 18, 1955, p. 46.

D'Emilio, John. "The Homosexual Menace: The Politics of Sexuality in Cold War America." In D'Emilio, *Making Trouble.* New York: Routledge, 1992.

Denney, Reuel. "Reactors of the Imagination." *Bulletin of the Atomic Scientists* 9 (July 1953), no. 6: 206–10, 224.

Dick, Bernard F. *Billy Wilder.* Boston: Twayne, 1980.

Doherty, Thomas. *Teenagers and Teenpics: The Juvenilization of American Movies in the 1950s.* Winchester, Mass.: Unwin Hyman, 1988.

Durgnat, Raymond. *The Crazy Mirror: Hollywood Comedy and the American Image.* New York: Dell, 1970.

Dyer, Richard. *Stars*. London: British Film Institute, 1979.

Eagleton, Terry. *Walter Benjamin; or, Towards a Revolutionary Criticism*. London: Verso, 1981.

Ebert, Roger. "Politics Goes to the Movies." *New York Times Book Review*, January 15, 1984, p. 12.

Elsaesser, Thomas. "Tales of Sound and Fury: Observations on the Family Melodrama." *Monogram* 4 (1972).

Farber, Stephen. "The Films of Billy Wilder." *Film Comment* 7 (Winter 1971/72), no. 4: 8–22.

Feuer, Jane. *The Hollywood Musical*. Bloomington: Indiana University Press, 1982.

Film Daily Yearbook (New York: 1960), p. 103.

"For Whom Are We Making Pictures?" *Variety*, September 27, 1950, p. 3.

French, Brandon. *On the Verge of Revolt*. New York: Frederick Ungar, 1978.

Freud, Sigmund. "'Civilized' Sexual Morality and Modern Nervousness." In Freud, *Sexuality and the Psychology of Love*. New York: Collier, 1972.

——. "Humor." In Freud, *Character and Culture*. New York: Collier, 1963.

——. *Jokes and Their Relation to the Unconscious*. Translated and edited by James Strachey. New York: W. W. Norton, 1963.

Frye, Northrop. *Anatomy of Criticism: Four Essays*. Princeton: Princeton University Press, 1973.

Gabbard, Krin, and Glen O. Gabbard, *Psychiatry and the Cinema*. Chicago: University of Chicago Press, 1987.

Garber, Marjorie. *Vested Interests: Cross-Dressing and Cultural Anxiety*. New York: HarperCollins, 1993.

Geist, Kenneth L. *Pictures Will Talk: The Life and Films of Joseph L. Mankiewicz*. New York: Scribners, 1978.

Gili, Jean A. *Howard Hawks*. Paris: Editions Seghers, 1971.

Gillett, Charlie. *The Sound of the City: The Rise of Rock and Roll*. New York: Pantheon, 1983.

Godard, Jean-Luc. *Godard on Godard*. Edited by Jean Narboni and Tom Milne. New York: Viking, 1972.

Gombrich, E. H. *Art and Illusion*. Princeton: Princeton University Press, 1960.

——. "The Wit of Saul Steinberg." *Art Journal* 43 (Winter 1983), no. 4: 377–80.

Gombrich, E. H., and E. Kris. *Caricature*. Harmondsworth, Middlesex: Penguin, 1940.

———. "The Principles of Caricature." *British Journal of Medical Psychology* 17 (1938): 319–41.

Goodman, Ezra. *The Fifty-year Decline and Fall of Hollywood*. New York: Simon and Schuster, 1961.

Gow, Gordon. *Hollywood in the Fifties*. New York: A. S. Barnes, 1971.

Guiles, Fred Lawrence. *Norma Jean: The Life of Marilyn Monroe*. New York: McGraw-Hill, 1969.

Haskell, Molly. *From Reverence to Rape: The Treatment of Women in the Movies*. New York: Holt, Rinehart and Winston, 1974.

Hayes, John Michael. *The Trouble with Harry* (first draft script dated July 27, 1954; shooting script dated September 14, 1954). Alfred Hitchcock Collection, Academy of Motion Picture Arts and Sciences, Beverly Hills, California.

Heath, Stephen. *Questions of Cinema*. Bloomington: Indiana University Press, 1981.

Higham, Charles. *Hollywood at Sunset*. New York: Saturday Review Press, 1972.

Hoberman, J., and Jonathan Rosenbaum. *Midnight Movies*. New York: Harper and Row, 1983.

Horton, Andrew S., ed. *Comedy/Cinema/Theory*. Berkeley: University of California Press, 1991.

Hughes, Richard, and Robert Brewin. *The Tranquilizing of America*. New York: Harcourt Brace Jovanovich, 1979.

Janet, Pierre. *The Mental State of Hystericals*. Translated by Caroline Rollin Corson. New York: G. P. Putnam's, 1901.

Jenkins, Henry III. "The Amazing Push-Me/Pull-You Text: Cognitive Processing, Narrational Play, and the Comic Film." *Wide Angle* 8 (1986), nos. 3–4: 35–44.

Johnston, Claire. "Feminist Politics and Film History." *Screen* 16 (Autumn 1975), no. 3: 115–24.

Johnston, Claire, and Paul Willamen, eds. *Frank Tashlin*. Edinburgh: Edinburgh Film Festival, 1973.

Johnston, Claire, Paul Willamen, and P. Hardy. "Introduction." *Edinburgh Magazine* 1 (London: British Film Institute, 1976).

Kael, Pauline. *5001 Nights at the Movies*. New York: Holt, Rinehart and Winston, 1984.

Kanfer, Stefan. *A Journal of the Plague Years*. New York: Atheneum, 1973.

Katz, Jonathan Ned. *Gay American History*. New York: Avon, 1976.

———. *The Gay/Lesbian Almanac*. New York: Harper and Row, 1983.

Kay, Karyn, and Gerald Peary. *Women and the Cinema*. New York: E. P. Dutton, 1977.

Kerouac, Jack. *On the Road*. New York: Penguin, 1977.

Kobler, John. "Gangway for the Atomic Garbageman!" *Saturday Evening Post* (January 25, 1958), pp. 36, 73.

Kris, Ernst. "The Psychology of Caricature." *International Journal of Psycho-Analysis* 17 (1936): 285–303.

Kundera, Milan. *The Book of Laughter and Forgetting*. Translated by Michael Henry Heim. New York: Alfred A. Knopf, 1981.

Labarthe, André S. "Lewis au pays de Carroll." *Cahiers du Cinéma* 132 (June 1962): 1–7.

Lacossit, Henry. "What a Way to Treat a Dog!" *Saturday Evening Post* (January 4, 1958), pp. 26–27, 52–54.

Langworth, Richard M., ed. *1957 Cars*. Secaucus, N.J.: Castle Books, 1980.

Laplanche, J., and J.-B. Pontalis. *The Language of Psychoanalysis*. Translated by Donald Nicholson-Smith. New York: W. W. Norton, 1973.

LaValley, Albert J., ed. *Focus on Hitchcock*. Englewood Cliffs, N.J.: Prentice-Hall, 1972.

Lemon, Lee T., and Marion J. Reis. *Russian Formalist Criticism*. Lincoln: University of Nebraska Press, 1965.

Lewes, Kenneth. *The Psychoanalytic Theory of Male Homosexuality*. New York: Simon and Schuster, 1988.

Lewis, Jerry. "Dialogue on Film." *American Film* 2 (September 1977), no. 10: 33–48.

———. *The Total Film Maker*. New York: Random House, 1971.

Lewis, Jerry, with Herb Gluck. *Jerry Lewis in Person*. New York: Atheneum, 1982.

"List of Security Separations." *New York Times*, January 4, 1955, p. 14.

Loos, Anita. *Gentlemen Prefer Blondes/But Gentlemen Marry Brunettes*. New York: Vintage, 1983.

Loos, Anita, and Joseph Fields. *Gentlemen Prefer Blondes*. Original typescript on file (Restricted Material #4388) at the New York Public Library, Library for the Performing Arts.

Madsen, Axel. *Billy Wilder*. Bloomington: Indiana University Press, 1969.

Marcuse, Herbert. *Eros and Civilization* (1955). Boston: Beacon Press, 1974.

Mast, Gerald. *The Comic Mind: Comedy and the Movies*. Chicago: University of Chicago Press, 1979.

———. *Howard Hawks, Storyteller*. New York: Oxford University Press, 1982.

Matthews, J. H. *Surrealism and American Feature Films*. Boston: Twayne, 1979.

Mayer, Martin. "Television's Lords of Creation, Part I: Strategic Thinking at NBC." *Harper's* (November 1956), pp. 25–32.

McBride, Joseph, ed. *Focus on Howard Hawks*. Englewood Cliffs, N.J.: Prentice-Hall, 1972.

McNeil, Alex. *Total Television*. New York: Penguin, 1980.

Mellen, Joan. *Marilyn Monroe*. New York: Galahad Books, 1973.

Miller, Douglas T., and Marion Nowak. *The Fifties: The Way We Really Were*. Garden City, N.Y.: Doubleday, 1977.

Miller, Gabriel. "Beyond the Frame: Hitchcock, Art, and the Ideal." *Post Script* 5 (1986), no. 2: 31–46.

Monroe, Marilyn. *My Story*. New York: Stein and Day, 1974.

Mulvey, Laura. "Visual Pleasure and Narrative Cinema." In Tony Bennett, Susan Boyd-Bowman, Colin Mercer, and Janet Woollacott, eds., *Popular Television and Film*. London: British Film Institute, 1981.

Mundy, Robert. "Frank Tashlin: A Tribute." In Johnston and Willamen, eds., *Frank Tashlin*. Edinburgh: Edinburgh Film Festival, 1973.

———. "Wilder Reappraised." *Cinema* (October 1969): 19–24 (London).

Nabokov, Vladimir. *Laughter in the Dark*. New York: New Directions, 1960.

Navasky, Victor. *Naming Names*. New York: Penguin, 1981.

Neale, Steve, and Frank Krutnik. *Popular Film and Television Comedy*. New York: Routledge, 1990.

New Scofield Reference Bible. New York: Oxford University Press, 1967.

Newman, Ralph M. "Screamin' Jay Hawkins." *Bim Bam Boom* 2 (September 1972), no. 1: 34–36.

"1929 Swanson Fiasco Is Finally Reviewed as a Museum Piece." *Variety*, July 26, 1950, p. 119.

Nugent, Frank S. "All About Joe." *Collier's* (March 24, 1951), pp. 24–25, 68–70.

Palmer, Jerry. "Enunciation and Comedy: 'Kind Hearts and Coronets.'" *Screen* 30 (1989), nos. 1–2: 144–58.

Partridge, Eric. *A Dictionary of Slang and Unconventional English*. Edited by Paul Beale. London: Routledge and Kegan Paul, 1984.

Paul, William. *Ernst Lubitsch's American Comedy*. New York: Columbia University Press, 1984.

———. *Laughing/Screaming*. New York: Columbia University Press, 1994.

Peale, Norman Vincent. *The Power of Positive Thinking*. New York: Prentice-Hall, 1952.

Perkins, V. F. "Comedies." *Movie* 5 (December 1962): 21–22.

Plant, Richard. *The Pink Triangle*. New York: Henry Holt, 1986.

Poague, Leland. *Howard Hawks*. Boston: Twayne, 1982.

Pryor, Thomas M. Review of *Yes, Sir, That's My Baby. New York Times*, November 11, 1949, p. 31.

Recasens, Gérard. "Jerry Lewis." *Cinéma d'aujourd'hui* 59. Paris: Editions Seghers, 1970.

Reik, Theodor. *Masochism in Modern Man*. Translated by Margaret H. Beigel and Gertrud M. Kruth. New York: Farrar, Straus, 1941.

Reisman, David. "Listening to Popular Music." *American Quarterly* 2 (Winter 1950), no. 4: 359–71.

Reisman, David, with Nathan Glazer and Reuel Denney. *The Lonely Crowd: A Study of the Changing American Character*. Garden City, N.Y.: Doubleday, 1953.

Rieff, Phillip. *Freud: The Mind of the Moralist*. Garden City, N.Y.: Doubleday, 1961.

——. *The Triumph of the Therapeutic*. New York: Harper and Row, 1968.

Rogin, Michael. *Ronald Reagan, the Movie*. Berkeley: University of California Press, 1987.

Rohmer, Eric, and Claude Chabrol. *Hitchcock: The First Fifty-four Films*. Translated by Stanley Hochman. New York: Frederick Ungar, 1979.

Rosenbaum, Jonathan. "Gold Diggers of 1953." *Sight and Sound* 5 (Winter 1984/85), no. 1: 45.

Rothman, William. *Hitchcock: The Murderous Gaze*. Cambridge: Harvard University Press, 1982.

Rubiner, Julia, ed. *Contemporary Musicians: Profiles of the People in Music*, vol. 9 (Washington, D.C.: Gale Research, 1993).

Russell, Jane. *Jane Russell: An Autobiography: My Paths and Detours*. New York: Franklin Watts, 1985.

Russo, Vito. *The Celluloid Closet*. New York: Harper and Row, 1981.

Sarris, Andrew. *The American Cinema*. New York: E. P. Dutton, 1968.

——. "A Few Kind Words for the Fifties." *Village Voice*, September 14, 1982, p. 47.

——. "The Trouble with Harry." *Film Culture* 5–6 (1955).

——. "The World of Howard Hawks." In Joseph McBride, ed., *Focus on Howard Hawks*. Englewood Cliffs, N.J.: Prentice-Hall, 1972.

Saxton, Martha. *Jayne Mansfield and the American Fifties*. Boston: Houghton Mifflin, 1975.

Sayre, Nora. *Running Time: Films of the Cold War*. New York: Dial, 1982.

Schiller, Greta (director). *Before Stonewall*. David Whitten Promotions, 1985.

Seidman, Steve. *The Film Career of Billy Wilder*. Boston: G. K. Hall, 1977.

"Senator Johnson Expected to Modify Certain Facets of Anti-Film Measure," *Variety*, March 22, 1950, p. 4.

Shelley, Percy Bysshe. "The Banquet of Plato." In Roger Ingpen and Walter E. Peck, eds., *The Complete Works of Percy Bysshe Shelley*, vol. 7. New York: Gordian Press, 1965.

"Showmanship Selling Seen Requiring More Personnel," *Hollywood Reporter*, March 13, 1950, p. 4.

Sinyard, Neil, and Adrian Turner. *Journey Down Sunset Boulevard: The Film Career of Billy Wilder*. Ryde, Isle of Wight: BCW Publishers, 1979.

Spectorsky, A. C. *The Exurbanites*. Philadelphia: Lippincott, 1954.

Spoto, Donald. *The Art of Alfred Hitchcock: Fifty Years of His Motion Pictures*. Garden City, N.Y.: Doubleday, 1959.

———. *The Dark Side of Genius: The Life of Alfred Hitchcock*. New York: Ballantine, 1983.

"Stars' Personals with Own Pix Pay Off Big in the Hinterlands on Publicity," *Variety*, October 11, 1950, p. 7, p. 53.

Steinberg, Saul. *The Passport*. New York: Harper, 1954.

Stern, Jane and Michael Stern. *The Encyclopedia of Bad Taste*. New York: Harper Perennial, 1991.

Stone, I. F. *The Haunted Fifties*. New York: Random House, 1963.

Story, J. Trevor. *The Trouble with Harry*. New York: Macmillan, 1950.

Studlar, Gaylyn. *In the Realm of Pleasure*. Chicago: University of Chicago Press, 1988.

"'Sunset' Looks to Music Hall Record," *Variety*, September 13, 1950, p. 7.

Swanson, Gloria. *Swanson on Swanson*. New York: Random House, 1980.

Teichmann, Howard, and George S. Kaufman. *The Solid Gold Cadillac*. New York: Random House, 1954.

Todorov, Tzvetan. *The Fantastic*. Translated by Richard Howard. Ithaca: Cornell University Press, 1975.

Truffaut, François. *Hitchcock*. New York: Simon and Schuster, 1967.

Turim, Maureen. "Designing Woman: The Emergence of the New Sweetheart Line." *Wide Angle* 6 (1984), no. 2: 4–11.

———. "Gentlemen Consume Blondes." *Wide Angle* 1 (1979), no. 1: 52–59.

Tynjanov, Ju. "On the Foundations of the Cinema." In *Russian Formalist Film Theory*. Translated by Zinaida Breschinsky and Herbert Eagle. Ann Arbor: Michigan Slavic Publications, 1981.

Van Hagen, (Mrs.) L. F. "Life in These United States" entry, *Reader's Digest* (October 1952), p. 52.

Variety, December 1949 through January 1960 (various issues).

Vidal, Gore. "Immortal Bird." *New York Review of Books*, June 13, 1985.

Walker, Janet. "Hollywood, Freud, and the Representation of Women." In Christine Gledhill, ed., *Home Is Where the Heart Is*. London: British Film Institute, 1987.

Warshow, Robert. *The Immediate Experience: Movies, Comics, Theatre, and Other Aspects of Popular Culture*. Garden City, N.Y.: Doubleday, 1962.

Wechsler, Judith. "Editor's Statement: The Issue of Caricature." *Art Journal* 43 (Winter 1983), no. 4: 317–18.

Wentworth, Harold, and Stuart Berg Flexner. *A Dictionary of American Slang*. New York: Thomas Y. Crowell, 1975.

Whitfield, Stephen J. *The Culture of the Cold War*. Baltimore: Johns Hopkins University Press, 1991.

Whyte, William H., Jr. *The Organization Man*. Garden City, N.Y.: Doubleday, 1957.

Wilde, Oscar. *The Picture of Dorian Gray* (1891). New York: New American Library, 1962.

Wilder, Billy. *Some Like It Hot: A Screenplay by Billy Wilder and I.A.L. Diamond*. New York: New American Library, 1959.

Wilder, Billy, and I.A.L. Diamond. "Dialogue on Film." *American Film* 1 (July–August 1976): 33–48.

Williamson, Judith. "Webfooted Friends." *New Statesman* (April 22, 1988), pp. 29–30.

Willis, Donald C. *The Films of Howard Hawks*. Metuchen, N.J.: Scarecrow Press, 1975.

Wilson, Earl. *The Show Business Nobody Knows*. New York: Cowles Book Co., 1971.

Wollen, Peter. *Readings and Writings*. London: Verso, 1982.

———. *Signs and Meaning in the Cinema*. Bloomington: Indiana University Press, 1973.

Wood, Robin. *Hitchcock's Films*. New York: A. S. Barnes, 1977.

———. *Howard Hawks*. London: British Film Institute, 1981.

——. "Introduction." *American Nightmare: Essays on the Horror Film*, pp. 7–28. Toronto: Festival of Festivals, 1979.

Wood, Tom. *The Bright Side of Billy Wilder, Primarily*. Garden City, N.Y.: Doubleday, 1970.

Zizek, Slavoj. "Hitchcock." Translated by Richard Miller. *October* 38 (Fall 1986): 99–111.

Zolotow, Maurice. *Billy Wilder in Hollywood*. New York: G. P. Putnam's, 1977.

——. *Marilyn Monroe*. New York: Harcourt, Brace, 1960.

index

Charters, Ann, 16
Chierichetti, David, 72
Chuckles, The, 216, 223
CinemaScope, 2, 180, 241, 244; and ideology of *Gentlemen Prefer Blondes* 75–77; in *The Girl Can't Help It*, 207–208, 221; compared to television, 198, 230
Cinerama, 2
Citizen Kane (1941), 107
Clark, Fred, 99
Clift, Montgomery: 2, 26, 44, 134
Coburn, Charles: 40–43; as representation of aging, 61–62, 78, 84; as representation of patriarchy, 76, 77–79
Coca, Imogene, 6
Cochran, Eddie, 210, 226–227
Colbert, Claudette, 188
Cold War, 5, 16; and fifties farce, 201–203; and homosexuality, 118–119, 202, 188–189; *See also* Atomic weapons
Colgate Comedy Hour, The, (1950–1955), 186
Collins, Joan, 201
Color: Deluxe: in *The Girl Can't Help It*, 207–208; in *Will Success Spoil Rock Hunter?*, 234; Technicolor: 105; in *Gentlemen Prefer Blondes*, 47, 69, 75, 78; in *Hollywood or Bust*, 224–225; in *The Trouble with Harry*, 149, 159
Comden, Betty, 5
Comedy: and believability, 31; black comedy in the fifties, 12, 122–124; and the body, 244; darkening of genre in fifties, 113–114, 123; and death, 102, 109–113, 122–123, 140–141, 150–151, 153–154; definition of genre, 28, 97–98; escapism in, 128–129; and inversion, 48, 57, 65–67, 77–82, 101–102, 128, 139; Jewish humor, 102; puns, 79, 206; and repression, 35; resolution and irresolution in, 63–64, 111–113, 172; safety of narrative mode, 21; screwball, 186–187; and sex in fifties films, 55–57, 61, 26–29, 181–182; as social critique, 6–7, 29–33; therapeutic function of, xii, xiv, 51–54, 244
Comics and comic books, 181; 191–192, 196–200, 210
Communism: comic representations of, 202–203; and Hollywood, 18–19, 27; and hysteria, 20, 202; and motherhood, 37
Comolli, Jean-Louis, 191–192
Congress, United States, 202
Cooper, Gary, 52, 107
Corliss, Richard, xvi, 97–98, 144–145
Corman, Roger, 17
Costumes: in *Gentlemen Prefer Blondes*, 68–69, 72–74, 78, 223; in *The Girl Can't Help It*, 223–225
"Crazy," as fifties slang, 13–16
Crist, Judith, 130–131
Crosby, Bing, 181
Cross-dressing, 7, 34; in Hawks's films, 46–47, 56; in *Money from Home*, 187–188; in *Some Like It Hot*, 130–134, 136, 145–148, 154; in *Stalag 17*, 116–117; in *Will Success Spoil Rock Hunter?*, 233–234; in *Yes, Sir, That's My Baby*, 41–43
Crowther, Bosley, 65–66, 217
Cukor, George, 47, 166, 196

Grant, Cary, xiv, 31, 133–134, 150, 152, 180, 186; comic persona of, 49–50, 52, 62; and cross-dressing, 46; parodied in *Some Like It Hot*, 145

Green, Adolph, 5

Gwenn, Edmund, 158

Haley, Bill, and his Comets, 14, 227

Hardy, Phil, 211

Hargitay, Mickey, 216, 236

Harris, Barbara, 169

Hart, Moss, 129

Has Anybody Seen My Gal? (1952), 61

Haskell, Molly, xvi, 66, 106, 135

Hathaway, Henry, 201

Hawkins, Screamin' Jay, 17–18, 20

Hawks, Howard, 27, 97, 180, 201, 226; and cross-dressing, 46; and gender inversion, 65–69; undermining film conventions, 43; as normative Hollywood director, 45–49; rationale for inclusion, xi–xiv; *See also* individual film titles

Hawthorne, Nathaniel, 125–126

Hayden, Richard, 188

Heath, Stephen, xvi, 169, 196–197

Hepburn, Audrey, 107

Hepburn, Katharine, 52, 186

High Noon (1952), 4, 7

High School Confidential (1958), 201

His Girl Friday (1940), 45

Hitchcock, Alfred, 55, 90, 149, 180, 244; and Addams, 154–156; and bathroom anxiety, 235–236; morbidity of, 153–154; rationale for inclusion, xi–xiv; and Steinberg, 156–157; as television personality, 174–175; *See also* individual film titles

Hitler, Adolf, 108, 123, 142, 199

Hogan's Heroes (1965–1971), 123–124

Holden, William, 89, 100, 119; on *Sunset Boulevard*'s original opening, 109–110

Hollywood or Bust (1956), 19, 31, 181, 224–225

Hollywood: blacklisting, 3, 18–19; conformism of, 2–3; formal film practice, 195, 197, 208–209; productivity in 1950s, 28; publicity and public relations, 93–95

Holt, Charlene, 44

Home Before Dark (1958), 22

Home of the Brave (1949), 22

Homosexuality: 28, 45, 139, 206; and the Cold War, 29, 202; fifties culture and, xv, 118–122, 134, 146–148, 188–189; in *Gentlemen Prefer Blondes*, 68, 74–77 83–85; hysteria and, 20; Jerry Lewis and, 185–190; Nazis and, 117–118; psychiatry and, 189; in *Some Like It Hot*, 130, 135–139, 143–148; in *Stalag 17*, 116–122

Hope, Bob, 5, 27, 56–57, 185

Horney, Karen, 35–36

Horwich, Dr. Frances, 39

House Committee on Un-American Activities (HUAC), 1, 3, 18, 93–94

How to Marry a Millionaire (1953), 3

Hudson, Rock, 128

Hughes, Howard, 73, 215–216

Hunter, Jeffrey, 134

Hunter, Tab, 134

Huston, John, 5

Hutton, Betty, 99

Hysteria: clinical, 19–21, 73, 193;

and Hollywood blacklisting, 18–19; Jerry Lewis as hysteric, 187, 190, 193

alytic structure of, 170–174; sexual symbolism in, 159–163

Trouble with Harry, The (novel) 158, 165, 167

Trzcinski, Edmund, 115, 119–120

Turim, Maureen, xvi, 65–68, 75, 183

Turner, Adrian, 100, 113–114, 130–131, 144

12 Angry Men (1957), 4, 7

Twentieth Century Fox, xiv, 82, 197, 215, 218, 233, 241

Underwater (1955), 215–216

United States Information Service, 29

Universal Pictures, 196n

Valentino, Rudolph, 89

Van Doren, Mamie, 201

Vertigo (1958), 55, 152, 157

Vidal, Gore, 182

Vincent, Gene, 17, 210, 226

VistaVision, 2, 156, 182–183, 198

Voice-over narration: as fifties convention, 115, 195–196

Wagner, Robert, 134

Walker, Hal, xi

Walker, Janet, 22

Ward, Jay, 203

Warner Bros., 94, 180

Warshow, Robert, 199

Waxman, Franz, 90

Wayne, John, 43–44, 52

Wellman, William, 3, 187

Whitfield, Stephen J., 118, 188–189, 202

Wilde, Oscar, 125–126

Wilder, Billy, 27, 87, 180, 187, 201, 209, 244; adapts plays, 113–116,

125–128; and female sexuality, 106–107, 142–143; and Freud, 102; and homosexuality, 119–122, 130–131, 136; ironic humor of, 88, 91–92, 98–103, 109–113, 122; rationale for inclusion, xi–xiv; on *Sunset Boulevard*'s original opening, 109

Will Success Spoil Rock Hunter? (1957), xii, 9, 37, 125, 181, 198, 225, 244–245; bathroom jokes in, 235–236; and dirt, 235–238; doggie fetish in, 233–234; marriage in, 239–240; psychoanalysis in, 238–239; self-consciousness of, 241–242

Will Success Spoil Rock Hunter? (stage play), 9, 231–232

Willemen, Paul, xvi, 195, 196–197, 211

Williams, John, 242

Wilmington, Michael, 113–114

Wilson, Michael, 18

Winnicott, D.W., 36

Winslow, George, 58, 62, 198–199, 217

Wise, Robert, 3

Witch hunts: *See* Hollywood: and blacklisting

Wolfe, Charles, 11

Wollen, Peter, 48, 98

Women: in cartoon form, 194, 203–204, 205, 244; and drugs and alcohol, 8–9; feminist issues represented in comedy, 41–43, 155–156, 176–178; and hysteria, 20–21; infantilized, 59–60, 62, 125; and motherhood, 36–39, 61–62; and psychoanalysis, 35–36; as spectacle, 33–35, 179–180,

Women (*continued*)
182–183, 214, 218–220, 224–225;
as temptresses, 85–86, 201; as
threat to patriarchy, 74–77,
127–128, 175–178, 224; *See also*
Breasts: women's; Cross-dressing
Wood, Edward D., Jr., 130
Wood, Robin, xvi, 43–45, 50, 57,
65, 83–85, 97
Wright, Will, 98
Written on the Wind (1956), 21, 201

Wylie, Philip, 36

Yes, Sir, That's My Baby (1949),
40–43, 49, 61, 64
You Can't Take It With You (1938),
129
You're Never Too Young (1955), 173,
187

Zizek, Slavoj, 171
Zugsmith, Albert, 201

Designer: Linda Secondari
Text: 11.5/14 Bembo
Compositor: Columbia University Press
Printer: Edwards Brothers
Binder: Edwards Brothers